A Theology of Cross and Kingdom

A Theology of Cross and Kingdom

Theologia Crucis after the Reformation, Modernity,
and Ultramodern Tribalistic Syncretism

D. K. MATTHEWS

With a contribution from J. Steven O'Malley

PICKWICK *Publications* · Eugene, Oregon

A THEOLOGY OF CROSS AND KINGDOM
Theologia Crucis after the Reformation, Modernity, and Ultramodern Syncretism

Pickwick Publications
An Imprint of Wipf and Stock Publishers
199 W. 8th Ave., Suite 3
Eugene, OR 97401

www.wipfandstock.com

PAPERBACK ISBN: 978-1-5326-4143-5
HARDCOVER ISBN: 978-1-5326-4144-2
EBOOK ISBN: 978-1-5326-4145-9

Cataloguing-in-Publication data:

Names: Matthews, D. K., author. | O'Malley, J. Steven, contributor.

Title: A theology of cross and kingdom : theologia crucis after the Reformation, modernity, and ultramodern sycretism / D. K. Matthews ; with a contribution from J. Steven O'Malley.

Description: Eugene, OR : Pickwick Publications, 2019 | Includes bibliographical references and indexes.

Identifiers: ISBN 978-1-5326-4143-5 (paperback) | ISBN 978-1-5326-4144-2 (hardcover) | ISBN 978-1-5326-4145-9 (ebook)

Subjects: LCSH: Theology of the cross.

Classification: BT453 .M38 2019 (paperback) | BT453 .M38 (ebook)

Manufactured in the U.S.A.   04/18/19

To my wife, Dr. Carol Matthews, who has truly made all things possible relative to serving and writing for time and eternity. Her gracious contribution to this project is incalculable and was made through much personal sacrifice in the shadow of the cross and the dawning of Christ's glorious kingdom.

Contents

Tables

Contributors

J. STEVEN O'MALLEY IS the John T. Seamands Professor of Methodist Holiness History at Asbury Theological Seminary. His publications include *Interpretive Trends in Christian Revitalization for the Early Twenty First Century; Pilgrimage of Faith: The Legacy of the Otterbeins; On the Journey Home: The History of Mission of the Evangelical United Brethren Church, 1946–1968; Early German-American Evangelicalism; Revitalization amid Diaspora, Consultation Three: Explorations in World Christian Revitalization Movements; John Seybert and the Evangelical Heritage; Pietist and Methodist* (with Jason Vickers); and *The Origin of the Wesleyan Theological Vision for Christian Globalization and the Pursuit of Pentecost in Early Pietist Revivalism.*

Preface

IF WE PROPERLY DEFINE and frame our theology of the cross and kingdom, then we will likely get it right on most of our theological reflections and applications, including missiology, ecclesiology, and theodicy. Similarly, we will chart a fruitful and biblical path for our social, political, cultural, and intellectual engagement. We will also birth a passion for God's mission that avoids the perils of triumphalism, theological accommodation, escapism, and separatism—to name a few theological and missional cul-de-sacs. For biblical Christians, the cross and kingdom are truly core and quintessential to our identity, and most relevant after modernity. The argument proffered in this work seeks to avoid less than helpful and disjunctive approaches to the interfacing theologies and philosophies of cross, kingdom, glory, modernity, postmodernity, and Christ and culture. To employ the vernacular at the applicable real world intersection of time and eternity, a proper theology of cross and kingdom rules and should rule our thought, passions, and action.

To gift this book and for additional resources please go to doctord.org
or millenniumfirst.org

Acknowledgments

IF THIS WORK, BY grace, contributes to kingdom advance, then gratitude to Divine Providence is the first and foremost acknowledgment. Christ's Trinitarian presence through Scripture, especially illuminated by countless hours reviewing Scripture for keys to formation, inspiration, and academic reflection, birthed a vibrant cross and kingdom passion. My wife, Dr. Carol Matthews, has been at my side as intellectual colleague, dialogical partner, best friend, and eternal love. Asbury Theological Seminary graciously allotted time for writing by the Provost at a very busy and energized seminary amidst countless initiatives. Numerous Asbury Seminary faculty and staff held down the fort, and often improved the seminary fortifications and ministry, during my absence. Asbury Seminary and academic guild faculty were most encouraging concerning the general direction of this work. Dr. J. Steven O'Malley filled a church history void in this project with predictable excellence. The faculty and staff of Spring Arbor University, Wheaton College, and Baylor University formed my heart, framed my intellectual journey, and birthed my love for the cross and the kingdom. Kelly Bixler, Judy Seitz, and the Reverend Andy Newman all made critical contributions to preparing the manuscript for publication. Dr. Daryl Diddle reliably preached and modeled Scripture as the Spirit fed and led our congregation during the critical years of finalizing this manuscript.

PART 1

Background, Assumptions, and Themes

1

Introduction and Major Trajectories

Jesus spoke these things; and lifting up His eyes to heaven, He said, "Father, the hour has come; glorify [from δόξα, glory] Your Son, that the Son may glorify You, even as You gave Him authority over all flesh, that to all whom You have given Him, He may give eternal life.

—JOHN 17:1–2

But the Lord said to him, "Go, for he is a chosen instrument of Mine,
to bear My name before the Gentiles and kings and the sons of Israel;
for I will show him how much he must suffer for My name's sake."

—ACTS 9:15–16

Now this He said, signifying by what kind of death he [Peter] would glorify [from δόξα, glory] God. And when He had spoken this, He said to him, "Follow Me!"

—JOHN 21:19

A PERSONAL JOURNEY TOWARD THE *VIA DOLOROSA*

Weeks after setting aside research on Luther's theology of the cross for another writing project, I was sitting in a hospital prayerfully holding the hand and, hopefully, comforting the last days and hours of a perishing, homeward bound loved one. This moment and related experiences seemed all too common in recent years. Echoing down the hallway from another hospital room was the frequent and almost hourly cry of, "Help, help, help." Lives were being saved, heroic and herculean efforts were evident by the medical staff, and the joyful yet somewhat ironic music of Brahms lullaby was heard every few hours to herald a new birth on a more celebratory floor. Only the term surreal captures the moment.

On our floor the culture included beeping monitors, uncomfortable tubes and unpredictable medications, troubling hallucinations, endless well-intended interruptions from helpful staff day and night, impossible end-of-life decisions, painful and life-threatening miscalculations by staff when attempts were made to provide comfort, less than needed sleep, loss of critical information between employee shifts, labored breathing, caring tears, and purgatorial endless nights. These are not the experiences most of us hope for or pursue. Some evangelicals view such experiences as the lack of divine blessing or faith. These are realities we sometimes, at least in part, pretend do not exist until the illusion finally vanishes in the crucible. And they are often not viewed as indispensable or defining of our discipleship and Christian formation.

In just a few short and endless years such sea billows ever rolled forward. The loss of multiple loved ones, including a centenarian whose memorial I officiated, failed and botched surgeries, repeat surgeries, endless tests and visits with physicians, the dynamics of hospice care, a daunting workload, and the challenging attempt to bring a healing salve to bear on the pain and sleep management of loved ones all converged.

My mind was certainly not on Luther or his theology of the cross during one of these long days and nights at the final bedside in the hospital. The bittersweet but agonizing and shadowy hours of losing a beloved was not a new experience. Then as I sat alone that dark night in the wee hours of the morning, playing classical hymns of the faith from my Bluetooth device with the hope of providing some encouragement to the suffering loved one, Luther's *theologia crucis* seemed unexpectedly relevant. In a world and church that often glories in and baptizes that which is not genuinely of God (a theology of glory), Luther contended that God is unexpectedly found in the hiddenness of the cross, suffering, pain, and shame. Somewhere in the middle of the night the entire room and my loved one seemingly became irradiated with the presence of the kenotic and cruciform Holy One. Perhaps it was a special visitation of the Spirit. Perhaps it was the reality of a loved one transitioning to another dimension and that deeper dimension fully enveloping the moment. Regardless, while the dark dagger in the heart was real, that sheer reality also lucidly conveyed the presence of the true future that forever redefined the present.

A few lessons were hopefully learned at these hospital and hospice deathbeds. Some of the worst days of my life and a loved one's life were surprised by a profound sense of God's presence. Spiritualizing and denial are ephemeral or short-lived. Years later these experiences continued to drive and frame my spiritual walk. I continued to wrestle with the dagger of loss, yet the dagger was the window to and mirror of reality. In over three decades of ministry, counseling, teaching, and chaplaincy, I have seen many responses to such trials and tribulation. Most become better, bitter, or land in seemingly endless spiritual vertigo and angst. Suffering is not simply marginal to a genuine, enduring, victorious and blessed Christian life and spiritual quest, or only distantly connected to the persecution or martyrdom of heroes of the faith in another time and place. Suffering and pain and loss are key conditions of authentic Christlikeness and spirituality given our fallen condition in an inverted world. Our response to suffering frames whether we will take up the cross of kingdom advance. Ministering to or being the one who suffers is not tangential or something to endure, but absolutely determinative of who we are in Christ as creatures seeking full and final redemption. Scripture does not call us to pursue suffering for the sake of suffering, yet these bedrock experiences must be integrated into our theology of the Christian life.

This work will argue that God certainly can be found in successes and a properly defined glory in this life, but if our response to suffering is removed from the kingdom equation then only the kingdom of spiritual fluff remains. The hope of heaven—as earth transformed according to N. T. Wright—for those suffering and for loved ones lost is not to be discounted in such situations. However, caution is in order lest this hope is little more than a flight from grieving, suffering, and a "spiritual" and psychologically unhealthy means of denial.

To be clear, such hospital sojourns and related hospice experiences with loved ones do not lie precisely at the soteriological core of Luther's theology of the cross, yet by way of analogy and existential relevance they certainly sparked reflection on Luther's influential construct. God's presence was especially evident amidst the seemingly endless last hours of suffering of the loved one and family member referenced at the very beginning of this chapter. However, this same loved one best embodied a theology of cross and kingdom years prior to this final hospice experience. A car with reckless young drivers, perhaps under the influence, had crossed the line and collided with our car. This elderly family member was driving our car, and stated that he turned the car at the last minute to take the full impact of the collision from the swerving car and protect other family members. I was in the back seat. After the accident our family member who was the driver, with a head injury, could not sleep in his own bed for a number of nights, as the head injury caused significant swelling, discomfort, and permanent scarring. He tried to sleep in a recliner. This accident also took place not long after his major open heart surgery. During this challenging season of life for the driver another family member who was also in the car accident was traversing great emotional distress, criticism, and marginalization at work—due to an unfortunate and seemingly prejudiced work and Christian ministry environment.

I will forever recall the lasting impact of the words of this loved one and driver, who was typically very quiet and non-expressive, with his head swollen and bandaged from the car accident. He sliced through the fog of his own pain and suffering while standing in the kitchen and offered powerful, bright, passionate, selfless, focused, and redemptive words of love and encouragement that comforted and strengthened the other family member. God's love and wisdom were mediated, and even more inspirational and memorable, via his tribulations. These words from the suffering driver and loved one helped to carry the other family member through some very difficult days, and through many key moments of ministry on life's journey. The kingdom truly had been embodied and advanced through cruciform love.[1]

Madsen underscores how Luther's Christocentrism and crucicentrism undergird and sustain all such authentic emobdiments of cruciform suffering, love, and kingdom advance:

> Luther sets up his essential proposition . . . that God is found only in death and abandonment, just as one finds Jesus on the cross. A theology of glory comforts, finding understandable solutions to the mysteries of life and God, and finding artificial [i.e., short-lived and misdirected] hope in the successes [glories] of this world. Luther rejected such a theology [of glory], asserting that God instead is found in the midst of death and despair.

---

1. However, see chapter 2 of this work where Luther does view human suffering as a means of soul purgation in this life. This work will reject Luther's deterministic conception of soul purgation, while also affirming that Divine Providence can harness human suffering for kingdom advance. No suffering ever needs to lack a positive kingdom impact in the divine economy.

> Any attempt to discover God on human terms results in further alienation from God.[2]

Luther's theological and soteriological cornerstone and firm conviction is that at the very end of numerous and failed "holy pilgrimages" seeking salvation—via mysticism, confession, good works, ecclesial and political glory, and actual physical pilgrimages—he unqualifiedly affirmed that God only can be truly known as Savior and Redeemer through the justifying forsakenness of the cross. True, passionate, transformational knowledge of God is *via dolorosa*.

Hence, for Luther, the practice of indulgences especially reflected a (false)[3] theology of glory "in direct opposition to the theology of the cross . . . finding comfort in the ease of giving money instead of the costly offering of one's life."[4] Indeed, without "appreciation of the Church's appeal for alms in the form of indulgences, one misses the entire catalyst for Luther's revolutionary theological advance. This sole element of the piety of Luther's day catapulted him into reflection about the nature of God, and the nature of humanity's relationship with God."[5] Therefore, "one finds the essential elements of Luther's theology of the cross—contrary to expectation, God abides in sinfulness, despair, helplessness, and persecution due to faith."[6]

From this theological wellspring of the theology of the cross, Luther also proffered a deterministic theology of the cross that included suffering.[7] For Luther, pain and suffering are sent by God for spiritual purgation.[8] This

---

2. Madsen, *Theology*, 77.

3. Luther primarily refers to the "theology of glory" as a negative or a distortion such as indulgences. Yet chapter 2 documents his more nuanced comments, which, like Scripture itself, distinguish between true and false wisdom. This work emphasizes that while the usage of a theology of glory can be restricted only to negatives, it is also important to acknowledge the biblical and positive usage of "glory"; a positive and possible biblical nuance of a theology of glory; the direct biblical and theological connection between a theology of cross and a theology of glory; and, a distorted, misused "theology of the cross" that actually morphs into a pseudo-theology of the cross. Such pseudo-theologies of the cross may bear more resemblance to Luther's negative definition of a theology of glory. For example, some utopian movements, in the name of compassionate solidarity with the marginalized and social justice, have specialized in the abuse of power, oppression, and an idolatrous and self-righteous self-definition. See chapters 11 and 12.

4. Madsen, *Theology*, 79.

5. Madsen, *Theology*, 80.

6. Madsen, *Theology*, 234.

7. Luther's deterministic formulation will be challenged especially in chapters 2 and 3.

8. Pain is used here to refer to the actual physical and sensory experience, whereas suffering is used to refer to the entire existential, psychological, and even spiritual interpretation and experience of the physical reality.

determinism will be assessed and reframed in chapters 3, 5, and 6. Nevertheless, determinism aside, such experiences of suffering have often proven to be surprisingly, and sometimes more profoundly and longitudinally, impactful and formative than well-crafted and glorious spiritual retreats, Christian conferences, or Christian concerts—events I cherish and some of which I have spent months and years planning. This is not to say that such events or worshipful music stood in total juxtaposition to God's unique presence that endless night in the hospital with a loved one. After all, the Bluetooth music referenced immediately above was playing softly in the background in the wee hours that morning, and Luther viewed music as the greatest thing next to the Word of God, since when we sing, he affirmed, we pray twice.

What is being maintained concerning such dark nights is that God's presence, frankly, oftentimes may be much more authentically intense, formative, enduring, and especially *real* than many of these other proffered means of Christian or spiritual formation.[9] To be clear, in an age of increasing spiritual sensualism and narcissism,[10] this spiritual progress in my life has not always included what Americans mean by "feeling good,"[11] but the

9. See chapter 4, but Luther often affirmed that the dark nights of the soul (*anfechtungen*) not only grounded his entire theology, but actually drove his theology to a more biblical soteriology and total reliance upon the God of grace. Yet Luther's dark nights were more about the medieval construct of the *spiritual* suffering of the pilgrim who sensed the unrelenting judgment of a holy God who could not be appeased by any attempts of the pilgrim to find peace with God. Strictly speaking, then, dark nights of pain and suffering in a hospital are not necessarily Luther's *anfechtungen*. Yet, as noted in this chapter previously, it will be argued that such dark nights are potentially and often the most significant loci of authentic divine and transformative encounter. Luther clearly did see such pain and suffering as deterministic means of soul purgation.

10. I am using spiritual sensualism intentionally here as a way of communicating that just as some rush after sensual pleasures, so others rush after spiritual pleasures. Neither reflects the kingdom of God. Spiritual narcissism refers to the usage of religion or experiences of God for self-serving reasons, which fits well with a "have it your way" consumerist culture.

11. While believers often and properly affirm the well known promises of a "peace that passeth all understanding" and the joyful "fruit of the Spirit," all of which certainly undergird truth and reality for the Christian walk, such affirmations also must be defined and synthesized consistent with biblical experiences such as the Garden of Gethsemane or the cross. Scripture must interpret and cohere with Scripture. In the book of Matthew, Jesus was "deeply grieved to the point of death," sweating as with drops of blood, and quoting biblical passages on God-forsakenness (see Matt 26:38; 27:46). Did the Christ lose his sanctification in those moments? Hardly. Perhaps his holiness was best incarnated in those dark moments and *anfechtung*. See the entire context, narrative, and specific and relevant references from Matt 26; 27; Gal 5; Phil 4 (a chapter that also references struggles, suffering, need, conflicts, contentment, and sacrifice). There are different seasons of the Christian life, and biblical joy and peace

change wrought has hopefully contributed substantially to *being* good. And, perhaps more importantly, such cruciform encounters have proven to be watersheds with *staying power*—sometimes troubling or even haunting, yet ever ameliorative, relative to the genuine pursuit of Christlikeness and kingdom advance. The cruciform experience seems to remove the veil of illusion and touch the very core of who we are—often referred to as volition, affection, passion, and imagination—and it creates the conditions that actually mediate and actualize real and longitudinal personal transformation: "Therefore I urge you, brethren, by the mercies of God, to present your bodies a living and holy sacrifice, acceptable to God, *which is* your spiritual service of worship. And do not be conformed to this world, but be transformed by the renewing of your mind, so that you may prove what the will of God is, that which is good and acceptable and perfect" (Rom 12:1–2). The crucible sparks such legitimate transformation.

Cruciform is here used in at least three senses: (1) taking on the form of the experience of the suffering of the cross, even if less intense, yet certainly not meritorious; (2) suffering and persecution that is directly the result of and facilitates kingdom advance, which is the most proper sense of the term; and, (3) suffering that is indirectly connected to kingdom advance (e.g., God works through someone's suffering, but the suffering was not directly caused by, say, persecution). This work will challenge Luther's determinism relative to suffering, including his deterministic rebuke of his suffering mother who was hesitant to accept such pain as God's purgation of her soul. Yet this work also contends for the potential cruciform, crucicentric, and kingdom-centric value of such suffering.

Luther is not alone in affirming that God is paradoxically found, especially, amidst suffering, weakness, and pain. To modify Andrew Root's insight slightly, "We [often best] discern God's presence next to human weakness, not human strength."[12] Many colleagues and relatives have concurred with this conviction. The family challenges of dealing with the advanced stages of cancer, or the death of a young child, or even the deathbed hours of a beloved centenarian, have especially served as windows of grace, mission, forgiveness, and an unparalleled sense of the divine presence. My student development and nontraditional chaplaincy experience dealing with various crises agrees with this poignant and piercing observation,[13]

were never intended to be a gnostic escape from reality, unrelated to grief and suffering, or an ephemeral emotional high. Biblical joy and peace will be viewed in this work as incarnational, eschatological, and foundational as opposed to a giddy and superficial happiness more consistent with media and marketing conceptualizations.

12. Root, *Christopraxis*, 108.

13. The nontraditional chaplaincy ministry of a few years was relevant to this

including the tragic, fiery, and nearly fatal automobile accident of a student, the imprisonment of that student, and the grief of the family.

Similarly, Krish Kandiah affirmed recently, "God turns up in all the wrong places at Christmas."[14] God self-reveals amidst military occupation, poverty, oppression, the seeming divine silence, the middle of night, the middle of nowhere, unclean foreigners, and straw in "a shed." Kandiah concludes, "God deliberately planned to turn up at the wrong time in the wrong place."[15]

The thesis that God unexpectedly shows up amidst pain, shame, and suffering neither entails Luther's affirmation that suffering is deterministic purgation, nor that all suffering is inherently kingdom-centric or due to faithful kingdom service. Consistent with the non-deterministic arguments made in this work (especially chapter 3), it will be asserted, however, that all suffering is *potentially* spiritually transformative and *potentially*, by grace, a means for kingdom advance.

I will also affirm a positive, biblical, useful, and appropriate definition of a theology of glory. Indeed, "The heavens declare the glory of God; and the firmament sheweth his handywork" (Ps 19:1, KJV). Luther rightly criticized the theology of glory that characterized the church-state edifice of his day and which eclipsed rather than revealed the saving God of Jesus Christ only found in the cross. That very cross, however, is also a primary conduit, in an inverted and fallen world, of authentic biblical glory and kingdom advance.

Concerning the surprising and sometimes bothersome theology of the cross, I must confess that much of my cultural nurturing has predisposed me toward finding or seeing God more in success than in suffering. This work will argue that perhaps God can be found both when we "abase" and when we "abound" (Phil 4:12).

Eric Liddel's most famous quotation, forever memorialized in *Chariots of Fire*, that God created him to be fast (and succeed at wining Olympic races), and "when I run I feel his pleasure," resonated for years far more than familiarity with "Why hast Thou forsaken me" (Matt 27:46) as the locus of God's presence. Recent years and experience have broadened my understanding. Indeed, the well-intended commitment in the American context to see truth and justice win out has sometimes morphed into the false belief that truth and justice *will* win out. Thus, pragmatism, or that which wins

---

discussion in view of a tragic incident with an unchurched student and family that involved much suffering and the eventual imprisonment of the student.

14. Kandiah, "God Turns Up."

15. Kandiah, "God Turns Up."

by some ill-defined unbiblical standard, becomes the arbiter of truth and justice. Believers look for cultural or civilizational confirmation of their efforts to make a difference, or become disillusioned when such efforts seem to backfire or fail. A theology of the cross is a helpful corrective and underscores that, from a kingdom perspective, winning is not always winning. We must faithfully and lovingly press on toward maximum kingdom influence and impact without ever assuming that such efforts will be well received or that truth and justice will win out prior to Christ's return. Kingdom advance may be met with a cross.

This work advocates for a properly defined theology of cross, glory, and kingdom capable of incorporating both success *and* forsakenness as proper and biblical means of experiencing God's transforming presence and kingdom advance. And, indeed, both success and shame can be received in such a manner that God's presence is eclipsed or muted.

Not all suffering is for righteous reasons (1 Pet 2:20), and this work contends that even social justice oriented theologies of cross, suffering, and liberation can be hijacked in any or all of these ways and more: as a self-preserving industry of victimhood that creates dependency and rewards liberators; as dangerous, self-righteous utopian movements that in the name of the cross and the marginalized morph into another form of oppression; and, as anti-cultural movements most adept at identifying the sins of those in power but not so adept at identifying the sins of those challenging power. Liberators often only apply the doctrine of human depravity to oppressors and not to themselves. Hence, movements claiming to align with the *theologia crucis* may indeed be hidden but critical illustrations of the false, unbiblical, and destructive theology of glory that riled Luther. It will be argued that even compassion and social justice, certainly biblical and virtuous in principle, can be transmuted into a Trojan horse for a cancerous theology of glory.

Emphases on suffering, compassion, and the cross inevitably relate to identification with the oppressed and marginalized. As a personal illustration, as a young skeptic of the faith I was always intrigued with how my mother would attempt to reach out to those who were sitting by themselves in social situations, those struggling with physical or emotional difficulties, or those who seemed to need encouragement. When the church finally hired her to serve as a visitation coordinator, I remember thinking, "It is about time they paid her!" This skeptic and son was not really sure what to make of it at the time, but it seemed that, somehow, Mom associated her "religion thing" with reaching out to those who were marginalized or in need of encouragement.

During the sunset of her life, I remember the countless and uncomfortable hours she spent in the hospital with a dear friend in anguish from terminal cancer. In the last weeks of my mother's earthly sojourn, due to pancreatic cancer, our family remembers with some awe that during her last frozen and icy winter in Michigan she was the one cheerfully encouraging and comforting hospital staff and others in the waiting room even as she was experiencing the most uncomfortable of symptoms and procedures. She had never heard of Luther's theology of the cross. I literally had to lift her out of the van to assist her getting into the hospital to take yet another nauseating test, and her response was to encourage the medical staff and others in the waiting room.

In the hospital with another perishing loved one, and that long night was already recounted above, Luther's theology of the cross became much more personal for this academic student of the cross amidst a culture that tends first to look for God elsewhere—in victory, or in fame, or in "success," or in Christian ministry "success" (often defined quantitatively by numbers), or in false "glory." And to be clear, the many dimensions of a full-orbed theology of the cross framed that bedside crucible and included gracious forgiveness, the blessed promise of eternal life, the truth that God in Christ shares and grounds our suffering, the reality that the cross is a statement about fallen humanity and a world yet fully redeemed, the ultimate defeat of darkness and disease by the cross and resurrection, and the somewhat ironic basis for healing by the Savior's stripes (Isa 53; Rom 6; 8). Luther was cognizant of all of these biblical verities and wrote many hymns to that effect. Yet his famous and prophetic contrast between the theology of glory and the theology of the cross is a specific and especially fertile and relevant theological application of the *theologia crucis* especially to soteriology, ecclesiology, authentic piety, and cultural analysis and engagement—and this application is the focus of this work. God is found in a manger. God is found in shame. God is found in suffering. God is not found in earthly or false glory—including false political or ecclesiological glory. God is found or best revealed in the cross. It is often only in the crucible of suffering that the reality of the true future is apprehended, manifest, incarnated, and made real.

My personal observations and experiences of suffering, of course, pale in comparison to the historic and contemporary persecution and suffering of the universal and global church. Whether the number of Christian martyrs today is 10,000 or 100,000 per year,[16] one does not have to look far

---

16. Alexander, "Are There Really"; Open Doors, "World Watch List"; Chiaramonte, "Christians"; "Quick Facts."

today for verified stories such as these: "Gunmen on motorcycles kill three people when they open fire on a wedding outside a Coptic Christian church in Cairo. A twin-suicide bombing outside a church in Pakistan kills at least 75 people."[17]

The persecution of Christians in Libya especially illustrates a theology of the cross where kingdom suffering sparks kingdom advance and reveals true kingdom glory. *Christianity Today* reported,

> Undaunted by the slaughter of 21 Christians in Libya, the director of the Bible Society of Egypt saw a golden gospel opportunity. "We must have a Scripture tract ready to distribute to the nation as soon as possible," Ramez Atallah told his staff the evening an ISIS-linked group released its gruesome propaganda video. Less than 36 hours later, *Two Rows by the Sea* was sent to the printer. One week later, 1.65 million copies have been distributed in the Bible Society's largest campaign ever. It eclipses even the 1 million tracts distributed after the 2012 death of Shenouda, the Coptic "Pope of the Bible." . . . The tract contains biblical quotations about the promise of blessing amid suffering, alongside a poignant poem in colloquial Arabic:
>
> > *Who fears the other?*
> > *The row in orange, watching paradise open?*
> > *Or the row in black, with minds evil and broken?*
>
> "The design is meant so that it can be given to any Egyptian without causing offense," said Atallah. "To comfort the mourning and challenge people to commit to Christ."[18]

Similarly, the martyrdom of the Japanese journalist Kenji Goto was viewed as cruciform and kingdom-centric by his loved ones:

> Goto's 78-year-old mother, Junko Ishido, told journalists following the news of his death, "It is my only hope that we can carry on with Kenji's mission to save the children from war and poverty." She added, "Kenji has left us on a journey."
>
> Goto's wife, Rinko, said in a statement via the Rory Peck Trust, "My family and I are devastated by the news of Kenji's death. He was not just my loving husband and father to our two beautiful children, but a son, brother and friend to many around the world. . . . I remain extremely proud of my husband who reported the plight of people in conflict areas like Iraq, Somalia, and Syria. It was his passion to highlight the effects on ordinary

17 Alexander, "Are There Really."
18. Casper, "How Libya's Martyrs."

people, especially through the eyes of children, and to inform the rest of us of the tragedies of war."[19]

The stories and list of martyrs from church history are endless, with estimates of multiple millions, from the apostles and Justin Martyr to Bonhoeffer, the ten Booms, Oscar Romero, Coptic Christians, and countless others. Yet the experiences of martyrs should not devalue the cruciform reality of chronic pain—some suffer years without relief—or the dagger of losing a child or loved one, or the heroic isolation of missionary heroes bringing the gospel to the unreached. The common experience of suffering and pain, if not self-manufactured, and the suffering because of kingdom obedience, while distinct, are also unified by a robust theology of cross and kingdom. The physical or emotional pain is often unbearable, but the potential for kingdom grace and advance in all such experiences is even greater still.

I remember one of my early sermons on the red hills of Georgia where I went out of my way to emphasize the promises and blessings of God and Scripture before also noting that God does not always deliver and that the cross is central to the authentic Christianity. After the service, one group performed the ritual shaking of hands and said "Thank you for your wonderful sermon," with enthusiasm. An elderly lady, very articulate, said I reminded her of Peter Marshall. I confess that I was clueless as to who he was but apparently that was a compliment. However, a week or so later, if I understood the pastor for which I was substituting, I was told that another group in the church had a debriefing on my sermon in which I was served as the "roast pastor" for Sunday dinner. I was stunned to find that, in this rather large and typical evangelical church, many were offended at the idea that the Christian life may well involve both blessings and a cruciform life.

Some dear saints apparently and improperly read biblical stories such as Joseph and Job as guarantees of final vindication and blessings in *this* life rather than as eschatological prolepsis. The vantage point of eschatological prolepsis would interpret these blessings and vindications as a foretaste of the eternal blessings and the vindication of all true believers. These stories recount that Joseph suffered but became Prime Minister of Egypt, and that Job's fortunes were eventually restored and multiplied. In contrast to an eschatologically proleptic view, many believers wrongly surmise from such stories or the promises of Proverbs that those who are faithful will *always* receive such final vindication and blessings in *this* present life or age.

In reality these eschatologically proleptic stories instruct us that the righteous will ultimately be blessed in the new creation, but these narratives certainly do not, from an integrated biblical standpoint, guarantee that

19. Casper, "How Libya's Martyrs."

this life ends in earthly blessings and fortune for *all* the righteous. Hebrews chapter 11 is crystal clear on this matter, that many suffer and are martyred and never receive an enduring earthly blessing or vindication in this life. Paul and almost all of the apostles were martyred. Jesus perished on what was perceived as a shameful cross then was resurrected after the crucifixion as the ultimate new creation prolepsis. The biblical stories of final blessings in this life are illustrative and proleptic, and not individualistic and universal guarantees for all believers prior to Christ's return. This argument will be advanced further below in this chapter and in subsequent chapters, but it is theologically sound to speak of Joseph and Job as proleptic heroes of the faith.

One individual in the congregation was particularly unconvinced by the suggestion that historical context is critical when applying the Old Testament corporate promises of blessing to every individual Christian in every possible historical context and situation. They seemed persuaded that the Bible teaches exemption from a cruciform life. They wondered if the Bible was simply wrong. The takeaway from this experience was just how widespread such suppositions about suffering and sacrifice might be in the evangelical world.

Such assumptions also seemed to be central to why so many of the thousands of American evangelical collegians I worked with as a professor or chaplain struggled so greatly with the problem of evil. Some landed in atheism after wrestling with this problem. Religion was not an opiate for most of these students, but they had thought they had heard all of their life that belief in Christ provided meaning, purpose, happiness, and a wonderful life where God would almost always protect believers, from harm, sometimes using angels, especially if one had true faith. I especially remember one conversation where a tragic car accident, brought on by the irresponsible behavior of the student who was suffering, was viewed as sufficient reason not to believe in God any longer.

Perhaps this is an unnecessary detour into Western evangelical spirituality, but these questions and concerns were certainly critical for many. One of my well-published professors at Wheaton temporarily threw out his faith after reflecting on the problem of suffering. Indeed, having been raised in a very supportive and nurturing but very American environment, I have at times wrestled with such questions. The questions are fair but often emerge from a cultural context that conditions some of us not to expect pain, shame, or suffering. The theology of cross, kingdom, and glory has been of great assistance with re-framing such experiences and providing some measure of liberation from the seeming spiritual narcissism so prevalent in the West.

This work is admittedly addressing cross, kingdom, and glory in a Western context but hopefully with global relevance and application.

The concept of martyrdom or taking up one's cross is not new. The theology of the cross is, naturally, rooted in the cross of Christ, but these stories of suffering illustrate how some forms of suffering today unite a theology of the cross, sacrifice, kingdom advance, and true kingdom glory. This present work seeks to clarify, integrate, augment, and apply (for twenty-first-century mission) key emphases of major theologies of the cross (and theologies of glory).

Hence, Luther's theology of the cross, always of great interest and often perplexing, has continued to take on new meaning and iterations, and sparked my continued research, writing, and reflection as well as those of a host of scholars—a half-millennium after the Reformation.

A TIMELY THEOLOGY THAT SUBSUMES SUFFERING AND THEODICY

It is important to emphasize at this juncture that the theology of the cross offers much more than comfort to the bereaved or inspiration for ministry to the marginalized. The references to suffering from physical illness discussed in this chapter are windows or even analogies to a comprehensive theology of the cross. All experience suffering and death, but not all suffering and death are kingdom-centric or necessarily facilitate kingdom advance. Yet this work concurs with Luther, however, that the physical suffering and death of believers—and this refers not only to persecution and martyrdom—certainly has the potential to be kingdom-centric.

As I am concluding this book another dear loved one is convalescing from recent surgery and still wrestling with lingering paralysis and pain, after also enduring a delayed surgery a few years ago that required corrective surgery followed by a repeat of the original failed surgery. This entire journey of multiple health challenges has created significant discomfort and sleep management issues over the period of a number of years. Another close family member had cancer surgery and the doctor operated on the wrong side of the body, even after clear instructions from the patient just prior to surgery. This relative also had to have a repeat surgery some four hours from her home, was drawn into endless paperwork, and the delayed surgery may have even shortened her earthly sojourn. A beloved in-law has had endless health issues and pain management issues for decades. A friend and colleague lost a young child. Sooner or later we all traverse these troubled waters. While these experiences do not qualify as persecution in the normal sense of the term, and certainly pale in comparison to the pain or suffering of many believers from time immemorial, this work will nevertheless contend that a sound and robust theology of cross and kingdom encompasses and illuminates such journeys.

As will be demonstrated in Part 2, the *theologia crucis* includes, but is far, far more than, a theodicy or theology of suffering and touches on the very nature of God, humanity, salvation, epistemology, history, evil, suffering, the mystery of evil, cultural and political engagement, the mission of the church, and, especially, the eschatology that frames this entire staurological, theological trajectory. A properly framed and sound theology of the cross and glory is multivalent.

A modified and refined theology of the cross, a theology largely associated with Martin Luther's famous *theologia crucis*, also has potent theological, philosophical relevance and ministry applicability for the twenty-first-century global context of post-Christendom and ultramodern syncretism.[20] This potency or relevance has only strengthened as forces increasingly gather to crush Christian influence and to marginalize or suppress the free exercise of speech and faith. The historic mega-trend in many areas of the West and throughout the globe is the increased diminishment of biblical beliefs and practices, including the torture and persecution of believers. Individuals or churches that only find God in numerical or cultural victories, or ecstatic and escapist praise and worship, may be less than prepared for twenty-first-century realties and ministry.

Edwin Lutzer shared a story from a German man who had resided in Nazi Germany as the anti-Semitic fires of hate swept through the nation and kindled brutal and heartless mass exterminations. The documentation of this story by Lutzer is less than desired, but the recollection vividly recounts how escapist spirituality, untethered from the reality and theology of the cross, ill prepares believers for authentic kingdom service:

> I lived in Germany during the Nazi Holocaust. I considered myself a Christian. We heard stories of what was happening to the Jews, but we tried to distance ourselves from it, because, what could anyone do to stop it?
>
> A railroad track ran behind our small church and each Sunday morning we could hear the whistle in the distance and then the wheels coming over the tracks. We became disturbed

20. Concerning the concept of "ultramodern" as the "last gasp" of modernism, and a better framework for understanding what often flies as postmodern, see Oden, "Long Journey," 77–92. This present work accepts much of Oden's argument but prefers to refer to this age not as primarily postmodern or ultramodern but as the age of either ultramodern or postmodern syncretism.

when we heard the cries coming from the train as it passed by. We realized that it was carrying Jews like cattle in the cars!

Week after week the whistle would blow. We dreaded to hear the sound of those wheels because we knew we would hear the cries of the Jews en route to a death camp. Their screams tormented us.

We knew the time the train was coming and when we heard the whistle blow we began singing hymns. By the time the train came past our church we were singing at the top of our voices. If we heard the screams, we sang more loudly and soon we heard them no more.

Years have passed and no one talks about it anymore. But I still hear that train whistle in my sleep. God forgive me; forgive all of us who called ourselves Christians yet did nothing to intervene.[21]

Dietrich Bonhoeffer's *Cost of Discipleship*, which applied Jesus' teaching on the kingdom from the Sermon on the Mount to this troubled historical context, concurs that countless Christians were more German or Nazi than Christian during these dark days. These Christians did not respond to the call of the cross: "When Christ calls a man . . . he bids him come and die."[22] The cross and the kingdom define biblical piety and Christlikeness.

Similarly, works and movements such as the *Confession of Belhar* or the *Kairos Document*,[23] birthed amidst apartheid, document and underscore Bonhoeffer's claim that countless "Christians" exhibit more loyalty to transient and unjust kingdoms than to the everlasting kingdom of God. This observation is not intended, however, to gloss over some of the naïve and liberationist assumptions of the *Kairos* movement, or the truism that liberationist movements are also and especially susceptible to being guilty of the same cultural accommodation and abuse of power as the very oppressors they critique or attempt to overthrow. The *Kairos Document*, via its critique of state theology and church theology, well illustrates a relevant, historic, and twentieth-century application of Luther's critique of the theology of glory.

21. Lutzer, *Hitler's Cross*, 99–100.
22. Bonhoeffer, *Cost of Discipleship*, 11.
23. Kairos Theologians, *Kairos Document*.

A THEMATIC, REPRESENTATIVE METHODOLOGY AND ESCHATOLOGICAL HEURISTIC

This book seeks to address the theology of the cross via the following: reviewing, evaluating, and modifying select and representative perspectives (e.g., Kadai, Brian, Saler, and Wright)[24] and classical themes of the *theologia crucis*; expanding the *theologia crucis* to include other key elements; proffering an alternative to deterministic assumptions often distorting this rich theology; integrating an enhanced theology of the cross with an eschatological theology of the kingdom; identifying normative themes for the future; and, applying a missional theology of the cross and kingdom to the contemporary and civilizational context. The review of Brian and Saler also directly touches on the thought of Barth and Moltmann.

This work focuses and builds upon the works of these selected authors that directly address and best articulate their theologies of the cross. This work does not pretend to offer a comprehensive theology of the cross—or a theology of the kingdom or glory for that matter—that encompasses all possible biblical and theological meanings of the cross or the atonement. This book focuses on key emphases in representative theologies of the cross as opposed to providing a comprehensive or historical overview and analysis of countless authors. Such fine overviews have been provided by others.[25] Wright was most helpful in his recent *Revolution*, but even he barely scratched the surface on all of these nuances and theories in a book exceeding four hundred pages. The axiom for this discussion, which interacts with the contemporary interpreters referenced in the prior paragraph, is Luther's cross and glory complex, with his largely negative presentation of the theology of glory and his positive presentation of the theology of the cross. This is not a work on Luther, but what were Luther's core emphases and how have our contemporary and representative authors responded, modified, or applied these concepts? What is or should be the future of these core concepts and themes?

I found it most helpful and particularly intriguing to approach the multiple themes associated with the theology of the cross from a philosophical, eschatological, and non-deterministic theological perspective. My PhD research focus at Baylor was in eschatology, with a major in religion or theology and an outside minor in political science—largely political philosophy. At the time of this writing, I served as Provost at a large interdenominational

---

24. Kadai, "Luther's Theology," 169–204; Brian, *Covering Up Luther*; Saler, *Theologia*; Wright, *Day the Revolution Began*. This work will flesh out the perspectives of these works that will serve as the springboard for the constructive work in Part 2.

25. See Madsen, *Theology*.

but Wesleyan-Arminian oriented theological seminary.[26] For some two decades I have taught and interacted with students on issues related to philosophy, theology, theological methodology, apologetics, and the possibility of the knowledge of God. Luther's *theologia crucis* is typically represented as discounting all knowledge of God not centered in the revelation of the cross while also critiquing any false knowledge of God—referred to as a theology of glory—derived apart from "by grace alone" (see Eph 2:8–10) and Christocentric and crucicentric revelation. Apologetics is marginal at best if Luther's theology of the cross is sound. Hence, the relationship between the theology of the cross and my theological and philosophical background fueled this research interest.

Additionally, scholars are increasingly exploring the relevance of the theology of the cross and glory to the post-Christian, post-Christendom, postmodern, post-critical, or ultramodern cultural and philosophical situation.[27] Such reflections also resonate with my personal and professional background, teaching experience, and involvement in apologetic inquiry and ministry.[28]

This book is not another text or article recounting or clarifying Luther's theology of the cross or Barth's view or any other specific scholarly perspective. Many such fine works exist. This book builds on those works, and such tasks have already been completed, and in the future such analyses of individual scholars should be left to specialists. *What follows is theological and philosophical reflection, exploration, and argument centered on the major emphases associated with representative and classical theologies of the cross.* Since this book is more of a theological and philosophical heuristic, I attempted to limit the size of the chapters when possible by focusing on the key arguments. Some chapters require considerable length in order to make the case for the theses of this book. The reader of this work should be able to grasp the arguments and preliminary evidence and reasoning more rapidly and then contribute to the scholarly community dialog on the *theologia crucis*. The hope is that this work assists to some degree with this valuable exploration. This book is also not an attempt to explore or construct Wesley's or a Wesleyan theology of the cross, which also should be left to leading Wesley scholars. Arminian assumptions will be compared and contrasted with Luther's assumptions, and a guest author, Dr. J. Steven O'Malley, will flesh out Wesleyan and pietistic connections. However, the

---

26. And, as always, this work and the work of professors at this institution are not officially endorsed by the institution.

27. See chapters 2 and 13.

28. Including a season of skepticism before coming to faith and a lifelong quest engaging such questions.

primary limitation of this work is that the importance of this topic surely requires the equivalent of three to five years of uninterrupted theological dialog, research, reflection, and writing. Such time, focus, and intensity simply was not congruent with the realities of my Provost responsibilities and other writing projects. However, the alternative of not attempting substantively to address this historically, culturally, and existentially relevant subject seemed more problematic than attempting this project. Hence, I hesitatingly rushed forward with this book, with the prayerful hope of making at least a slight contribution, by grace, to the dialog on the cross and kingdom.

One of the key challenges addressed in this work is the lack of precision concerning exactly what constitutes a theology of the cross or Luther's theology of the cross. An attempt has been made to *identify and clarify the primary and relevant themes for today in Luther and other representative writers*. What is certain and which will be argued throughout this work is that the key motifs associated with Luther's theology of the cross, as mediated through select scholars reviewed in this work, are philosophically, theologically, and historically timely at this juncture of world history, church history, and mission.

Personal Suffering

My passion for this project especially emerged from multiple sources. Christian leaders, pastors, academics, and laity often lack a theology-of-the-cross framework for intense personal suffering—for self or others. Our individualistic culture asks, "Why me," or, "Why her," or, "Why him," which is understandable, but the query is often disconnected from a robust theology of cross and kingdom, much less a robust ecclesiology. This disconnection has been conspicuous in over two decades of dialog with evangelical college students and evangelical laity struggling with the problem of evil and suffering. Without attempting to be the least bit pejorative, the problem-of-evil questions I have often encountered seem to be rooted in a culturally conditioned and hyper-individualistic form of narcissism and spiritual consumerism. This narcissism is in the air we breathe in many quarters of the globe. The problem of evil cannot possibly be resolved or meliorated in such a flawed theological and philosophical context.

In contrast, a broader cross and kingdom framework made sense in recent years, inasmuch as making experiential and emotional sense is possible in such situations, of the multiple losses and suffering of loved ones. While theodicy and suffering overlap, it is important to distinguish between a theology of evil and suffering (or a theodicy) and a theology of the cross, with the latter most helpfully informing, grounding, and framing the former. Suffering connected to a comprehensive theological vision and optimistic kingdom *telos* is much preferred to endless existential and hyper-individualistic angst and "why me!" wrestlings with theodicy.

Corporate, Non-Individualistic, and Proleptic Theodicy

Indeed, while not the focus, this work will assume and proffer a corporate, non-individualistic, and proleptic theodicy rooted in a missional theology of cross and kingdom. The countless biblical promises of divine deliverance from captivity (e.g., the Psalms) and suffering are devastating to individual lives and the mission of the church when distorted through the lens of individualism—that *I* will always be protected and delivered from all suffering and pain in the present in every possible historical and cultural context.

Deliverance from suffering and pain in this age is always kingdom-centric and initiatory or proleptic rather than egocentric and universal. Careful reviewers of the recently released film *Darkest Hour* cannot miss how this film grippingly portrays Churchill and England's non-individualistic and anti-accommodationist response to the blitzkrieg pace at which Hitler's shadow was engulfing and inflaming the world in genocide, death, and destruction.

The evil Reich was countered with the sheer faith and eschatological confidence that Light would ultimately triumph over darkness and bring a great deliverance, often at the cost of the ultimate sacrifice for hundreds of thousands of individuals, families, and communities. The mission and eschatological vision of never, never, never compromising with darkness only advances in a fashion analogous to *via dolorosa*.

Some will be amazingly and miraculously delivered, such as the soldiers trapped at Dunkirk in 1940. Some will not be delivered in the present age, such as the tens of thousands who delayed the German advance to Dunkirk and who saved hundreds of thousands of lives if not the world and saved the British forces needed to continue the fight as Europe staggered. These cruciform heroes who survived and were not evacuated at Dunkirk experienced mistreatment, abuse, shame, forced consumption of putrid food and ditch water, death marches, slave labor, salt mines, and summary executions.[29] For many, if not most, deliverance was only in the age to come.

Theologia crucis means that deliverance is *not* of every individual life in this present age. The eschatological element is essential to theologies of cross, kingdom, evil, and suffering. *Theodicy without eschatology is*

29. Boissoneault, "True Story of Dunkirk."

preposterous. The Psalms regularly speak of deliverance from captivity and evil (e.g., Ps 121; 125), yet clearly not every faithful individual or family was delivered—some were martyred (see Heb 11). In the Pentateuch, not every individual reached the Promised Land. Not every individual was spared in all battles. The apostles experienced protection, deliverance, and also stoning and crucifixion. Some who were miraculously delivered (e.g., Paul) to advance the mission were also executed—and even beheaded.

Deliverance, in the present age, is not from all suffering, weakness, torture, the sense of forsakenness, *Anfechtung*, and death. The deliverance of some, and the advance of Light, is a proleptic mission coupled with a non-utopian vision. To repeat, not all are healed. Not all are delivered. Not all are spared in the present age. All will be delivered in the *eschaton*. Those who "hath" no "greater love" (John 15:13, KJV) proleptically envelop the present, bring the future into the present, save many, reveal the future, and mediate the victorious God of the future. They sow the seeds of final deliverance for God's creatures and good creation. Deliverance is proleptic, initiatory, penultimate, and ultimate.

Dietrich Bonhoeffer, famous for proclaiming, "When Christ calls a man, he bids him come and die," cited immediately above, penned these most relevant words on July 28, 1944:

> Now, is it right to see the Old Testament blessing against the cross? That is what Kierkegaard did. That makes the cross, or at least suffering, an abstract principle; and that is just what gives rise to an unhealthy Methodism, which deprives suffering of its element of contingency as a divine ordinance. It's true that in the Old Testament the person who receives the blessing has to endure a great deal of suffering (e.g., Abraham, Isaac, Jacob, and Joseph), but this never leads to the idea that fortune and suffering, blessing and cross are mutually exclusive and contradictory—nor does it in the New Testament. Indeed, the only difference between the Old and New Testaments in this respect is that in the Old the blessing includes the cross, and in the New the cross includes the blessing.
>
> To turn to a different point: not only action, but also suffering is a way to freedom. In suffering, the deliverance consists in our being allowed to put the matter out of our own hands into God's hands. In this sense death is the crowning of human freedom. Whether the human died as a matter of faith or not depends on whether we understand our suffering as an extension

of our action and a completion of freedom. I think that is very important and very comforting.[30]

This reading of theodicy and the theology of the cross is well suited for the present age—or perhaps the present age is well suited for this theology?

Theological Math

Sometimes we simply need to do the theological math concerning the theology of the cross. In an upside-down world, civilization, or community, authentic kingdom Christians will oft suffer shame, ridicule, and persecution. The intensity of that opposition will depend upon the specific historical, cultural, and spiritual context. The suggestion that the waves of persecution in the early church had more to do with the lack of faith of the persecuted kingdom Christians rather than the lack of faith of the Emperor or various rulers and religious leaders seems rather mindless. In contexts more favorable to the gospel and Christian values, Christians may actually flourish. Perhaps Billy Graham's reception in many quarters is illustrative. Again, and this merits repeating in our narcissistic age, the math of the cross, kingdom, and glory means that kingdom Christians will suffer or flourish based on the specific historical and spiritual context. Perhaps this math is also reflected in how Matt 10:14 discriminates between towns that merit the shaking of the dust from one's feet and those that do not.

John Wesley's ministry underscores this critical and hermeneutical concept of cruciform context. Wesley marveled in his later years at the respectability he had achieved in English society after being banned from Oxford, jeered, threatened, banned from churches, and even shunned from his own father's church—and as most know, he concluded it best to preach from his father's tomb just outside since he had been denied access to his father's pulpit. Wesley recounts how the Methodist revival emerged from the prior Arminian movement where an Arminian was often viewed as a mad dog. Many who heard Arminians speak were "put into fright at once: They run away from him [the Arminian] with all speed and diligence; and will hardly stop, unless it be to throw a stone at the dreadful and mischievous animal." Indeed, according to Wesley, Arminians (and Wesley founded a magazine inspired by that name) "were put to death, some banished, some imprisoned for life, all turned out of their employments, and made incapable of holding any office, either in Church or State."[31] Hence, there

30. Bonhoeffer, *Letters*, 374.
31. Wesley, "What Is an Arminian," 193–95.

should be no surprise at John Wesley achieving a measure of respectability late in life, *after* the historical, cultural, and cruciform context had been greatly impacted by revival. Wesley's experience of persecution, and even Luther's, was mild compared to countless heroes of the faith, especially in prior centuries and other regions of the globe, but such experiences likely describe and foretell the experience of Christlike and cruiciform believers as the West decays and post-Christian and post-Christendom morphs toward an anti-Christian cruciform context.

Age of Post

The age of "post" (i.e., post-Christian, militant post-Christian, post-Christendom, postmodern, post-critical, ultramodern, syncretistic) especially connects with a theology and theodicy of cross and glory. With some three decades of experience with apologetics and philosophy, and working with countless "post" students and skeptics, relevant issues leap from the pages of themes associated with the theology of the cross. The theology of the kingdom has dominated evangelicalism for centuries, and hopefully a full-orbed theology of cross, kingdom, and glory will guide the future.

Apologetics

Luther and Barth both, as is suggested in chapters 2 and 6, essentially destroyed a biblical and intellectually defensible approach to apologetics in part because of distortions and false dichotomies in their understanding of the theology and the revelatory or epistemological status of the cross. In subjection to the Word of God, this distortion hopefully can be countered while also preserving critical insights of the theology of the cross related to epistemology and apologetics. The cross does not destroy philosophy and apologetics; the cross redeems apologetics and philosophy.

Eschatology

As noted, my PhD research focused on eschatology. Rather than running from eschatology because of myriad and ill-informed eschatological distortions (dubbed eschatomania by Millard Erickson),[32] eschatology has been, during important moments in church history, and should be passionate fuel for genuine and shrewd kingdom advance.

32. Millard Erickson, *Christian Theology*, 1152.

The profound implications of eschatology for the theology of the cross first began to crystalize in my thinking and writings during my PhD studies decades prior to the publication, popularization, and proliferation of many great works by others on new creation eschatology or theologies of the cross. After immersing myself in eschatological literature, it became rather lucid that kingdom impact and influence were fundamentally theological and eschatological and that such impact, "revolves around the effectiveness of the church of the cross. Crucifixion and sacrifice precede resurrection and transformation."[33] The biblical theology of cross and kingdom includes but is far more relevant, compelling, theologically rich, and missionally comprehensive than the willingness to endure scorn, persecution, and martyrdom. Kingdom advance is cruciform.

First, the classical liberal removal of the scandal of the cross from authentic kingdom advance was most evident in contemporary theological literature of the late nineteenth and early twentieth centuries: "H. R. Niebuhr's criticism of classical liberal theology . . . [encapsulated] the vulnerability of what his brother Reinhold also viewed as a faulty theological anthropology: 'A God without wrath brought men without sin into a kingdom without judgment through the ministrations of a Christ without a cross.'"[34] An effective theology of cross and kingdom illuminates the theological, cultural, and philosophical context.

Second, apart from the eschatological Christ-event of the cross and resurrection—a radical statement about human and civilizational depravity and a radical statement about the victory of the cross—kingdom advance is theologically incoherent[35]: "The *Parousia* is not yet, but the cross and resurrection mean that already 'Christ rules as Lord over all things on heaven and on earth!'"[36] This victory means that "racism, power struggles, and unjust usage of force are antichrist, for these powers already have been judged at the cross and ultimately have no future."[37] The synoptic and incarnational "It is finished" Christ-event of cross and resurrection births the proleptic new creation mission of the called-out ones, meaning the church. Through

33. Matthews, "Approximating," 414–15.

34. Matthews, "Approximating," 49; Niebuhr, *Kingdom*, 193. The Niebuhr quote was taken directly from Niebuhr's writings, but it was also cited in Matthews, "Approximating."

35. The singular use of *event* is used intentionally here as the biblical perspective views the multifaceted Christ-event (i.e., incarnation, birth, life, teaching, death, resurrection, ascension, sending of the Spirit) as a singular eschatological Christ-event.

36. Matthews, "Approximating," 363, introducing then citing Cullmann, *Christ and Time*, 211. The Cullmann citation is directly from the primary source.

37. Matthews, "Approximating," 40–42.

the cross alone, grace alone, and faith in Christ alone, the reborn are now, in this age, the non-utopian agents of the proleptic new creation.

Third, it became evident that cruciform and kenotic *agape* "requires the church, the body of Christ, to experience the cross as it empties itself in the strain to avert another Auschwitz [as a symbol of all genocide, enslavement, abuse and oppression]."[38] Cruciform *agape* is central to a biblical theology of the cross. Surely kenotic *agape* requires that, as a goal, "there must be no more gas chambers or killing fields."[39] Surely a theology of the cross means that the unexpected presence of God is somehow surprisingly present amidst genocide, as with the ministry of Betsie and Corrie ten Boom during World War II in occupied Holland and the concentration camps. Betsie often commented, "There is no pit so deep that God's love is not deeper still."[40]

Surely the presence of the future "demands the liberation of the [truly] oppressed." Surely "the presence of the future requires the preservation and restoration of the present creation that will be the locus of the future."[41] This future may be partially realized in the current age.

Fourth, "Christianity's transformational way of the cross . . . loves the world while ever urging the present misguided world order toward its true telos."[42] The theology of cross and kingdom are both prophetic and lovingly engaged with the fallen world that God loves.

Fifth, and a lengthy quote is helpful as this juncture, these cruciform eschatological reflections implied that, for many churches,

> the adoption of a global and transformational [cruciform and eschatologically approximative] vista would constitute nothing less than an ecclesial reformation. Church piety too often degenerates into a spiritual narcissism [or even a spiritual sensualism], hedonism, and egocentrism. The meeting of individual needs, through proclamation, counsel, worship, and singing is biblically sound but can become the exclusive or nearly exclusive preoccupation of the church. [It has been humorously noted that in many churches prayers are rarely connected to global, cruciform kingdom advance and sound like "organ recitals." In other words, while personal physical needs are most appropriate prayer petitions, the absence of passionate petitions for kingdom work around the world or cultural and civilizational

38. Matthews, "Approximating," 413.
39. Matthews, "Approximating," 413.
40. For a relevant summary of this story, see Radcliff, "War Story."
41. Matthews, "Approximating," 413.
42. Matthews, "Approximating," 346.

crises and opportunities for amelioration are symptomatic of a rather flawed eschatology. In addition, the] . . . voluntaristic nature of the American churches, where the popular pastor who meets needs or best entertains is viewed as the successful pastor, only encourages this spiritual hedonism. This spiritual sensualism may reflect the mentality of a larger culture that ceaselessly strives for some new emotional, sexual [or romantic], drug-induced, [adrenaline-driven] or experiential high. People may attend church for the same types of reasons they attend [a rock concert or] a self-help class—not to follow Christ and Him crucified but to chase after personal fulfillment [and good feelings]. A church that is entirely turned in upon itself and fixated with the personal benefits of belief in God is idolatrous. In contrast, the journey towards global transformation is Theocentric, Christocentric, Creation-centered, and other-centered, without ignoring the meeting of personal needs. The journey usually if not always involves the cross. The church is the community of the crucified—crucified so that others might participate in millennial approximation in the present and millennial realization in the future. The journey requires a shrewd involvement in the world under the telos of the future world. Such involvement is the antithesis of a spiritually narcissistic [eschatology] . . . that ceaselessly chases after spiritual blessings [or escape, or good feelings] in the name of worship or devotion to God. Unfortunately, such egocentrism is only natural in a church that is passively waiting for the collapse of civilization.[43]

If your church seems more like Starbucks, a movie experience, or a rock concert than a biblical church experience, it probably is. And I make this observation as one who loves good movies, grew up on hard rock and massive rock concerts, and truly enjoys a well-made vanilla steamer.

The primary shift in my thinking in recent decades relative to this quotation, rooted somewhat in a theology of the cross, is that the use of "transformation" or "social transformation" needs to be markedly qualified or consistently replaced with terms such as the following: impact, influence, proleptic, or approximation.[44] The aforementioned eschatological reformation of conservative to moderate American evangelical churches still seems less than fully realized, in spite of the heroic work of many scholars, including Wright.[45] Perhaps this failure is, in part, because we have pursued

43. Matthews, "Approximating," 431–32.

44. See especially chapters 11 and 12.

45. See chapter 11.

transformation rather than influence and impact, resulting in sporadic, incoherent cultural engagement and frequent disillusionment.

Hence, over two decades ago, it became most evident that the theology of the cross is better articulated within an eschatological framework as a theology of cross and kingdom. It also became evident that this eschatological framework for the cross included emphases such as the new creation, heaven as inclusive of an incarnational and earthly paradise lost now being regained, the well-known already-not-yet conception of the kingdom, and, issuing forth from the already-not-yet theology, kingdom approximation rather than any form of kingdom utopianism. This argument also included rejection of the rather Platonic understanding of a universe completely abolished rather than redeemed by Christ's return. Yet while the kingdom can be approximated now, and the redeemed cosmos may well be our eternal future, accelerated or sluggish, naïve or shrewd utopianisms all are biblically suspect, run counter to sound theological anthropology, and all utopianisms ultimately mislead the church and fail.

In subsequent years of ministry and research, it has become most evident that the theological norm of "cross and kingdom" must replace "cross" relative to future theologies of the cross. This is not to say that the phrase "theology of the cross" cannot be used appropriately and biblically in isolation. This is to say that the theological norm for such references should always be tethered to the unitary theology of cross and kingdom. It will be argued, especially in chapters 8–10, that the general eschatological framework of Oscar Cullmann is especially helpful and precise relative to this unitary task, and he both lays the foundation for and clarifies Wright's more recent theology of the cross and theology of heaven—with heaven defined as earth transformed.

The cross is a central eschatological event inseparable from the larger Christ-event (the incarnation, birth, life, teaching, death, resurrection, ascension, and sending of the Spirit). For Jesus, the cross is framed within his central, repetitive, constant teaching on the already-not-yet kingdom enveloping of the present and the kingdom's future total victory. It will be maintained, especially in chapter 12, that this eschatological or new creation framework should guide and ground the cruciform holiness, mission, and ecclesiology of the church.

Holiness and Christlikeness

For personal and theological reasons, what is often referred to in various ways as holiness, Christlikeness, Christian formation, and spiritual formation has been a passionate and lifelong journey. As a college student, I even requested and completed a four semester-hour independent study on spiritual formation under a Wesleyan scholar. While this book is not a work on Christian holiness, I am increasingly convinced that many of the contemporary options and movements for spiritual formation, holiness, Christlikeness, sacramental spirituality, spiritual power, signs and wonders, or renewal, while not completely flawed, all need to traverse deeply through the waters of a theology of cross and kingdom. This recommendation includes, as noted earlier in this chapter, the cross and kingdom filtering of activities and experiences such as retreats, ecstatic worship, new movements, Christian concerts and conferences, proffered steps to Christian maturity, models of Christian community, and sacramental theology and worship.

The way of the cross brings a needed reality to all such models and means for holiness or Christlikeness. The wartime journey of the ten Booms courageously rescuing God's people and being carted off to minister, yes minister, at Scheveningen, Herzogenbusch, and Ravensbrück, reflected and formed an authentic holiness that contrasts greatly with the seeming unreality of much of what passes today for spirituality and Christlikeness: For "we also exult [or glory] in our tribulations, knowing that tribulation brings about perseverance; and perseverance, proven character; and proven character, hope; and hope does not disappoint, because the love of God has been poured out within our hearts through the Holy Spirit who was given to us" (Rom 5:3–4). As noted already, the tribulations of the early church or evangelical believers across the globe today, such as in Africa, Syria, Iraq, or North Korea, also bring this same reality check to our theological table talk.

Luther's theology of the cross and his critique of the theology of glory need refinement yet forever keep in check all triumphalist, human, ecclesial, missional, civilizational hubris and eschatological envisioning. The seemingly uncontrollable non-cruciform urges, even in Christian quarters, to engage in addictive image management, or to defend reputations rudely, or to desire or demand to receive glory, honor, and praise and always be proven right, or to view worldly weakness, suffering, or health as a curse rather than a potential blessing, or only to seek the voice and counsel of the successful—all fall away at the foot of the cross. While there is certainly a time and place for the reluctant and missional defense of one's reputation and ministry (2 Cor 11–12), the current cultural context of proliferating, militant, and rude self-advocacy stands in stark contrast to the silence of Christ on trial on the eve of his publicly displayed suffering (Acts 1:3) and incarnational *theologia crucis*.

For Luther, the theology of the cross must be starkly contrasted with this self-absorbed or culturally idolatrous theology of glory. For Luther, this distinction is a nonnegotiable and major theological watershed.

Luther's point is well taken and lauded, yet for the Johanine literature the cross of Christ and the cross of Peter also eschatologically *glorify* the Son and the Father through the Spirit.[46] Hence, cross and glory, properly and biblically defined, are ultimately united and unleash the authentic and proleptic kingdom of God via the Spirit.

It will be argued that a properly framed and approximative theology of the kingdom unifies the theology of the cross and the theology of glory. This unified and proleptic theology of cross, glory, and kingdom properly defines our pursuit of Christlikeness (or holiness) and, likewise, animates, clarifies, guides, and disciplines our cultural and civilizational engagement. A biblical theology of the cross is kingdom-centric and focused, yet it is also philosophically full-orbed, biblically comprehensive, theologically comprehensive, and multi-complex, enveloping multiple layers and emphases. The theology of the cross is more than one affirmation or nuance. Reducing a theology of the cross to a single emphasis, e.g., that it is in opposition to a theology of glory, or that it only has to do with epistemology, distorts both Scripture and the *theologia crucis.*

The theology of the cross is no passing fancy, as demonstrated by the literature referenced in this work, and it "belongs to the beginnings of the Church, the reformation of the Church, and the modernization [and postmodernization] of the Church."[47] It should also be added that it is certainly rooted in Scripture and, as noted, especially belongs to and is relevant to an era experiencing the postmodernization or ultramodernization of the church and culture. The church typically accommodates to culture, and much of contemporary culture worships health, wealth, feelings, and experience and suppresses the reality of suffering and the cross. Indeed, a properly framed theology of cross and glory may never have been more relevant.

A SUMMARY AND OVERVIEW OF THEOLOGICAL TRAJECTORIES

Hence, one half-millennium after Wittenberg, philosophical and theological reflection on key elements of Luther's *theologia crucis* and his attendant theology of glory—and subsequent iterations of both theological emphases— serve as most fertile ground for relevant and impactful kingdom theology,

46. See the italicized Scriptures in this chapter.

47. Madsen, *Theology*, 231.

ministry, and constructive civilizational engagement. This theological orientation has many nuances, even in Luther, with a recurring emphasis on how the hiddenness of God amidst the scandal of the cross is the locus of God's work in the world and actual, authentic, saving knowledge of God and God's nature. For Luther, this anchor (for the whole of theology) is also an essential cruciform context for spiritual growth through suffering. Kadai argues that the *theologia crucis* is also a core and foundational constant in the whole of Luther's theology.[48]

Luther's masterful theological proposal, once filtered and modified,[49] has countless and profound biblical applications amidst post-Christendom and syncretistic postmodernity or ultramodernity.[50] Such applications are addressed throughout the work, especially in chapter 13.

Theologia crucis is most applicable to this increasingly post-Christendom cultural and philosophical context where orthodox Christianity and the evangelical movement[51] in the West are progressively marginalized from centers of power and sometimes persecuted. Reformed theology has often advocated for the cultural or creation mandate. Segments of American evangelicalism have often lamented the decline of civilization and the need to save America or the West, often coterminous with predicting the end of civilization. Wesley preached hopefully of the "General Spread of the Gospel" (in a bimillennial fashion),[52] and in recent centuries many Wesleyan, Reformed, and even liberal theological leaders were postmillennial to some degree and hopeful of a coming *Christian Century*.[53] The new reality today,

48. Kadai, "Luther's Theology," 183.

49. E.g., from salient hermeneutical and epistemological flaw, which is partially the task of this work. See chapters 3 and 5–7.

50. For a clarification of terminology related to postmodernity, see chapter 13.

51. The debate concerning how to define *evangelical* and *evangelicalism* has become somewhat overworked. Evangelicalism here is used to refer to American evangelicalism and American-influenced evangelicalism in Europe and across the globe, from some continuity from the American colonial era to the present, but especially referring to the post-fundamentalist evangelicalism emerging after World War II. It is more than common knowledge that the definition of evangelicalism or American evangelicalism is fraught with challenges. See Dochuk et al., *American Evangelicalism*; "Quick Facts." Note that chapter 3 addresses the influence of both Jonathan Edwards and Francis Asbury, thus broadening the definition of American evangelicalism

52. Wesley, "General Spread of the Gospel."

53. This magazine aimed more at progressive, classical liberal, and neoorthodox constituents, yet it symbolized widespread utopianism and the vision of Christendom. Also see, concerning the prevalence, power, and influence of postmillennial eschatology: Smith, *Revivalism*. Eschatology is jet fuel for world changers, and the dynamism of powerful and influential social movements. Martin Luther King Jr.'s well-known envisioning or dream is yet another classic example.

to one degree or another depending on the global region, regional demographics, or even local demographics, is an era increasingly characterized by diminishing Christian influence or even anti-Christian influence.

The global evangelical movement is increasingly in tension with any theology of glory that emphasizes human ability, human knowledge, political success, or cultural presence and impact. God's work in the West after Christendom, though the United States has not completely followed suit or pace in emulating Europe, often seems *absconditus* and culturally peripheral. This theology is especially relevant in an ultramodern syncretistic context where non-individualistic knowledge claims and any religious metanarrative for culture or civilization are most suspect or met with extreme *animus*. Preaching, teaching, and evangelistic efforts that move beyond "this is just my opinion," or "it makes me feel good," or "it works for me," or suggest a normative truth that is more than "true for me" are increasingly and quickly crucified by the hegemonic cultural consensus.

As the church experiences culturally and governmentally enforced privatization or persecution in many quarters of the globe, a theology properly defined and rooted in the forsakenness of the cross and the hiddenness of God self-evidently has immediate and potent application.

In addition to mandated and voluntary privatization, many megachurches and Christian organizations seem increasingly obsessed with a consumerist-oriented mission and culture, success, happiness, health, and wealth. Even Christian organizations not espousing health and wealth often emphasize fiscal and numerical health as the primary metric or evidence for kingdom success and divine blessing.

Luther, no doubt, is turning in his grave and concerned that his warnings about the theology of glory are going unheeded in the global *evangelische kirche*.[54] While conservative American evangelical cultural engagement has often been less than tactful or less than "speaking the truth in love," the "wild boar loose in the vineyard,"[55] who championed the theology of the cross, would doubtless be humored and irritated by the supposition of some evangelicals that cultural losses suggest that it is time for cultural withdrawal.[56] The cross also speaks to human depravity and opposition to the gospel.

Luther no doubt would also be suspicious that compassionate social concern or social justice will somehow win over most of the evangelical

54. This is an intentional reference to the global evangelical movement as opposed to a specific denomination in Deutschland by referring to the etymological root of the Lutheran Church in Germany.

55. A critical reference to Luther during the heated days of the Reformation.

56. See "Is It Time."

critics and remove the scandal of the cross. This supposition that "they hate us solely because of our tactless political and cultural engagement" is rooted in a profoundly anemic and unbiblical theological anthropology and unfamiliarity with the theology of the cross. Lack of loving tactfulness is certainly unwise and unbiblical (John 13; 1 Cor 13) and invites criticism, yet there are many other reasons for anti-evangelical sentiments, including nearly a century (in some quarters) of escalating anti-Christian educational indoctrination.

Additionally, I might add, why believers living in relatively democratic states, who presumably love their progeny, would forfeit the freedom of speech and assembly, religious expression, political and cultural engagement based on a total misunderstanding and misapplication of Luther's theology of cross and glory is perplexing. Indeed, such withdrawal is misguided and falls far short of neighborly love. The false supposition that the marginalization of the cross requires us to disengage from the glory of human culture and civilization is both bewildering and invites further cultural decay. Luther may have viewed biblical Christianity and culture in tension, but he was no separatist. Kingdom advance, even loving kingdom advance, requires such tension.[57]

The cross means that even infinite love will be crucified. The cross means that doing everything right, healing the blind, restoring the lame, reaching out to the oppressed, touching the leper, and caring for the spiritually and materially poor may well lead to Golgotha. The cross means that teaching and living out Scripture in some cultural contexts, even religious contexts, means rejection, scorn, and death. Tact, love, good works, good lives, and compassion are essential (John 13:35; 1 Pet 2:12) to Christian mission, yet the not yet of the kingdom and the *Parousia* remain, and even a perfect church will not change human nature, establish utopia, or remove the scandal of being a follower of the cross in this present age. Total allegiance to the Lordship of the crucified Lamb is simply not allowed by multiple centers of power in the present age. Only the return of Christ will finally crush such powers.

This current and increasingly post-Christian murky cultural and philosophical context includes the ivory tower, the halls of justice, the downloads of social media, and the lights of Hollywood. The omnipresent cloud of suspicion now enshrouds the culturally acceptable limits of human reason and jettisons any normative claims to truth and morality. Luther's

---

57. The whole of Scripture confirms this argument, especially the Gospels, Acts, and Hebrews 11.

sixteenth-century staurological and epistemological questions certainly appear *au courant*.

This work will further develop the thesis that Luther's theology of the cross is much better articulated and contextualized in dialog with Christ's central *catechesis* of the kingdom of God. The cross is certainly central to Scripture and soteriology, but biblical soteriology is robust and, in the teaching of Jesus, certainly framed within the theology of the eschatological kingdom. If Christ grounds the central saving event of the cross within his theological didactic and ministry of the kingdom, shall we do any less? It seems odd to reference a theology of the cross rather than a theology of cross and kingdom.

A theology of the cross applied in isolation from the entire Christ-event (i.e., incarnation, birth, life, teaching, death, resurrection, ascension, exaltation, and sending of the Spirit) easily falters. A theology of the cross presented apart from Christ's central teaching on the kingdom of God is especially vulnerable to distortion. A theologically quarantined theology of the cross is easily misconstrued and morphed into a misapplied and typically negative affirmation concerning good works, culture, and civilization as opposed to a theology of the cross that is both a prophetic critique and a constructive theology leading to limited but proleptic kingdom approximation in the lives of individuals, church, and state. A robust theology of cross and kingdom, as will be documented in Part 2, is certainly biblical, integrative, and can serve as a mainstay and safeguard for all theological reflection.

Nevertheless, as noted, I suggest that the elements of current and representative theologies of the cross might be refined and enhanced due to methodological, theological, philosophical, biblical, hermeneutical, and epistemological shortcomings; flawed deterministic theological assumptions; and, a number of logical fallacies in the prior expressions of this rich theology. This filtering process and an expansion of the scope of this theology will hopefully add even more depth and coherence to the *theologia crucis*. Philosophical reflection on this theology in view of a philosophical and hermeneutical analysis of the contemporary cultural, philosophical, and civilizational context should also assist with the application of this theology today.

While charts and tables are always somewhat misleading due to their brevity, and analysis of this entire book is essential for understanding, Table 1 highlights the major trajectories that frame the chapter content pursued in this work.

Table 1. Cross and Kingdom Options

Major Themes of Representative Theologies of the Cross	Modified Themes of a Theology of Cross and Kingdom
Deterministic soteriological singularity	Sovereignly good soteriological singularity
Deterministic epistemological singularity	Sovereignly good epistemological singularity
Contra theology of glory	*Contra* theology of glory and self-glorification
Theological anchor and singularity	Integrative, conjunctive, theological anchor
Deterministic, spiritually purging cruciform suffering	Kenotic cruciform kingdom holiness
Liberation and identification with weakness	Cruciform liberation and kingdom approximation

As noted earlier in this chapter, the purpose of this book is not to rehearse or evaluate the theology of the cross as articulated by Luther, Althaus, Barth, Bonhoeffer (largely theodicy), Bradbury, Moltmann, Pannenberg, and countless others, not to mention an analysis of Nietzsche's well-known scorn and antipathy for any *theologia crucis*.[58] Major nuances of the *theologia crucis* will be identified and evaluated via interaction with select representatives.

Kadai's succinct summary of Luther's approach in the *Concordia Theological Quarterly*, referenced previously, is sufficient and possibly unrivalled as a concise late twentieth and early twenty-first-century classical articulation of Luther's position and key emphases regarding the cross. Brian's recent work referenced previously, *Covering up Luther*, endorsed by Radical Orthodoxy's John Milbank, is an excellent recent expression (2013) not only of a Barthian perspective, but of how the Barthian view is most applicable given the present cultural, theological, and postmodern philosophical context. Saler's 2016 publication,[59] *Theologia Crucis*, referenced previously, is a helpful review of Luther's theology of the cross from a Lutheran and pastoral perspective and contains abridged content that represent and carefully apply a more liberationist perspective (e.g., elements of Moltmann's *Crucified God*) on the cross to current realities. Wright's *The Day the Revolution Began: Reconsidering the Meaning of Jesus's Crucifixion* (2016), also referenced

---

58. Nietzsche, *Antichrist*.

59. In 2018, Saler was serving as the Research Professor of Lutheran Studies and Executive Director of the Center for Pastoral Excellence and the Lilly Endowment Clergy Renewal Program at Christian Theological Seminary in Indianapolis.

previously, views the cross not only as the way for the individual to "get to heaven"[60] but also as the revolutionary way to get heaven to earth.

Hence, this present book seeks to identify, contextualize, enhance, and contemporize key themes and nuances regarding a theology of cross. A relatively brief review of seven key and representative themes in the next chapter should lay the foundation for the constructive analysis later in this work.

A PRACTICAL UTILIZATION OF CROSS, GLORY, AND KINGDOM

On the practical level, much more can and will be affirmed, but this work is hopefully for believers who are experiencing suffering, marginalization, persecution, apologetic challenges, and soul-wrenching challenges with theodicy and suffering (the problem of evil). This book is intended for those who resonate with Wright's affirmation that the cross is more than a ticket to heaven but a radical call to new creation revolution.[61] This work is for those who preach and teach prophetically and biblically yet with cultural relevance and a clarion call to constructive civilizational engagement. This book is for those who appreciate Luther's *theologia crucis* yet yearn for clarity and a robust refinement of this potent and signature theology and a direct application to the twenty-first century. This work is for those seeking a different and very grounded, "in the trenches," even earthy or incarnational framework, for Christian formation, spirituality, and holiness. This book is for those who sometimes sense that there may have been more authentic spirituality and Christlikeness on the beaches of Normandy and in the liberation of the concentration camps—or in the Confessing Church or the Confession of Belhar, or among cruciform believers in the killing fields of southeast Asia, or in those who remained faithful in the brutal and insect-infested Nazi concentration camps—than in many church pews today. This work is for those who have experienced the forsakenness and isolation of the cross. This book may be for those gripped by seemingly endless suffering and unanswered prayers and who sense that the cross may somehow lift that bewildering fog and provide a theological framework for fortitude and kingdom advance. This work may resonate with those who graciously and

60. Or to the way to be truly justified (in the broad sense) and saved. As is well known, Wright bristles at individualistic and escapist conceptions of "getting to heaven."

61. Concerning the usage and association of the term revolution in the contemporary cultural context and in view of a shrewd eschatology, see especially chapters 11 and 12.

sacrificially take up the often unrecognized and seemingly invisible mantle of caregiving for weeks if not years, often with disdain from the needy and anguished loved one, and discern that only a theology of the cross and kingdom can ground and sustain such servant leadership. This work is for those who have been deafened by the seeming and overwhelming silence and hiddenness of God amidst the dark nights of the soul. This book is for those accustomed to success who are learning, by grace, to deeply and sincerely empathize with those on the margins who live under the stark reality of endless suffering, the calling of the cross, and the sometimes crushing weight of an inverted world. This work is for those who sense that the cross has everything to do with courageous, cruciform, and sacrificial cultural and civilizational engagement and melioration. This book is for believers who fully grasp that we live in a fallen world, yet still yearn for a theological framework that makes sense of the apparent long-lived success of religious and non-religious luminaries who trample on biblical justice, integrity, ethics, and character. This work is for those who live daily in the shadow of others who abscond with and take credit for their labor, ideas, and accomplishments. This book is for those willing to pattern their spiritual walk and Christian mission after the Savior: "He was despised and forsaken of men, A man of sorrows and acquainted with grief; And like one from whom men hide their face He was despised, and we did not esteem Him" (Isa 53:3). This work is for those who perceive the grief-stricken grace and mercy of Joseph as a quintessential and most relevant illustration of cross and kingdom advance and authentic and earthly spirituality, when Joseph made a kingdom proclamation for the ages: "As for you, you meant evil against me, *but* God meant it for good in order to bring about this present result, to preserve many people alive" (Gen 50:20). This book is for those who sense that the way of the cross and kingdom may properly define ecclesiology, as well as Christian mission, cultural and political engagement, in an age increasingly characterized by self-serving spin, outrage, insults, and barbarism. Yet this book is ultimately for those who are unquenchably and indomitably passionate for a cruciform vision of "thy kingdom come, thy will be done, on earth as it is in heaven."

2

Classical Themes of Theologies of the Cross

THEOLOGIA CRUCIS AS A DETERMINISTIC SOTERIOLOGICAL SINGULARITY

PERSPECTIVES VARY CONCERNING THE precise extent of Luther's theological determinism, and that debate is not the focus of this book. It will be argued, however, that an evident deterministic dimension of Luther's thought is essential for comprehending Luther's theology of the cross. Douglas Sweeney, professor at Trinity Evangelical Divinity School, provided a fairly recent (2014) concise summary challenging an iron clad deterministic view of Luther and Lutheranism and affirms:

> The wrong thing to conclude from this evidence is that Lutherans are hesitant Calvinists, or two-and-a-half-point Calvinists, or imperfect Arminians. Lutherans are Lutherans. Their theological frame of reference is not closely related to the Calvinist-Arminian continuum. Lutherans have their own theological history, one that has contributed in major ways to the evangelical movement.[1]

In contrast, while conceding the uniqueness of the Lutheran context for this discussion, Linwood Urban, who served as Professor Emeritus of Religion at the prestigious Swarthmore College, provided a classic and thorough

1. Sweeney, "Was Luther a Calvinist?"

review of the deterministic debate and argued "that the earlier commentators [on Luther] are correct with regard to Luther's final position and that the evidence that he was a thoroughgoing Determinist is conclusive."[2]

Kenneth Grider, a Wesleyan scholar, did not classify Luther as affirming the most extreme Calvinistic perspective concerning God's decrees but was unequivocal concerning a strong deterministic element in Luther's thought: "Besides Augustine, Martin Luther taught sublapsarian predestination. Luther even said that he did not know which eternal destiny he himself was predestined to. He said it would undermine our being justified by faith if we could know, or have knowledge of, our predestined destiny."[3] Luther was most clear that "original sin [entirely] enslaves us."[4] This assumption was, of course, central to Luther's *sola gratia* and *sola fide*, as evidenced by Luther's well-known debate with Erasmus concerning the bondage of the will.

Kadai's classic presentation of Luther's theology of the cross certainly demonstrated that a strong measure of determinism was operative at the level of theological and philosophical assumptions. God places the cross of suffering on Christians so they might learn humility. Christians need to experience this divinely imposed terror in order to crucify the old man. The proper response for the Christian is to "be still; let God rule."[5] Luther's advice to his own dying mother in 1531 was to receive the suffering as gracious and fatherly chastisement. Luther's consolation to a friend who had lost his wife included reference to the hidden goodness of the will of God in such situations that should spark abandonment to God's will, and pleasure in God's will, and joy.[6] In contrast to Luther, while suffering certainly can reflect discipline in select cases (Heb 12), among other reasons, such counsel to one's mother and a friend either requires intimate knowledge of the mind of God and/or the ability to speak for God—otherwise this counsel by Luther reflects a profound commitment to and theological assumption of the divine determinism of all events. The latter option for understanding Luther seems persuasive. Regardless of precisely how iron clad Luther's determinism was, or how many decrees he or subsequent Lutherans affirmed, or to what degree Luther found systematic speculation on decrees and determinism helpful, it would be difficult to overemphasize how significant

---

2. Urban, "Was Luther?," 113.
3. Grider, *Wesleyan Holiness Theology*, 247–48.
4. Grider, *Wesleyan Holiness Theology*, 276.
5. Kadai, "Luther's Theology," 194.
6. Kadai, "Luther's Theology," 194.

Luther's determinism is for comprehending his rendition of the theology of the cross.

The cross, for Luther, is a divinely determined soteriological singularity. Luther's well-known reaction to what he perceived as a terrifying works righteousness, a reaction that led him to have canonical concerns even about biblical books such as James, is central to his theology of the cross. Salvation *via dolorosa* is a divinely determined gift and singularity, meaning that the cross is the only way of and to salvation, period, and the only way to encounter the true God of Jesus Christ.

Luther personally experienced and passionately articulated the key assumptions of his theology of the cross in these classic quotes:

> [From *Bondage of the Will*] Free-will is plainly a divine term, and can be applicable to none but the divine Majesty only. . . . Wherefore, it becomes Theologians to refrain from the use of this term altogether, whenever they wish to speak of human ability, and leave it to be applied to God only.
>
> "Free-will" is overruled by the Free-will of God alone, just as he pleases: but that, God-ward, or in things which pertain unto salvation and damnation, he [humanity] has no "Free-will," is but a captive, slave, and servant, either to the will of God, or to the will of Satan.
>
> Thus the human will is, as it were, a beast between the two. If God sit thereon, it wills and goes where God will. . . . If Satan sit thereon, it wills and goes as Satan will. Nor is it in the owner of its own will to choose, to which rider it will run, nor which it will seek; but the riders themselves contend, which shall have and hold it.[7]

> [From *Table-talk* #CCLXII] This is my absolute opinion: he that will maintain that man's free-will is able to do or work anything in spiritual cases be they never so small, denies Christ.[8]

> [From *Heidelberg Theses* # 18] It is certain that human beings must utterly despair of their own ability before they are prepared to receive the grace of Christ.[9]

This is a deterministic and aggressive theology, soteriology, and staurology of *sola fide, sola gratia,* and non-synergistic alien righteousness. This also

---

7. Luther, *Compend*, 88, 90.

8. Luther, *Compend*, 90.

9. Luther, "Heidelberg Disputation," *Martin Luther's Basic Theological Writings*, 15.

implies another *sola,* which is the *cross alone.* Luther, rooted in Scripture, recovered biblical soteriology, but the messenger was (understandably) flawed, troubled, reactive, and militantly committed to abolishing works righteousness and ecclesial overreach from the face of the earth.

My father-in-law, who was a farmer, used to note that sometimes when a farmer tries to pull a farm implement out of the ditch the farmer ends up in the ditch on the other side of the road. Luther's determinism was reactionary. The question of whether Luther erred when correcting the error of works righteousness exceeds the scope of this present work, yet some degree of determinism by Luther is an unavoidable conclusion. Yet Luther was ultimately right: The cross is a singularity. Christ is the only way, truth, and life, and the only way to Christ and God is through the cross. Luther's advocacy went on to add the possible accretion that this way of salvation through the cross was applied to humanity in a monergistic and deterministic fashion at every step and every level of the *ordo salutis.* Human ability—and ecclesial power and glory—must be completely set aside and the mystery of salvation through the weakness of the cross must be fully and unqualifiedly embraced. Period. For Luther, this corrective includes mammoth theological, philosophical, and epistemological assumptions and affirmations, and this corrective saves theology, a biblical conception of salvation and the church.

THEOLOGIA CRUCIS AS A DETERMINISTIC EPISTEMOLOGICAL SINGULARITY

Luther believes that this soteriological singularity is also an epistemological singularity. Given humanity's fallen predicament and obsession with false glory, authentic knowledge of God is only through the divinely determined soteriological singularity: "Luther claimed that one knows God not through conjecture and subjective sense, but rather through the cross of Christ."[10] The complexity, multiple nuances and even divisiveness of Luther's position will require significant analysis. What follows in this chapter is all too brief, but brevity is necessary to maintain the larger argument of this present work.

For Luther, the "devil's bride" (i.e., reason) and the "blind heathen master" (namely Aristotle, that "stinking philosopher") were not only of little help but absolutely useless relative to salvation and the true knowledge of God. Lest one conclude that such disparagement by Luther was isolated, Table 2 should be of some assistance.[11]

10. Madsen, *Theology,* 71.

11. The material for this table is well-known but comes from Rogers and McKim, *Authority,* 80.

Table 2. Luther on Reason

Luther on Reason	Luther on Aristotle
Beast	Destroyer of pious doctrine
Enemy of God	Mere sophist and quibbler
Devil's whore	Inventor of fable
Source of mischief	Ungodly public enemy of the truth
Devil's bride	Stinking philosopher, blind heathen master, pagan, beast, and billy goat

The argument that Luther is only concerned about Aristotelian and medieval "reason" simply has failed to consider Luther's theological and philosophical methodology, his somewhat stark staurology, his sharp criticisms of the theology of glory, and his persistent advocacy for the *Deus Absconditus* (or hiddenness of God). Luther retains a role for philosophy and reason, but relative to salvation and the true knowledge of God the cross is a divinely determined epistemological singularity. David Whitford succinctly summarizes Luther's use of reason in the following intentionally extensive but critical quote.[12] This material should greatly assist with much of the epistemological analysis in this book. The sentences and long phrases in italics are added to highlight questionable conclusions that will be assessed in this chapter and chapter 6:

> Another fundamental aspect of Luther's theology is his understanding of God. In rejecting much of scholastic thought Luther rejected the scholastic belief in continuity between revelation and perception. Luther notes that *revelation must be indirect and concealed.* Luther's theology is based in the Word of God (thus his phrase *sola scriptura*). It is based not in speculation or philosophical principles, but in revelation.
>
> Because of humanity's fallen condition, one can neither understand the redemptive word nor can one see God face to face. Here Luther's exposition on number twenty of his *Heidelberg Disputation* is important. It is an allusion to Exodus 33, where Moses seeks to see the Glory of the Lord but instead sees only God's backside. No one can see God face-to-face and live,

---

12. Whitford has been associated with Baylor University and Claflin University.

so God reveals himself on the backside, that is to say, where it seems he should not be. For Luther this meant in the human nature of Christ, in his weakness, his suffering, and his foolishness.

Thus revelation is seen in the suffering of Christ rather than in moral activity or created order and is addressed to faith. The *Deus Absconditus* is actually quite simple. It is a rejection of philosophy as the starting point for theology. Why? Because if one begins with philosophical categories for God one begins with the attributes of God: i.e., omniscient, omnipresent, omnipotent, impassible, etc. For Luther, *it was impossible to begin there and by using syllogisms or other logical means to end up with a God who suffers on the cross on behalf of humanity.* It simply does not work. *The God revealed in and through the cross is not the God of philosophy but the God of revelation.* Only faith can understand and appreciate this, logic and reason—to quote St. Paul—become a stumbling block to belief instead of a helpmate. . . .

Given Luther's critique of philosophy and his famous phrase that philosophy is the "devil's whore," it would be easy to assume that Luther had only contempt for philosophy and reason. Nothing could be further from the truth. Luther believed, rather, that philosophy and reason had important roles to play in our lives and in the life of the community. However, he also felt that it was important to remember what those roles were and not to confuse the proper use of philosophy with an improper one.

Properly understood and used, philosophy and reason are a great aid to individuals and society. Improperly used, they become a great threat to both. Likewise, revelation and the gospel when used properly are an aid to society, but when misused also have sad and profound implications.

The proper role of philosophy is organizational and as an aid in governance. When Cardinal Cajetan first demanded Luther's recantation of the *Ninety-Five Theses*, Luther appealed to scripture and right reason. Reason can be an aid to faith in that it helps to clarify and organize, but it is always second-order discourse. It is, following St. Anselm, *fides quarenes intellectum* (faith seeking understanding) and never the reverse. Philosophy tells us that God is omnipotent and impassible; revelation tells us that Jesus Christ died for humanity's sin. *The two cannot be reconciled.* Reason is the devil's whore precisely because [it] asks the wrong questions and looks in the wrong direction for answers. Revelation is the only proper place for theology to begin. Reason must always take a back seat.

Reason does play a primary role in governance and in most human interaction. Reason, Luther argued, is necessary for a good and just society. In fact, unlike most of his contemporaries, Luther did not believe that a ruler had to be Christian, only reasonable. Here, opposite to his discussion of theology, it is revelation that is improper. *Trying to govern using the gospel as one's model would either corrupt the government or corrupt the gospel.* The gospel's fundamental message is forgiveness, government must maintain justice. To confuse the two here is just as troubling as confusing them when discussing theology. If forgiveness becomes the dominant model in government, people being sinful, chaos will increase. If however, the government claims the gospel but acts on the basis of justice, then people will be misled as to the proper nature of the gospel.

Luther was self-consciously trying to carve out proper realms for revelation and philosophy or reason. Each had a proper role that enables humanity to thrive. Chaos only became a problem when the two got confused. One cannot understand Luther's relationship to philosophy and his discussions of philosophy without understanding that key concept.[13]

Brian, affirming Barth, is much less hopeful concerning the assumptions and implications of Luther's *Deus absconditus*. Brian affirms, "The overwhelming amount of material [from Barth], and the consistency of Barth's arguments therein, prove that Barth's God is not . . . [Luther's] *Deus absconditus*, and that he rejects the logic of such a theological position." Brian contends that "*Deus absconditus* became, unintentionally, the dominant theological position of modernity, and . . . this was accomplished through the logic of dialectic." For Brian and Barth, "God is not veiled. . . . God is revealed once and for all, definitively in Christ Jesus." Theology proper and Scripture retain some elements of hiddenness concerning God, yet hiddenness "or veiling is [initiatory and] only a way to begin the discussion of the knowledge of God, particularly in the context of pagans." Divine revelation of God in Christ has lifted the veil whereas modernity basked in and remained behind the veil. God is "hidden and yet always already revealed God, a tenuous position that is held together not by dialectic but by . . . the logic of paradox."[14] Brian elaborates as follows:

> Barth's mature theology, which most assuredly begins with Romans II, is accurately characterized as a theology of tension, difference, and distinction between God and humanity. This

13. Whitford, "Martin Luther."

14. Brian, *Covering Up*, 3, 108.

difference, however, is definitely not the tension of dialectic, but rather it is a different kind of tension; it is the resolved and yet persistent tension that is paradox. It is the tension of two seeming opposites coinciding in a noncontradictory matter, in which an overall meaning is achieved through a fundamental unity that both is beyond and yet contains within itself, all distinction.[15]

Brian, echoing Barth, is arguing that Luther's epistemology, premised on the *Deus absconditus* and philosophical nominalism, ultimately led to the *No Exit* dead end cul-de-sac of modernity. The hidden God, and nominalism,[16] "became the dominant theological and philosophical framework for burgeoning modernity and would eventually lead to, among other [undesirable] things, nihilism."[17]

Hence, the title of Brian's intriguing work, *Covering up Luther*, was selected because Barth literally covered up the works of Luther in his library with an ornate rug due to Luther's *Deus absconditus* and Luther's tragic and "lingering" impact on the modern world.[18] Barth repositioned *Deus revalatus* in Christ at the center, in contrast to the modernity and classical liberal theology that was crumbling all around him. Barth rejected cultural accommodation and returned to Scripture. Barth and Luther both pursued staurology and anchored the whole of theology in Christology, for "the fundamental revelation of God . . . [is] the incarnation, death, resurrection, and ascension of the Son in the person of Jesus of Nazareth."[19]

So Brian's critique is that the *Deus absconditus* leads to liberalism, modernism, and nihilism. Whitford's more sympathetic appraisal is that Luther was mostly advocating for the Anselmian *fides quarenes intellectum* or faith seeking understanding. Which is preferred? It is not the purpose of this book to resolve such a multi-complex issue, but in order to set up the recommended trajectories of this present work, a few comments are in order.

Luther's staurology is famously expressed in the *Heidelberg Disputation Theses*, classified as theological or philosophical, and subsequent comments on or proofs of the theses.[20] Space disallows a review of all of

---

15. Brian, *Covering Up*, 56.

16. Resulting in an epistemological and perceptual gap between the knower and the known, between the knower and the world, and, for Luther, ultimately between the knower and God apart from the cross.

17. Brian, *Covering Up*, 32.

18. Brian, *Covering Up*, 2.

19. Brian, *Covering Up*, 1.

20. Luther, "Heidelberg Disputation," 14–25.

these theses, but a selected few should assist with determining what can be affirmed about Luther's epistemological staurology. The first eighteen theses revolve around a militant reaction to works righteousness, ecclesial overreach, and an affirmation of the deterministic soteriological singularity motif. Beginning with thesis nineteen, Luther includes a number of theses with immense implications for his deterministic epistemological singularity and the *Deus absconditus*.

19. That person does not deserve to be called a theologian who looks upon the invisible things of God as though they were clearly perceptible in those things which have actually happened.

20. One deserves to be called a theologian, however, who comprehends the visible and manifest things of God seen through suffering and the cross.

21. A theologian of glory calls evil good and good evil. A theologian of the cross calls the thing what it actually is.

22. That wisdom that sees the invisible things of God in works as perceived by humans is completely puffed up, blinded, and hardened.

29. Whoever wishes to philosophize by using Aristotle without danger to their soul must first become thoroughly foolish in Christ.

30. Just as persons do not use the evil of passion well unless they are married, so no one philosophizes well unless they are fools, that is, Christian.

36. Aristotle wrongly finds fault with and derides the ideas of Plato, which actually are better than his own.

37. The mathematical order of material things is ingeniously maintained by Pythagoras, but more ingenious is the interaction of ideas maintained by Plato.[21]

The failure to integrate references to the theological theses (1–28) with the philosophical theses (29–40) greatly undermines the hermeneutical task in Luther studies, as does the neglect of Luther's comments on and proofs of the theses. Given this bulleted evidence and Luther's nuanced comments, perhaps Barth could have partially removed his rug from the Luther section of his library.

---

21. Luther, "Heidelberg Disputation," 14–25.

Luther clearly does not reject philosophy in total, includes substantive philosophical preferences, commends Pythagoras, lauds the ingenious and creative coherence of Plato, and with much passion articulates the theological hermeneutic of faith seeking understanding. In his proof of Thesis 19, Luther defends his approach by Paul's reference to theologians as fools in Romans 1 and by insisting that the invisible things such as virtue, godliness, and true wisdom do not make one worthy or wise. *Fallen* humanity cannot see through the visible to the invisible. Luther does not deny a natural knowledge of God, only that such knowledge cannot lead to a true grasp of God's saving intentions apprehended *sola fide*. Luther does not appear to condemn human wisdom in terms of ontology—that human wisdom, knowledge, or theology is impossible—but in terms of theological anthropology. Fallen humanity's use of reason must kneel at the foot of the cross. Hence, Luther explains further in his proof of Thesis 20,

> The "back" and visible things of God are placed in opposition to the invisible, namely, his human nature, weakness, foolishness. The Apostle in 1 Cor 1 [v. 25] calls them the weakness and folly of God. *Because humans misused the knowledge of God through works,* God wished again to be recognized in suffering, and to condemn wisdom concerning invisible things by means of wisdom concerning visible things, *so that those who did not honor God* as manifested in the Divine works should honor him God hidden in [his] suffering. As the Apostle says in 1 Cor 1 [v. 21], "For since, in the wisdom of God, the world did not know God through wisdom, it pleased God through the folly of what we preach to save those who believe." Now it is not sufficient for anyone, and *it does one no good to recognize God in Divine glory and majesty, unless one recognizes God in the humility and shame of the cross.* Thus God destroys the wisdom of the wise, as Isaiah [45:15] says, "Truly, thou art a God who hides yourself."
>
> So, also, in John 14 [v. 8], where Philip spoke according to the theology of glory: "Show us the Father." Christ forthwith set aside his flighty thought about seeing God elsewhere and led him to himself, saying, "Philip, he who has seen me has seen the Father" [John 14:9]. For this reason true theology and recognition of God are in the crucified Christ, as it is also stated in John 10 [14:6]: "No one comes to the Father, but by me." "I am the door" [John 10:9], and so forth.[22]

22. Luther, "Heidelberg Disputation," 14–25. Emphasis added to underscore Luther's understanding of the reason for emphasizing the epistemological singularity. Fallen humanity's use of reason creates the context that requires the epistemological singularity in order for fallen humanity to encounter the saving God.

McGrath calls this translation of Thesis 20 "seriously inaccurate." He renders it thusly: "The man who perceives the visible rearward parts of God as seen in suffering and the cross does, however, deserve to be called a theologian" (*Sed qui visibilia et posteriora Dei per passiones et crucem conspecta intellgit*). To translate *posteriora Dei* as "manifest things of God" is to miss both the allusion to Exodus 33:23 and the concept of a "hidden revelation."[23]

Thesis 21 amplifies Luther's thought by affirming that the theologian of glory subverts good and evil:

> He who does not know Christ does not know God hidden in suffering. Therefore he prefers works to suffering, glory to the cross, strength to weakness, wisdom to folly, and, in general, good to evil. . . . [Such "theologians" are not theologians because they] hate the cross and suffering and love works and the glory of works. Thus they call the good of the cross evil and the evil of a deed good. God can be found only in suffering and the cross, as has already been said. Therefore the friends of the cross say that the cross is good and works are evil, for through the cross works are destroyed.[24]

Luther is especially nuanced when referencing wisdom, glory, and power while commenting on Thesis 22:

> Because humans do not know the cross and hate it, they necessarily love the opposite, namely, wisdom, glory, power, and so on. Therefore they become increasingly blinded and hardened by such love, for desire cannot be satisfied by the acquisition of those things which it desires. Just as the love of money grows in proportion to the increase of the money itself, so the dropsy of the soul becomes thirstier the more it drinks. . . .
>
> Thus also the desire for knowledge is not satisfied by the acquisition of wisdom but is stimulated that much more. Likewise the desire for glory is not satisfied by the acquisition of glory, nor is the desire to rule satisfied by power and authority, nor is the desire for praise satisfied by praise, and so on. . . .
>
> The remedy for curing desire does not lie in satisfying it, but in extinguishing it. In other words, he who wishes to become wise does not seek wisdom by progressing toward it but becomes a fool by retrogressing into seeking folly. Likewise he who wishes to have much power, honor, pleasure, satisfaction in all things must flee rather than seek power, honor, pleasure,

23. McGrath, *Luther's Theology*, 148–49.
24. Luther, "Heidelberg Disputation," 22.

and satisfaction in all things. This is the wisdom which is folly to the world.[25]

This passage is significant. Luther seems, somewhat unfairly, to be fully associated with the onus of irrationalism or extreme representations of his *Deus absconditus*. Luther is engaging in semantic nuancing, just as the apostle Paul did when chastising the Corinthians in 1 Cor 1–2 relative to wisdom and folly. For Luther, there is legitimate wisdom and illegitimate wisdom. For Luther, there is legitimate power, honor, and, by logical extension, glory, and there is also illegitimate power, honor, and glory. In principle, Luther's trajectory should accommodate the thesis of this work that there is also a legitimate theology of the cross and glory and an illegitimate theology of the cross and glory.

Paul's regular missional pattern in Acts, where he first attempts to reason and persuade the Jews, then do the same with the Gentiles, was also the pattern in Corinth (Acts 18). This apologetic and evangelistic pattern birthed the Corinthian church. Paul used reason and wisdom, properly defined, in Corinth while rejecting reason and wisdom, improperly defined, by some in Corinth. And reason and wisdom, properly defined, are Christocentric. Paul, a well-educated rabbinic Jew grounded in the exaltation of godly wisdom in tradition and Scripture (e.g., Proverbs) clearly values reason and proclaims "God's wisdom"—a mystery rejected by those claiming to be wise but now fully revealed in Christ (1 Cor 2:6–16). Paul is not rejecting wisdom per se but arrogant, elitist Corinthian false wisdom in dire need of crucifixion.

Hence, Paul is engaging in the nuanced, perceptual, contextual, or even phenomenological analysis of terms. The Corinthians' perception of "wisdom" and "folly" is wrong and inverted. In actuality, some Corinthians were engaging in folly and rejecting true wisdom rooted in the Christ-event. Paul rejects pretentious and false wisdom but uses genuine wisdom, reason, and persuasion while intentionally focusing on the cross to strike at the heart of Corinthian arrogance and spiritual blindness. Paul's custom was to reason with and try to persuade Jews and Gentiles, even in Corinth (Acts 17:2, 17; 18:4). For Paul, no authentic wisdom conflicts with the Christ-event. Likewise, for Luther, wisdom, folly, and power have multiple definitions, and Luther is simply advocating not for a total renunciation of reason or wisdom but simply for a christologically governed theological methodology and priority rooted in revelation and sound theological anthropology. Reason must be subjugated to revelation, and humanity's fallen condition must be the starting point for doing theology.

25. Luther, "Heidelberg Disputation," 23.

This all too brief review suggests that Luther's theological theses and proofs, taken together with his philosophical theses and proofs, preserve a place for reason properly defined and philosophy properly exercised. Whitford's "faith seeking understanding" hermeneutic for Luther, though flawed (see chapter 6), may have more merit than the extreme claim that Luther's *Deus absconditus* created the modernity that birthed nihilism. Even if the nihilistic thesis has some merit, countless other factors—theological, historical, theological, philosophical, and psychological—moved the West from Luther to Nietzsche.

The claim that Luther's theology produced cultural nihilism would be exceedingly difficult to prove in terms of a direct cause and effect relationship traced through the layers and complexities and centuries of history. Such a claim is also exceedingly modernist in nature, suggesting that sociological, historical, psychological, and other factors (e.g., simple weariness with seventeenth-century religious wars) had little relevance to the birth of modernity and subsequent nihilism. This faith seeking understanding interpretation, though incomplete,[26] seems especially worthy of consideration given that Luther was an explosive, emotionally mercurial counter-puncher who was in a virtual war with works righteousness, ecclesial overreach, and a powerful and corrupt Christendom empire. Luther's battle with Christendom is yet another reason for the relevance of *theologia crucis* in an age witnessing the decline of Christendom.

For Luther, partial knowledge of God is possible via reason, but fallen humanity cannot pierce the veil and uncover the full truth about humanity and the gracious truth concerning God's saving intentions and the means of salvation. Hence, even partial knowledge can become an idol of glory that obscures rather than reveals. Kadai notes that Luther

> pointed out that philosophers argue and speculate about the existence of God and arrive at some sort of knowledge of Him. This, however, is limited to what Luther called objective knowledge. It falls short of the true knowledge of God, which entails comprehension of His nature and will. . . . God wants to be a personal Lord and merciful Father. This is beyond metaphysical knowledge.[27]

God's epistemological singularity for fallen humanity—emphasize fallen—is masked, clothed, and hidden in the cross largely because of fallen humanity's phenomenological and ontological realities. Saving revelation and knowledge, because of humanity's ontological condition, is via the

26. See chapter 6.
27. Kadai, "Luther's Theology," 191.

backside of God (see Gen 45; Exod 33). Kadai concludes: "To know God, one must learn to understand *His* ways, His masks, His gospel, his cross."[28]

Yet conjunctive or synthetic theology may assist in evaluating both Brian and Whitford. Brian and Barth had it partially right concerning God's revelation in Christ. In Scripture, the mystery of the Christ-event is properly described as the following: That which was concealed is now fully revealed. The knowledge of God is hidden not because reasoning is inherently or ontologically flawed or because such knowledge had no ontological reality prior to the cross but because humanity is flawed and the divine *kairos* and initiative must come first. Eph 3:3–10 affirms

> that by revelation there was made known to me the mystery, as I wrote before in brief. By referring to this, when you read you can understand my insight into the mystery of Christ, which in other generations was not made known to the sons of men, as it has now been revealed to His holy apostles and prophets in the Spirit; *to be specific*, that the Gentiles are fellow heirs and fellow members of the body, and fellow partakers of the promise in Christ Jesus through the gospel, of which I was made a minister, according to the gift of God's grace which was given to me according to the working of His power. To me, the very least of all saints, this grace was given, to preach to the Gentiles the unfathomable riches of Christ, and to bring to light what is the administration of the mystery which for ages has been hidden in God who created all things; so that the manifold wisdom of God might now be made known through the church to the rulers and the authorities in the heavenly *places*.

If Barth and Luther are being properly interpreted in this chapter, then the implications for the knowledge of God and apologetics are displayed in Table 3.

Table 3. Luther and Barth on Apologetics

Subject	Luther	Barth
Apologetics or Natural Theology as a means to the true knowledge of God	Negated	Negated

---

28. Kadai, "Luther's Theology," 191 (emphasis added).

Deus Absconditus	Affirmed, relative to knowledge of the saving God	Replaced with an emphasis upon revelation
Knowledge of God	Extremely limited apart from the cross; no true or saving knowledge of the saving God	Unqualified rejection of knowledge of God apart from revelation
Modernity	Qualified rejection of emerging modernity (Barth views Luther as fueling modernity via *absconditus*)	Rejection of most/all of modernity, rejection of *Deus absconditus* as a key assumption of modernity
Wisdom of the world	Utterly fails	Utterly fails
Aristotle and Aquinas	Their epistemologies fail	Their epistemologies fail

Theologies of the cross have often espoused a non-nuanced and unrefined theology of the cross premised upon a very extreme, fideistic, and even irrationalistic understanding of the cross and the *Deus absconditus* as an epistemological singularity that devalues, subverts, or entirely replaces the need for reason. Further assessment and modification follows in this chapter and chapter 6, and Luther certainly provided fodder for such an interpretation and leaned in this fideistic direction at times.[29] Yet Luther's key point relative to this discussion seemed to be the complete exaltation of the soteriological priority of revelatory Christocentric reasoning and wisdom. Kadai sums up Luther's posture very well: "To the human eye [fallen human and often arrogant perception] Christ looked powerless on the cross, yet

---

29. Kadai summarizes Luther as follows: "One might wonder about proof. Hardly! God's word and work do not demand proof of reason; man must know in free and pure faith alone" (Kadai, "Luther's Theology," 186). However, it is important to remember that it is one thing to be a fideist or a presuppositionalist relative to evangelism and apologetics, and quite another to renounce truly all nuances of reason and wisdom entirely. Luther is close to the edge but seemingly did not succumb. He also rejected the mystical soteriological and epistemological options in favor of revelatory content and cognition. "For the mystic, sin is creatureliness that ultimately must be overcome. For a faith-centered theologian like Luther sin is unbelief, disobedience to God's will. Systematically speaking, Luther was no mystic; in fact his theology was in many respects sharply opposed to mysticism. . . . [Luther] never abrogates the difference between the creature and the Creator. . . . [Hence] mysticism and faith are independent religious orientations proposing different ways of [and epistemologies for] comprehending God" (Kadai, "Luther's Theology," 197–98).

it was there that He performed his mightiest work. So [fallen humanity's] sense and reason must close their eyes and faith must take over."[30]

Luther admitted, "Philosophers argue and speculate about the existence of God and arrive at some sort of knowledge of Him. This, however, is limited to what Luther called objective knowledge. It falls short of the true knowledge of God, which entails the comprehension of His nature and will [and loving intention and power to save].... [Hence] God wants to be a personal Lord and merciful Father. This is beyond metaphysical knowledge."[31] Relational knowledge should not be confused with theological knowledge. Faith and reason are not entirely polarized or entirely ontologically and atomistically distinct. Instead, reason is baptized by grace through faith. To be fair to all interpreters, Luther's view is not crystal clear, but in the realm of apologetics he may have more in common with philosophical presuppositionalism than total, irrational, radical, or extreme fideism.

Regardless, while Luther's gift of communication included his stark contrasts and counter-punching, this gift sometimes created false dichotomies. This present work does not attempt to assess all of these false dichotomies, but a few comments are in order:

- Why could not revelation be both indirect or concealed as well as public and revealed, depending on the content and the recipient? Luther even hints—see his theses already mentioned—at different types of revelation and different types of recipients. Why cannot images from the Hubble space telescope prepare the way for and reinforce majestic kenosis? Is not the failure to see God in the cross a limitation of the recipient rather than a limitation of revelation? After all, some did see God in the cross and certainly the triune God could see and foresee the cross.

- Why cannot different emphases and nuances in knowledge and reason be acknowledged? Some knowledge is more relational, though involving more general knowledge. A healthy marriage includes general knowledge of each other that is necessary but not central to relational knowledge and intimacy. Must relational and propositional knowledge only be framed as either/or? That false dichotomy is not how reason functions in daily life and may presuppose a shallow and dated definition of reason.

- Why cannot revelation be seen both in the sufferings of Christ as well as moral activity and the created order?

30. Kadai, "Luther's Theology," 186.
31. Kadai, "Luther's Theology," 191.

- Why cannot the move from the attributes of God revealed in creation (Rom 1–2) to the revelatory cross be conjunctive rather than disjunctive?

- Why cannot the God of the cross be the God of the true philosophers, true wisdom, and the God of authentic revelation? Justin Martyr viewed Socrates noble execution not as of the same kind or category as the triune cross of Christ, but it was, for Justin, a helpful analogy when communicating with a non-Christian audience.

- Why cannot the stumbling blocks of logic and reason be viewed as the stumbling blocks of false logic, fallen reason, and a hard heart? As discussed previously in this chapter, does not reason sometimes point some outside the faith to an affirmation of human depravity and the need for sacrifice and transformation?

- Does not the affirmation that God's attributes are irreconcilable with the cross, unless intended to describe the condition or perception of the fallen mind, ultimately destroy Christian theology? Do we really want to try to vacate God's attributes from God's revelation in Christ's cross and resurrection? Does not the cross actually reveal attributes such as holy, sovereign, omnipresent, omnipotent, just, righteous, loving, unchanging, faithful, and merciful? Perhaps a few select attributes (e.g., impassibility) would be most troubling for some theological perspectives (yet not for others, e.g., Process thought) attempting to develop a theology of the cross, and certainly the cross is unexpected from the fallen human vantage point but are not the attributes of God essential to and also revealed in the Christ-event? Are not God's nature and attributes the very source of the cross?

Perhaps the real point here is that given human depravity and *hubris*, the cross is the last place one would expect to find the triune God. From the divine vantage point, however, was this not the Lamb slain from the foundation of the world (Rev 13:8)? From the divine vantage point, is not the cross the first place one would expect to find the triune God in a dying world? Fallen human wisdom, and certainly carnal Corinthian wisdom, should not serve as the arbiter or definition of true wisdom.

THEOLOGIA CRUCIS AS CONTRA THE THEOLOGY OF GLORY

Hence, this critical and extended epistemological discussion and Luther's Heidelberg theses are suggestive that the negative construct for a theology of glory be primarily viewed as arrogant, volitional, and intellectual works righteousness as well as overreaching reason. This negative understanding of glory includes pseudo-reason and pseudo-wisdom. This so-called glory is especially incarnated and systemically institutionalized in the ecclesial and statist powers that are in opposition to the gracious gospel of Jesus Christ. Luther's concern here is primarily soteriological, and his epistemology is soteriologically driven. The true God is only to be found in the cross.

To modify Althaus slightly yet consistent with my prior observations,

> God cannot meet us [fallen humanity] when he is clothed in his majesty. If he came thus, we [as fallen] could not grasp him and we would find the brilliance of his glory too terrible to bear. [Fallen] Man and God in his majesty are enemies. . . . [Luther affirms that the arrogant, moralistic, depraved, culturally en-throned] theology of glory seeks to know God directly in his obviously divine power, wisdom, and glory; whereas the theology of the cross [in an inverted world] paradoxically recognizes him precisely where he has hidden himself, in his sufferings and in all that which the [false] theology of glory considers to be weakness and foolishness.[32]

McGrath elaborates, "Christian thinking about God comes to an abrupt halt at the foot of the cross. The Christian is forced, by the very existence of the crucified Christ, to make a momentous decision. Either he will [falsely] seek God elsewhere, or he will make the cross the foundation and criterion of his thought about God."[33] Indeed, "Any attempt to seek God elsewhere than in the cross of Christ is to be rejected out of hand."[34]

Saler goes so far as to represent Luther as follows: "What is at stake between the theology of the cross and the theology of glory is a fight between two very different 'Gods': one who is present most directly in that which the

---

32. Althaus, *Theology*, 21. And do note the presence of the phrase "that which the world calls good." As mentioned previously, the very movements for what the world or a less-than-perfect church views as good, just, compassionate, and consistent with a theology of the cross may actually be coopted by a destructive theology of glory.

33. McGrath, *Luther's Theology*, 1.

34. McGrath, *Luther's Theology*, 161.

world calls good and powerful, and one who is hidden under the contradiction (*sub contrario*, as Luther would say) of weakness and death."[35]

Why? Because the world looks for a god who affirms depraved human wisdom and achievement and does not require either a cross or a radically transformed new heart. The gracious gift of the cross and the new heart lies at the core of the New Covenant salvation, and thus the cross is the anchor for the whole of biblical and Christian theology.

THEOLOGIA CRUCIS AS THEOLOGICAL ANCHOR FOR THE WHOLE OF THEOLOGY

It then naturally follows that theology begins with and is fundamentally anchored to Christology and staurology. This method is more than cognitive. The real theologian (see the Heidelberg theses discussed previously in this chapter) begins the theological task with a bent knee before the cross. Luther is recognizing the noetic impact of the fall, the necessity of transformational grace, and the revelatory singularity of the cross. How can one theologize about God when not in orbit around the cross? This orbit must be both intellectual and in the heart or core of one's being and desires: "Dogmatics is possible only as a *theologia crucis*, in the act of obedience which is certain in faith, but which for this very reason is humble."[36] We cannot "bypass or overcome the man-God Jesus Christ, but Jesus confronts, condemns and overcomes them. This occurs most immediately and most shockingly in the cross, being God's final 'No!' to modern pride, arrogance, and the self-empowered pursuit of glory."[37] For Luther and Scripture, "God humbled the proud and gave grace to the humble."[38] Luther's "conception of God, Christology, anthropology, soteriology, doctrine of the word, sacraments, the church, ministry, and ethics all stand in the context of the cross."[39]

The analogy of faith for Luther is staurological and soteriological. By way of contrast, Wesley is more broadly soteriological:

> What helped Wesley avoid fragmentary proof texting was another of his exegetical principles: that any particular Scripture must be interpreted according to the "analogy of faith." For Wesley, this term referred to a "connected chain of Scripture truths."

35. Saler, *Theologia Crucis*, 33.
36. Barth, *Doctrine of the Word*, 14.
37. Bradbury, *Cross Theology*, 155.
38. Kadai, "Luther's Theology," 185.
39. Kadai, "Luther's Theology," 200.

He highlighted four soteriological truths in particular: the corruption of sin, justification by faith, the new birth, and present inward and outward holiness. He believed that it was the shared articulation of these truths that gave the diverse components of Scripture their unity. Accordingly, he required that all passages be read in light of these truths.[40]

Luther does not ignore the broad scope of soteriology in his analogy of faith; he simply locates the core in the cross and focuses on the cross: "Luther's theology is—and Lutherans would do well to heed this—Christocentric. Man's relationship to God depends on the saving event of the cross of Christ."[41] In addition, "Luther's theology is revelation oriented. God meets man in the cross of Jesus Christ. Now His gracious revelation continues in the word, the Holy Scriptures. God also offers His gracious forgiveness in the sacraments of baptism and the Eucharist."[42] The theology of the cross views the cross as the theological anchor for theology and practice.

THEOLOGIA CRUCIS AS DETERMINISTIC AND SPIRITUALLY FORMATIVE SUFFERING AND PURGATION

Within this broader theological context of Christocentric staurology and soteriology, Luther pivots away from the theology of glory, mysticism, *ascecis*, and asceticism—all of which he personally tried in his failed quest—to articulate a very earthy theology of the cross as divinely determined spiritually formative cruciform suffering. This aspect of Luther's theology, very capable of abuse, can certainly preach in certain theological quarters.

The real object of praise for Luther is "God's own work which He performs in the believer; it is joyful suffering. Of course this does not agree with those who are ready to praise God only when He does well to them." God "places the cross of Christ on them [believers] in order to help them maintain their humble spirit. Humility . . . is a truly Christian virtue. God cannot condone the proud, powerful and smart-alecky [reflective of the theology of glory]." The "Christian must remain humble, truly humble. He should be the last person to recognize his own humility, let alone boast about it. But even a humble Christian must accept the cross of suffering." While faith is properly tested, the Christian "surrenders patiently [to] that which God

---

40. Maddox, *Responsible Grace*, 38.

41. Kadai, "Luther's Theology," 200.

42. Kadai, "Luther's Theology," 200.

sees fit to deprive him of." The Christian, much in contrast to contemporary entitlement culture is not to demand rights "because in God's sight man has no rights. He will patiently suffer wrong if necessary, endure shame if that is his lot. All this he will do for Christ's sake and in so doing will cling to Him alone." In some cases the believer's suffering will be "for the sake of the community in which he lives."[43]

The hidden God often "acts as a tyrant, who in Joseph's story deserts the father and hurls the son into slavery." The hidden God appears as death and hell, and often "it seems that only groanings, tears, troubles, and oppression for the poor prevail. Rather than seeing God's face, man gazes at the devil's [rather than God's] behind." The proper and learned response of the believer is to "trust that behind the mask is the true face of God, according to which He is the God of life, glory, salvation, joy and peace." Hidden behind the terror of the holy and these "frightening faces" is the God who "provides salvation. This a Christian can and must know, but only by God's grace, and in faith. So a Christian dutifully bears burdens, endures ill and pain, and lets God act as he pleases." The believer is to "hope, pray, listen to the word of God, and cling to it." And "no matter how angry God seems, men should believe that He is their personal Savior and Father."[44]

This cruciform suffering is essential: "Spiritual trials, struggles of conscience, sorrow, and anguish must also occur. The heart must be smitten by terror; the old man must be destroyed [or crucified]. Struggles with unbelief, indignation against God, even despair plague the Christian because he often cannot see the will of God and His counsel in time of suffering." Suffering is sent by God to deal with pride, purge of sin, punish for sin, "or as chastisement for the benefit of others who see and hear about it." Regardless of the situation, even though "the affairs of the world may often confound the Christian . . . he can—and this in spite of what he may see or hear—believe by grace in God's gracious presence."[45] Kadai contends, "There are no more profound answers to the perennial [and most contemporary question] 'Why did this have to happen to me?' than those based on the *theologia crucis.*"[46]

Luther's final and direct counsel to the suffering "is clear: Be still; let God rule."[47]

43. Kadai, "Luther's Theology," 188–90.

44. Kadai, "Luther's Theology," 192–93.

45. Kadai, "Luther's Theology," 193–94, 200.

46. Kadai, "Luther's Theology," 203.

47. Kadai, "Luther's Theology," 194.

Hence, we have Luther's strong advice to his own dying mother and to his grieving friend illustrative of his deterministic framing of suffering and theodicy. Much could be said concerning the psychological and contextual dynamics at work here, but that exceeds the purpose of this book.

Most salient in this discussion of suffering are these elements: (1) divine determinism and patient surrender to the will of God, (2) non-meritorious identification with the cross of Christ, (3) God's hiddenness in suffering and the need for eyes of faith, (4) the purging of the soul of negative affections and intentions and the nurturing of humility, and (5) discipline for the sake of community.

Yet these conspicuous elements certainly can be abused, thus enabling the abusers of the suffering, so the question emerges, especially in our day, as to whether the theology of the cross offers any real hope for those suffering from systemic evil. Does the cross spark any motivation to liberate the oppressed? Kadai affirms that viewing Luther's teaching "in terms of *imitatio Christi* is too simple. God calls on Christians to accept the cross in hope and faith. This may have implications for contemporary social concerns. It may even suggest guiding principles in charting out the Christian quest for ameliorating social injustices . . . [and speak to] Luther's understanding of the concept of vocation . . . [in view of a *theologia crucis* that clearly] demands a radical reevaluation of all values."[48]

THEOLOGIA CRUCIS AS LIBERATION VIA IDENTIFICATION WITH WEAKNESS AND SUFFERING

Saler, greatly influenced by Moltmann, provides a fresh, concise, and fairly recent (2016) articulation of how the theology of the cross challenges contemporary values and propels believers into the marketplace of social injustice. This work is particularly helpful given its goal of service, as it is presented in a form easily comprehensible by pastors and laity.

Saler's application of Luther begins with a reorientation of vision:

> A central claim of Christianity is that the God of Jesus Christ is manifest to the world, not primarily in the form of theophany and power, but in the form of weakness and suffering; thus, in order to "find God" and God's actions in the world, it is precisely in the everyday suffering of humanity and creation—even the most terrible suffering—that one should look. Indeed, it is precisely because suffering is so ubiquitous (including suffering at the hands of injustice, the "passions" of those who are victims

48. Kadai, "Luther's Theology," 201.

of theological and political lust for domination no less than was Christ himself) that the centrality of the cross to faith remains . . . compelling to many. . . . Theology of the cross invokes the cross in order to try to speak rightly about the pain of the world and the God who, in Christ, involves the divine life in that pain—even unto death.[49]

In the background of this vision are, of course, the twentieth-century experiences and theological reflections of Bonhoeffer, Moltmann, and Pannenberg, especially the journey through Nazi terror and oppression and the search for God amidst asking, "Why hast thou forsaken me?" (Matt 27:46, KJV). This vision finds "God's truth and God's actions in the least likely places—the battered body of a crucified criminal, the ugly and marginalized places of our own worlds . . . [thus] keeping our projections of our own agendas [theology of glory] onto God in check. . . . [While the] theology of the cross has lent itself to abuse and the support of oppression . . . [the symbol of the cross has also] been taken up and utilized as a tool against oppressive concepts of God. . . . [The *theologia cruces*] can either be deadly or life-giving."[50]

A most intriguing discussion emerged some years ago when I was attending an American Academy of Religion meeting in Chicago. Feminist theologians were concerned that the cross, especially the satisfaction theory of the atonement—though the critique was much broader than one theory—justified child abuse and therefore the abuse of women. James Cone, whose thought on this eventually *culminated in The Cross and the Lynching Tree* (2011), pointed out that in the black experience the cross was an absolutely essential symbol and theology representing liberation and redemption for victims of lynching on crosses—also known as trees. And this is Saler's point: The *theologia crucis* needs to be handled with care and not superficially dismissed. Proper deployment of this theology should cause theological "'stammer' by interrupting overconfident and projective speech about God . . . [and] providing the basis by Christians and others can understand how God chooses to interact with the ugliness of our world, and do so salvifically. The cross is what allows theology to talk, but it is also what forces theology to stammer."[51]

Luther's theology of the cross helps us stammer by serving as a powerful model and prophetic critique of "human pretension and politically oppressive theology." Luther challenged the "arrogance of [the] theology [of

49. Saler, *Theologia Crucis*, 6.
50. Saler, *Theologia Crucis*, 9.
51. Saler, *Theologia Crucis*, 10.

glory]" of his day by going after the medieval theological consensus that justified "the power of the church to impose the implications of this theology [e.g., indulgences, merits]." For Saler, "there is no one set of tenets or propositions that makes up the *theologia crucis*; it is more a kind of methodological bearing centered on the theologian's positioning vis-a-vis the scandal of God's choosing to reveal saving truth in the form of brokenness and scandal. The cross gives us lenses to see . . . [that which is] very different from what is on display in theologies of 'glory.'" Luther challenged "a kind of theo-politico edifice" in his day, and so should we.[52]

In our own day, "theology unchastened by the cross" has "located obedience to God's will in earthly success rather than fidelity to the crucified Messiah. . . . Bad thinking about God leads to exploitative churches built in God's name." Hence, based on Luther's writings, Saler affirms that a true theologian of the cross "must be subject to persecution." Persecution "suffered by the true theologian is itself part of the formation by which correct perception and proclamation of the gospel can happen."[53]

For Saler, Moltmann and Bonhoeffer got it right on the theology of the cross and arm us with a "combat theology" application. Believers are to combat "oppressive political and church structures," and any "god who serves as the religious supplement of the status quo." Even within the church, "not all Christian conceptions of God are worthy of the name." And some are arguably worse than atheism. In the West, a church that has increasingly lost its power, status, and cozy espousal of a theology of glory, and which no longer serves as the "cultural broker of society's morals," may now be freed "to pursue the countercultural path of the cross to be among those that society deems disreputable or weak."[54] This last quote reinforces the contention of this work that the perennially relevant theology of the cross is a theology whose time especially has arrived.

Hence, as Saler's argument progresses, he increasingly identifies with what, in the West, would be described as the more politically (contemporary not classical) liberal and socialist political spectrum and definitions of compassion and justice. As with so many advocates of contemporary liberal political theory, the optics of and trust in big government are unexplainably preferable to the optics of and trust in big corporations. The optics of centralized governmental power and compassion are also preferred over the optics of and trust in some form of what Michael Novak refers to as the charitable freedom of the citizenry in trinitarian democratic capitalism.

52. Saler, *Theologia Crucis*, 17–23.

53. Saler, *Theologia Crucis*, 24–26.

54. Saler, *Theologia Crucis*, 45–46.

Novak believes that such freedom is far less dangerous and much more generous, sustainable, and truly more ameliorative than centralized statist solutions.[55] Marvin Olaskey made a similar argument in his classic work, *The Tragedy of American Compassion* some years ago. This debate will not be settled in this work, but it does clearly illuminate how theologies of the cross can course in varied or even opposite directions.

For example, Saler's suspicion of capitalism is clear when noting the "optics of the cross" that resist "the optics of the marketplace."[56] Yet, before we conclude that a theology of the cross today must take on a particular socio-political agenda, surely at least one question is in order. After endless wars and genocides by powerful governments, could it be that fallen humanity at least has the potential for much greater harm via unchecked governments, police forces, and brutal military actions than big corporations, even when taking into account the sometimes deleterious influence of the corporate world on governments? Indeed, any sound theology of the cross today must remember that the vast majority of genocides—if not all—have been justified in the name of social justice. Might truly fair and truly free markets serve to check both the abusive power of governments and the abusive power and influence of monopolistic corporations and perhaps encourage the promotion of the general welfare? In view of profound human depravity, perhaps the civilizational key is to provide checks and balances to fallen human centers of power in any form (government, law, education, media, and corporations), harness self-interest for the common good, and exalt principles and values of truth and justice (*Lex Rex*) over any self-appointed sovereigns. Kings, government, corporations, education, media, and even social justice movements often seem to claim to speak and act on behalf of God and may function as yet another disastrous *Rex Lex*.[57] This observation is not intended as a fixed conclusion for this present work

55. Novak, *Spirit*.

56. Saler, *Theologia Crucis*, 82.

57. This is an intentional expansion of the dualistic "Law is King" versus the "King is Law" framework of Samuel Rutherford's seventeenth-century *The Law and the Prince*. In Rutherford's day the conflict was between the divine rights of kings and the subjection of kings to laws rooted in justice. Rutherford wanted all governments to be subject to eternal, transcultural laws and principles. In our day Rutheford's insights require much more complex analysis and application. For example, Stalinist-Leninist communism claimed to be a manifestation of social justice for the working class and opposed to the divine right of the kings or Czars. This version of communism claimed to be placing a liberationist ideology ("for the people" or working class, of course) above human rulers. In reality, this genocidal global movement was far more tyrannical than many, if not most, kings in history with the Politburo functioning as an elitist, self-serving *Rex Lex* and compassionate justice for the marginalized (the people of the cross) being used as a *cause celebre* and ideology that tortured, murdered, and crushed those very people.

but simply as a check and balance to the presumptive identification of the theology of the cross with any unchecked definition of compassionate justice, including contemporary politically liberal social justice movements.

In any event, Saler's concern is for the optics of the marketplace, not the optics of Leviathan government, relative to identification with the poor and the oppressed. Saler believes

> the theology of the cross has, within the last several decades, proven itself to be a potent weapon in the hands of those who seek to subvert theologies that support unjust status quos, and to replace them with alternatives that are more faithful to the gospel by being more attuned to the power of that gospel to subvert human domination of the poor and of the earth. . . . This dual attack upon bad theology and bad politics was at the heart of Luther's own *theologia crucis*, and it is the aspect of his legacy that has endured and grown most significantly in our own day.[58]

Needless to say, it is somewhat speculative to attempt to speak for a Luther today who certainly challenged the status quo at times but also penned *Against the Murderous, Thieving Hordes of Peasants* (1525) written after his Heidelberg theses, which emphasized the theology of the cross versus the theology of glory. Yet this debate will have to be left to others. The key plea for the present moment is not to identify easily any formulation of the theology of the cross or a theology of glory with a contemporary sociopolitical agenda.

Wright's *The Day the Revolution Began: Reconsidering the Meaning of Jesus's Crucifixion*, referenced previously in this work, has a connection to the liberationist thread in Saler. The profoundly eschatological nature of *The Day the Revolution Began* will be addressed in chapters 11 and 12 when dealing with the constructive theological task of this present work regarding eschatology, liberation, approximation, and doxology. Wright argues that his approach is truly a paradigm-shifting conceptualization of the cross and eschatology for many believers today—especially for American believers.

58. Saler, *Theologia Crucis*, 54.

3

Deterministic versus Non-Deterministic Staurology

SOVEREIGN GOODNESS AND PREVENIENT GRACE

PRIOR TO MOVING TOWARD the constructive task of assessing and modifying key themes in the representative theologies of the cross, the deterministic flavor of much of Luther's thought will be contrasted with an alternative theological option. Reviewing the whole of non-deterministic theological options relative to the implications for the theology of the cross would exceed the limitations of multiple volumes, much less this present book. Given that some theologies of the cross have been premised upon a divine determinism, it should be useful to review a select few of Arminius's key counter-deterministic or non-deterministic emphases and explore the possible staurological implications as a precursor to the constructive and summative arguments and conclusions in Part 2. This chapter presents Arminius's well-known views but also attempts to elucidate how, while moving beyond Arminius, Arminian thought might interface with the theology of the cross. This chapter also serves as preparatory for the next chapter concerning the cross, Wesley, and the pietistic tradition.

Luther lived from 1483 to 1546, and Arminius, originally a staunch defender of deterministic theology, lived from 1560 to 1609. The mother and a number of relatives of Arminius perished in a religiously and politically motivated massacre at Oudewater. Perhaps this massacre, which was part of the Eighty Years' War, reflects behavior inspired by a very fatal theology of glory. Perhaps this event also influenced the later theology of Arminius. In any event, Arminius's modification of deterministic theology ultimately launched a theology of religious and political toleration, or liberation from oppression, that likely even coursed its way through the writings of John Locke and the American *Declaration of Independence*.[1] This observation raises the possibility that one could see a logical and historical connection between a constructive staurology and the rejection of an anemic or cancerous theology of glory, including a rejection of a false theology of God's glory, and movements emphasizing the harnessing of governmental power, the God-given right to associate freely, the right to protest, and the right to political freedom.

Arminius viewed himself as still Reformed even after modifying key reformed assumptions. He wanted to reform the Reformed church via a return to Scripture and a better application of reason to foundational theological assumptions concerning God and salvation. Hence, Arminius argued that it was possible to affirm God's glorious sovereignty and glory along with God's infinite goodness while preserving a biblical doctrine of election, human depravity, and the total failure of works righteousness. *Sola scriptura, sola fide, sola gratia, soli Deo Gloria,* and *solus Christus,* for Arminius, could all be preserved without making God a tyrant or humanity a puppet.

For Arminius, humanity can do no good "without the continued aids of Divine Grace"[2] or without prevenient or preventing grace. Arminian humanity was actually a greater sinner because of the freedom of responsibility that came with grace.

Sovereign goodness in the form of grace is the source of, and is prior to, all human goodness. The priority of grace is consistently maintained: "In this manner, I ascribe to grace The Commencement, The Continuance, and the Consummation of All Good. . . . [Even regenerate man] can neither conceive, will, nor do any good at all, nor resist any evil temptation, without this preventing [prevenient] and exciting, this following and co-operating grace."[3] And "justification is by grace alone, there being no meritoriousness in our faith that occasions justification since it is only through prevenient grace that fallen humanity can exercise that faith."[4]

Arminius's conceptualization of theological anthropology, justification by faith alone, and prevenient grace touched the very edges of Calvinism

---

1. See the section in this chapter on "Sovereign Goodness, Toleration, and Liberation."

2. Arminius, *Writings*, 1:253–54.

3. Arminius, *Writings*, 1:253–54.

4. Grider, "Arminianism," 79.

and attempted to preserve the divine sovereignty *and* goodness. Prevenient grace, which enabled the entire fallen world to respond to the gospel of the cross, issued forth from divine sovereignty while avoiding divine tyranny and reflecting divine goodness. God's sovereignty was, for Arminius, glorious and good. Prevenient grace also meant that even fallen humanity was personally responsible for *hamartia*. All of these emphases run counter to a false and oppressive theology of glory.

Arminius sought a via media or "a middle way . . . neither inflicting an injury on Grace, as the Pelagians do, nor on Free Will as do the Manichees."[5] He planted the seeds amidst the often blood-soaked soil of Europe for a new framework for a theology of the cross and glory, as well as for the conjunctive theology of John Wesley. Outler brilliantly summarizes Wesley's conjunctive theology:

> [Wesley] glimpsed the underlying unity of Christian truth in both the Catholic and Protestant traditions and . . . turned this recognition to the services of a great popular religious reform and renewal. In the name of Christianity both Biblical and patristic, he managed to transcend the stark doctrinal disjunctions [and theologies of glory?] which had spilled so much ink and blood since Augsburg [Reformation] and Trent [Counter-Reformation]. In their stead, he proceeded to develop a theological fusion of faith and good works, Scripture and tradition, revelation and reason, God's sovereignty and human freedom, universal redemption and conditional election, Christian liberty and an ordered polity, the assurance of pardon and the risks of "falling from grace," original sin and Christian perfection. In each of these conjunctions, as he insisted almost tediously, the initiative is with God, the response with man.[6]

This work argues that this approach is a helpful conjunctive methodology or framework for a biblically and theologically sound theology of glory and theology of the cross. In particular, overemphasizing arbitrariness as a key component of sovereignty, or shrouding sovereignty with mystery such that God's goodness is tertiary at best, or essentially redefined out of existence, lays the foundation for a distorted theology of glory—both in reference to the glory of God and the glory of creation and humanity. Likewise, this work contends that a sound theology of cross, kingdom, and glory is also conjunctive to the major millennial or eschatological views.[7]

5. Arminius, *Writings*, 1:372.

6. Outler, *John Wesley*, iv.

7. See chapters 9–12.

Calvin fostered heteronomy, Pelagianism fostered self-sufficient autonomy, and Arminius fostered a grace-based autotheonomy: "An ultimate dependency on divine grace which does not abrogate, but rather grounds, limits and fulfills autonomy."[8] Heteronomy moves toward a false theology of God's glory or the glory of the elect, where some who are weak and marginalized are either viewed as reprobate or predetermined victims, and God is viewed as arbitrary rather than the source of goodness and the ground of ethics. Autonomy likewise moves toward a false theology of glory, where humanity only sees the cross as folly, a scandal, or a stumbling block, and humans exalt themselves—even through religion. Autotheonomy truly glorifies God and both condemns and eschatologically glorifies humanity through the cross.

SOVEREIGN GOODNESS, ELECTION, AND DAMNATION

For Arminius, prior reformers had disordered the divine decrees and departed from Scripture by starting with election and reprobation, which were often arbitrary decrees. For Arminius the first decree was the appointment of Christ as Savior via the cross, followed by the decree to receive favorably those who, by grace alone, repent and believe. This repentance and belief unitary complex is only possible in view of the third decree to provide the necessary means or grace to make possible and allow for repentance and faith. The fourth decree (election and reprobation) followed the first three in terms of knowing God's heart and mind and was based on foreknowledge of the grace-assisted acceptance or rejection of Christ. Hence, we have a sovereignly good *sola gratia* contingency or conditionalism.[9] The cross is for us and for everyone. Arminius did not develop a specific theology of the cross *per se*, but his conception of the cross levels all of humanity in the shadow and luminescence of the cross. Justice is not "just us" but is rooted in sovereign goodness and the amazing gift of freedom. Any church, government, or leader who abrogates grace-based freedom clearly illustrates a destructive and manipulative theology of glory. It is hard to resist the conjecture that Arminius was battling toxic theologies of glory in the Reformed and Roman Catholic traditions under the banner of the cross defined as an unlimited atonement. These toxic theologies personally impacted his family.

Arminius believed that some prior and very deterministic reformers had made Christ and the cross a subordinate cause of salvation, thereby diminishing Christ's work and the cross and consequently elevating the

8. Adams, "Arminius," 88–112.

9. Arminius, *Writings*, 1:241–45.

deterministic decrees. This inversion or subversion led to advocacy for an irresistible grace that also subverted ethics. If ethics is centered in the nature of God and the goal of the Christian life is to be Christlike, and Christ is the exact representation of the Father, then irresistible grace is a deficient model for how we should treat each other. Is it not the case that a dark theology of glory lies at the core of oppression? If Arminian thought is faithfully represented here, then irresistible grace is the ultimate grounding and expression of what Luther referred to as the manipulative and oppressive theology of glory. Hence, from an Arminian vantage point, it would seem that Luther's determinism undermines his own theology of cross and glory.

SOVEREIGN GOODNESS AND THE ATONEMENT

The sovereignly good "Lord of peace" (2 Thess 3:16) and the Christ who is the Prince of Peace thus provided an atonement on the cross that was not limited only to the elect, but which especially targeted the meek, weak, oppressed and marginalized. Blessed are the lost sheep, the poor, the meek, and those who are persecuted. For Arminian thought, God's sovereignly good grace seeks to save all who will believe because of prevenient grace and by grace alone. The cross and prevenient grace includes or targets everyone and excludes no one. God's sovereign goodness is directed towards all; therefore, there is no place for self-righteousness or self-glorification by the elect. The elect are forgiven, infinite debtors. Freedom exclusively flows out of sovereign goodness and is a divine gift requiring enormous responsibility.

– All are created profoundly equal and all are equally and profoundly fallen. –

Even pagans are responsible because of the cross, which is a form of prevenient grace. Prevenient grace also levels all because all are the objects of redemption via the triune Spirit. Arminius is much more hopeful about non-Christians doing good works, even if the motives for such works are mixed, than his deterministic contemporaries. Arminius places a much greater emphasis on universal moral responsibility via grace in spite of universal depravity. Political and religious oppression and massacres thus reflect, to borrow Luther's terms, not the theology of the cross but the theo-political edifice birthed by the cancerous theology of glory.

Hence, Arminius would side more with Barth and Brian regarding the *Deus absconditus*. The glorious mystery of Christ and the cross, once concealed, is now fully revealed and is being globally proclaimed through gospel preaching and the convicting work of the triune Holy Spirit. Arminius is arguably a major theological contributor to the modern missions' movement and fervor, since Christ truly died for all and "who desires all people to be saved and to come to the knowledge of the truth" (1 Tim 2:4, ESV). The cross of Arminius, by definition, counters elitist theologies of glory.

There is no place in Arminius for a mysterious, still hidden will of God that grounds and justifies oppression, manipulation of others, theopolitical tyranny, ethical subversion, neglect of the marginalized, or which views human suffering as directly, specifically, and divinely determined. For Arminius, since sovereignty is infinitely good, Luther's "Be still and let God rule" is entirely reframed within the context of the following: sovereign goodness; a just, revealed, and caring heavenly father; human depravity; human fallenness; unlimited atonement; prevenient grace; responsible human freedom; trust in sovereignly good divine Providence; and, the ardent quest for holiness.

Arminian thought will not, based on this conception of God and the cross, torment the suffering and dying by claiming to know that such experiences are divine punishment and chastisement or purgation. Such experiences could be used by God for discipline, but the assumption that the suffering are somehow predetermined to suffer runs counter to Arminian intuitions. A true follower of Arminius will not console his suffering mother by referencing divine determinism and divinely determined purgation. Instead, Arminian thought, in the face of tribulations, will encourage trust in sovereignly good Providence while calling the faithful to serve as conduits of overflowing love via personal immersion in and identification with the suffering. In contrast to purgation consolation to those in pain, Mother Theresa's self-sacrifice for the physically and spiritually needy is a more fitting model of an Arminian theology of the cross applied to the suffering. Theologies of glory that classify the rich, poor, black, white, or any race or demographic as reprobate or *untermensch* emerge from reprobate theologies of glory.

Hence, it is of great importance to the present discussion, regarding the Arminian corrective, that Christ died for all. In addition to leveling all of humanity, and providing hope for all, such a *theologia crucis* allows for "Arminian" prevenient grace to all, which makes missions, evangelism, kingdom advance, holiness, and civilizational influence possible. The eschatological Arminian cross brings the Abrahamic blessing to the whole world for which Christ suffered and died. The crucified Christ crucified the present age and initiated the coming kingdom already.

SOVEREIGN GOODNESS, TOLERATION, AND LIBERATION

James Luther Adams, one-time professor of Christian Ethics at Harvard, suggests that the tolerance impulse in Arminius and the Remonstrants (followers of Arminius), emanating from sovereign goodness, prevenient grace, and unlimited atonement, has significantly affected the very structure of society and politics in the West:

> Arminianism has been a major force in the development of . . . what is called freedom of association. . . . This sort of freedom of association is a watershed between the left and right wing of the Reformation, between territorialism and voluntarism. It is the harbinger of the modern conception of the multi-group society. . . . The Arminian thrust in history has been in the direction of pluralism, on the presupposition that flexibility and openness make way for the appropriate reception of divine grace and for the fuller response to the gospel. Freedom within associations and freedom of associations thus become the social-organizational consequences. . . . Just as God had given [humanity] . . . freedom to choose, so [Arminius and the Remonstrants] . . . felt [they] should give others freedom also—freedom not only to choose but freedom also to associate."[10]

This approach clearly counters both a deterministic theology of the cross and a theo-politico state complex rooted in a corrupted theology of glory. Most importantly, this frame of reference for a theology of the cross and kingdom presupposes individual, communal, social, cultural, historical, and civilizational fluidity—as opposed to determinism. All can significantly change for the better—or the worse—contingent upon the response to grace. This is why Arminians and Wesleyans speak often of the realism of human nature and the optimism of grace. The whole world can be saved, and those who are being saved can be saved wholly or entirely—even to the uttermost (Heb 7:25). Individuals and civilizations can be greatly impacted by kingdom advance. Slave owners can walk away from the despicable practice of slavery. Wesley can draw upon Arminian theology and Wesleyan revivalism to encourage Wilberforce to press on in the way of the cross by risking everything and seeking to liberate the slaves. Wilberforce, via the British Parliament, patiently, and under much duress and ridicule from the fraudulent theologians and philosophers of glory in the church, the media,

---

10. Adams, "Arminius," 92, 101, 109–10.

and Parliament, can and did spark the abolition of the slave trade and the eventual abolition of slavery.

Personal and social holiness are not only possible but unified and inseparable within an approximative, non-utopian, or proleptic understanding of future kingdom cruciform advance. A fluid rather than fatalistic or deterministic future allows for many visitations of transformational grace in the twilight of the Second Coming.

It is not inconsequential or mere coincidence that "John Locke wrote his Letter on Toleration after reading Grotius,"[11] a follower of Arminius, or that the earliest and most effective defense of universal redemption by the Quakers (and written by Samuel Fisher), very early advocates of abolitionism, quoted from and referred to Arminius.[12] Arminianism at its best is a liberating theology of the cross and a sound theology of glory! According to Adams, Arminius himself became a symbol for toleration.[13]

Arminian humanity is, therefore, more sinful, more dignified, more fluid or indeterminate, and more liberated via an Arminian conception of the cross and kingdom inclusive of the Arminian assumptions presented in this chapter. And God is more sovereign and glorious because of his infinite Goodness and his gift of grace-birthed spiritual and political freedom. Cross and glory are thus theocentric and Christocentric. Arminian thought became the framework for John and Charles Wesley and the eighteenth-century Wesleyan revivals that ultimately swept the globe and became an important influencer on and dimension of the American religious experience. It is no wonder that Wesley founded and edited *The Arminian Magazine.*

Prior to turning to the constructive section of this present work in Part 2, contextualizing the theology of the cross in relationship to critical data from church history and historical theology should be of great value. The pietist and Wesleyan awakenings are instructive, reinforce arguments in this present work, and foster a deepening and broadening of the applicability of Luther's signature cross and glory doctrine today. While this book is more of a theological argument, and chapter 4 might be superficially viewed as a church history excursus, a careful reading will uncover core theological principles and absolutely essential historical, contextual, and substantive content.

A few examples of the importance of the next chapter relevant to our conversation will have to suffice:

11. Hoonderdaal, "Dutch Theology," 455.

12. Hoonderdaal, "Dutch Theology," 455.

13. Adams, "Arminius," 92, 101, 109–10.

- Significant evidence is presented that Luther's posture is *contra* modernity and *contra* nominalism, which reinforces the thesis of this work that Luther is not to blame for modernity or nihilism. Chapter 4 maintains that *the outlook of modernity* stands as the polar antithesis to Luther's discovery.

- Compelling documentation is presented suggesting that Luther's theology of the cross did indeed have what we might refer to today as a holiness emphasis and did not end with only alien righteousness. Luther's rejection of antinomianism and alien righteousness reductionism was rooted in the theology of the cross, especially the expected, automatic, symbiotic, or spontaneous gratitude for the cross.[14] The pietistic and Wesleyan revivals, as with Arminius, elevated the connection among cross, holiness, and kingdom. These revivals particularly connected the cross to the multiple stages of grace supportive of many Wesleyan themes regarding sanctification and holiness, including world-changing holiness.

- The Silesian revival, in general, the amazing children's revival, in particular, and the Wesleyan revivals all advanced the *theologia crucis* in a more pneumatic, Trinitarian, and kingdom-centric direction. Luther influenced Wesley through these historic awakenings or revivals. Cross, Spirit, and kingdom became more organic after Luther and certainly bridged or pointed to the kingdom eschatological arguments of chapters 9–12 of this work. Chapter 4 evidences this fact by pointing out how the cross became more significant, theologically robust, and pneumatic for the Wesleyan revival subsequent to Aldersgate.

The historical information alone in the next chapter is superb and provides an enormously helpful context for the theological argumentation of this work. The comparative work (Luther, pietist leaders, Wesleyan leaders) greatly illumines the discussion of cross and kingdom.

Dr. J. Steve O'Malley is the distinguished guest author of the next chapter and is an accomplished scholar with expertise in theology, church history, pietism, renewal and discipleship theology, as well as the historical and theological foundations for Wesleyan thought. He served as the founding director of the Center for the Study of World Christian Revitalization Movements at Asbury Theological Seminary, which received a research grant in

14. I would add that Luther's overall tone on what sanctification or holiness is possible in this life, however, is more suppression than eradication or even longitudinal transformation, as well illustrated by his famous beard analogy for the persistence of sin in the Christian life. On sanctification, Luther is more in the suppression camp not the eradication, Keswickian, or entire sanctification camp.

2007 from the Henry Luce Foundation. This center engaged in cutting-edge research and produced many helpful resources and manuscripts on global Christian revitalization movements. His graduate degrees are from the Yale and Drew Universities. Dr. O'Malley is the author of many books and articles, including a forthcoming volume on *The Origin of the Wesleyan Theological Vision for Christian Globalization and the Pursuit of Pentecost in Early Pietist Revivalism*. In 2017 he received the Distinguished Scholar Award by the prestigious Wesleyan Theological Society.

This next chapter will serve as an effective bridge between the core Arminian emphases relevant to a discussion of the *theologia crucis* and pietist and Wesleyan thought as we move toward the enduring themes of a twenty-first-century theology of the cross and kingdom. O'Malley will carefully make such connections and helpfully conclude the following,

> Hence, a parallel trajectory appears between the stirrings of revival in central Europe and among the Methodists in Britain in the early modern era. There was the Kingdom theme of the Silesian revival, whose purpose, beginning with the children, Steinmetz called the "Building of the Kingdom of God on Earth," and that was matched by the homilies and hymns of the Wesleys on behalf of the "grand Pentecost" which was coming from the "General Spread of the Gospel" on earth.

4

Theology of the Cross in Luther and Its Reconfiguration in the Pietistic and Wesleyan Awakenings

J. Steven O'Malley

IN LIGHT OF THE recent celebration of the five hundredth anniversary of the Reformation, the moment has arrived to consider what happened to Luther's theology of the cross in the annals of the first awakening (revival) in the Protestant tradition, which occurred in Silesia. There, two centuries after Luther announced the doctrine, it resurfaced in altered form and, in that form, became a grid upon which John Wesley adapted its content to function as the staple for the early Methodist revival in England.

This investigation proceeds from a fresh interpretation of the doctrine in Luther to the reconstruction of the doctrine by Johann Adam Steinmetz (1690–1761) in the context of the awakening that grew out of the Silesian children's revival (1707/8). Then, we examine the adaptation of that message by Christian David in his extensive interactions at the Moravian center of Herrnhut with the visiting John Wesley. That visit occurred in August 1738 on the heels of his Aldersgate conversion on May 25 of that year. Wesley stated in his journal that he was decisively influenced by David's presentation, even regarding it as providing him with the missing piece that would complete his theology of revival. It is noteworthy that Wesley's interaction with David on this matter directly preceded his return to England and the start of the evangelical revival in England in 1739, which occurred under Wesley's preaching at Bristol.[1]

Luther's theology of the cross was a development from his reported act of posting his 95 theses on his church door in the Saxon town of Wittenberg on October 17, 1517. They would become the herald heard round the church and the world of that day, signaling a new era was now at hand— the day of God's appearing. It was made possible by Luther's recovery of the living Word of God and its central message of personal salvation by grace through faith in Jesus Christ. He articulated this message as part of his protest against the prevailing practices of the Roman Catholic Church in linking salvation to the purchase of certificates of indulgence. This practice had effectively tied salvation to the church's quest for worldly influence and glory. At the cost of burdening an already impoverished and oppressed laity with the obligation of seeking absolution from the guilt penalty of sin, it was offered in return for the monetary purchase of papal-approved certificates of indulgence. This practice effectively tied salvation to the church's quest for worldly influence and glory. It came at the cost of burdening an already impoverished laity with the obligation of seeking absolution from the guilt penalty of sin in return for the monetary purchase of papal-approved certificates of indulgence.

In one of his three landmark treatises of 1520, the now maligned Luther boldly published his *Freedom of a Christian*, which first introduced German-speaking Europeans to the message of a personal God of grace and freedom in what became known as his "theology of the cross."

LUTHER AND THE PROBLEM OF MODERNITY

In another of my recent studies, Luther's development of this Pauline theme is viewed as the antithesis of the cultural ethos of modernity. In a notable treatment of that topic published in the early post-World War II era, the author, Richard Weaver, with the title *Ideas Have Consequences*,[2] identified as a core problem of modernity the sense of cultural malaise—a perception of Western culture as being inherently hollow with a void of moral authority to which nations might successfully appeal in addressing the catastrophes born of totalitarian regimes, which were then threatening human existence. His diagnosis: The postwar society was one that had lost moral compass,

---

1. A full treatment of this development is found in my current project, which provides a full translation of Steinmetz's *Pentecost Addresses*, and the larger historical context. See O'Malley, *Pietism*.

2. Weaver, *Ideas*, vi, 14.

one that desired to believe again in value and obligation but was not willing to recognize how it has lost that foundation nor to face what is required to recover it.

Weaver traced the source of this problem to the misuse of human freedom thanks to the triumph of nominalism in Western culture in the fourteenth century when "the denial of universals carried with it the denial of everything transcending experience."[3] This meant, inevitably, the denial of truth as truth. "Whereas nature had formerly been regarded as imitating a transcendent model" (which is called realism in philosophy), with the triumph of nominalism, "nature was now looked upon as containing all the principles of its own constitution and behavior."[4] Defects of nature cannot be thought of as suffering from any constitutional evil. And so human defects "are attributed to ignorance or social deprivation."[5] So much for the Augustinian doctrine of original sin and its concern for understanding man as one who always exists *coram Deo*.

Luther, in his declaration of human freedom, was inappropriately regarded in the post-Enlightenment era as representing the forerunner of a long line of modernist thinkers,[6] rather than having offered a strong word of protest to this slippery slope. That represents a reading of Luther that contradicts his intentions, which, as this study intends to demonstrate, stands squarely counter to such a reading.

As a consequence of critiquing the claims made for Luther's modernity, the present study demonstrates the greater feasibility of regarding Luther's theology of the cross, embodied in that 1520 treatise, as precursor to a quite different line of interpretation that occurred in one subsequent and influential expression of Lutheran theology.

That era will take us to the beginning of the eighteenth century, in the era of Pietism and the birth of revival in the larger Protestant tradition on the European continent. As a sequel to this study, the interface of John Wesley with this reconstituted Lutheran theology of the cross will be regarded, perhaps ironically, as an important incentive for the development of Wesley's doctrine of Pentecost and sanctification. The latter theme in Wesley studies has gained recent prominence in the landmark study on this subject by Professor Laurence Wood.[7]

3. Weaver, *Ideas*, vi, 14.

4. Weaver, *Ideas*, vi, 14.

5. Weaver, *Ideas*, vi, 14.

6. Since it is not our intent to decry all modern authors, *modernist* is deployed to characterize those authors who write within the ideology presented here, whose influence has been robust in modern liberal, political, and intellectual thought.

7. Wood, *Pentecost*.

Luther's Theology of the Cross within Its Historical Context

Those who favor Luther's affinities for modernity have sought evidence in his collegiate education. He graduated from Erfurt, a German university that chose to follow the *via moderna* (modern way) in early sixteenth-century Catholicism. This designation identified it as a center of nominalist thinking in late medieval Christendom. Instead of focusing on the great mysteries of the faith, Erfurt's faculty chose to emphasize a practical approach to theology based on helping persons negotiate the steps to salvation. It worked this way: the learner was repeatedly confronted with the assertion, "*facere quod in se est* (do your best, or to begin by doing what lies within you)!"[8] Today this same thing might be stated, "God helps those who help themselves." Focusing on the particulars known to exist, nominalists dismissed universals as mental fictions, acknowledging them only on the basis of fideism (blind faith)—a reductionism that anticipated that of modern theological liberalism.

Luther's exposure to the *via moderna* of modernism, although he was immersed in one version of its teachings, did not really "take" simply because its argument did not address his acute spiritual crisis. He wondered how he could ever know when he had arrived at the point where he was doing his best (*facere quod in se est*), where he had done all that lay within him for his salvation to meet God's expectations of righteousness. Here was the theological basis for his *Anfechtungen*, or moments of despair, which were only dispelled by his illumination through his rereading of the Pauline epistles.[9]

His critique of the nominalists at Erfurt was the intellectual expression of his existential struggle for faith. The biblical resource to which he turned to make his case is Paul's distinction of law and gospel. This distinction supplied the biblical grounding for his anthropology, including the various polarities concerning the meaning of righteousness, which he derives from those biblical texts.

Luther's first response to this nominalist challenge was rather bleak. His *Anfechtung*, an almost untranslatable word in German depicting Luther's mortal despair, suggests he had experienced God only as a punishing

8. Biel's explanation of the possibility of this *facere quod in se est* means everyone is by nature in a position to discharge this first duty. For God, however, the *facere quod in se est* means only one thing: "He is obliged, because he has placed the obligation on himself, to infuse his grace in everyone who has done his very best" (Oberman, *Harvest of Medieval Theology*, 132).

9. For an in-depth discussion of these early developments in Luther's life, see Bainton, *Here I Stand*, 15–44.

wrathful Deity, and Christ as the stern instrument of the Father's judgment. This darker side of Luther would align him with an apocalyptic worldview contrary to modern optimism and more akin to a prolonged state of penitential despair.[10] His God, rooted as it was in that austere culture, required a plenary righteousness from sinners that could come only through a painful, prolonged task of meriting sacramental grace, unaccompanied by any likelihood of its success in procuring assurance of personal acceptance by a holy God. It was like being consigned to eternal penance without absolution.

A seeker without hope of peace with God, he remained a tormented human being, putting on a brave front even as he prepared to begin his new vocation as a teacher of biblical studies. It would be pursued under his Augustinian monastic orders. His despair of finding peace of soul through religious observance and even through monastic vows, led him in desperation to seek access to an inaccessible book in those late medieval days, the holy Bible. His first serious sighting of a Bible may have been the one he saw chained to the library desk at the University of Erfurt. At that moment he determined his vocation to be the extrication of the Word of God from its entrapment in ecclesial bondage.[11]

This condition persisted through early lectures presented to his students at the University of Wittenberg. As Luther prepared to lecture on Romans, he encountered numerous instances of that dreaded phrase *iustita Dei* (the righteousness of God). Romans 1:16–17a was both the point of his despair and of his illumination. Please note, from his reading of the Vulgate of that day he understood this text as saying, "In the gospel a righteousness from God is required,"[12] a rendering that compounded Luther's dread of God's judgment upon him as a sinner, only deepening his *Anfechtung*.

Providentially, he then procured a copy of the recently published *koine* Greek text of the New Testament, which had recently been completed by the renowned Renaissance humanist, Erasmus. The text in Greek clearly declared that "the righteousness of God" is not required but is "revealed" (i.e., made known). It is gift, not a sentence, and it is revealed not unto damnation but unto faith as it reads, "It is a righteousness that is by faith from first to last" (Rom 1:17, NIV).[13] In brief, the good news in this moment of truth was the discovery that this dreaded *iustitia Dei* was, to Luther's

10. Gabriel Biel cited in Bornkamm, *Harvest of Medieval Theology*, 128.

11. For Luther, *Word of God* may reference Christ or God's entire redemptive activity with humanity through Christ as displayed in law, "in which God speaks against me," and gospel, "in which God speaks for me." See Bayer's description of Luther's interpretation of the gospel as a "different word" in Bayer, *Martin Luther's Theology*, 61.

12. See Bainton, *Here I Stand*, 49–51.

13. Bainton, *Here I Stand*, 49.

amazement, not an impossible requirement imposed on him by God on pain of death. Instead, it was instead an unbelievable, undeserved gift from the One who holds our salvation in his hands. This was the exegetical basis for his spiritual illumination.

His illumination led to his *theology of the cross*,[14] which, in turn, became his basis for a new theological anthropology and for a challenge of the hegemony of the *via moderna*. Our concern is to fathom, from this Reformer's perspective, the meaning of being a human being who is also Christian. And, if not a modern view of humanity, then what, pray tell, do we have here?

It is also not sixteenth-century Catholicism: His biblical assertions stood over against the Roman view of righteousness as one accrued through works of merit by the penitent and as supplemented by infusions of sacramental grace to enhance and facilitate their completion. With their view, growth in righteousness is also growth in sanctification, there being no substantial difference between the two. The righteousness achieved by the penitent and confirmed by the absolution of the church then becomes a meritorious ascent toward fulfillment of the law of God through the guidance and participation of the church and its means of grace.

In countering such a position, we turn to the critical biblical resource by which he made his case, namely, the Pauline distinction of law and gospel viewed here as grounding for his anthropology.[15]

Being able to distinguish correctly law from gospel is, according to the Tübingen Luther scholar Oswald Bayer, what makes a theologian a theologian.[16] This biblical polarity is vital for his understanding of Luther's theological man—humanity *coram Deo*. Luther stated that what happened in his breakthrough moment was, in theological terms, a shift from living under law to living under gospel: "The law is for the old Adam, and the gospel is for my despairing, terrified conscience."[17] Luther writes this is the difference between works and faith, between a Christian and a heathen as Paul talked about when he commanded Timothy to "divide correctly the word of truth" (2 Tim 2:15).[18]

Luther's spiritual illumination, followed by his reported posting of the *Ninety-Five Theses*, directed against that corruption of catholic penitential practice called indulgences, enabled Luther to formulate his mature

14. Luther cited in Dillenberger, *Martin Luther*, 80.

15. Bayer, *Martin Luther's Theology*, 74–77.

16. Based on Luther's own words (cited in Bayer, *Martin Luther's Theology*, 65).

17. Luther cited in Bayer, *Martin Luther's Theology*, 59.

18. Luther cited in Bayer, *Martin Luther's Theology*, 59.

theological anthropology. The clearest statement of this position is the seminal treatise of 1520, "On the Freedom of a Christian."[19] This document also helped seal his fate with Rome since Pope Leo X edict of excommunication of the Reformer was among its consequences. It appears as the virtual *magna carta* of the Protestant Reformation. In this treatise he grounds the identity of a Christian in a crisp pair of dialectical propositions. Luther proceeds by confessing that his intent was "to make the way smoother for the unlearned—for only them do I serve, and so I shall set down following two propositions concerning the freedom and bondage of the spirit:

1. A Christian is a perfectly free Lord over all, subject to none.

2. A Christian is a perfectly dutiful servant of all, subject to all."[20]

And then he follows with this afterthought: "These two themes seem to contradict one another. If they should be found to fit together, they would serve our purpose beautifully. They are Paul's statements: 'for though I am free from all men, I have made myself a slave to all' (1 Cor 9:19)."[21] Just how did Luther go about fitting together these two contradictory propositions? He does so by articulating a group of polarity statements analogous to these two propositions. Each one came in a pair, intended to clarify one aspect of the mystery of the human person, existing *coram Deo*. These appear in other texts produced during this critical period of his theological formation based in his first public exposition of his theology in the Heidelberg Disputation of 1518 through the three major theological treatises of 1521.[22]

The first pair of polarity statements appears to be the earliest public exposition of his evangelical theology in the Heidelberg Disputation (1518) conducted with his Augustinian monastic brothers the year following the posting of the theses.[23] Here Luther explicitly links the meaning of human existence to God's intention for humanity as demonstrated in the cross. This is the distinction between the *theologia crucis,* or the theology of the

---

19. The version used here is found in Dillenberger, *Martin Luther.*

20. Luther cited in Dillenberger, *Martin Luther,* 50.

21. Luther cited in Dillenberger, *Martin Luther,* 50.

22. His first opportunity to offer public exposition of his developing evangelical theology was before his fellow Augustinian monks in 1518, followed by the *Address to the German Nobility* (his critique of papal usurpation of authority over the interpretation of the Bible), the *Babylonian Captivity of the Church* (his critique of the seven Catholic sacraments), and the *Freedom of a Christian,* all in 1521.

23. Righteousness in this sense relates to *justification,* as "legal acquittal and vindication," and this is "because God's creative word brings into being, his verdict in practice is also transformative." See the commentary on Rom 1:16–17 in Keener, *IVP Bible Background Commentary,* 427.

cross, as opposed to the *theologia gloria,* or the theology of glory. The former locates where faith meets God's redemptive love while the latter denotes the triumphal, self-justifying ways the flesh behaves toward God out of a sense of superiority, even to God himself: "We Christians are *not* to become "theologians of glory, which calls the bad good and the good bad . . . [but] theologians of the cross, who say what a thing is."[24]

Theological man for Luther is the person who exists before God only on the ground of his or her acceptance of Christ's righteousness as an undeserved gift: God is the actor; we are the recipient, not vice versa as Luther detects in the clerical abuses of his day. The one who inverts or flips this polarity is not a theologian in the evangelical sense and is bound for self-destruction, since the first shall be last while the last shall be first (Matt 19:30).

The second pair, building upon the first, appears in a sermon from 1519, where he asserted, "The first kind of righteousness is *alien righteousness,* that is the righteousness of another, instilled from without. This is the righteousness of Christ by which he justifies through faith. . . . [Through that faith,] Christ's righteousness becomes our righteousness, and all that he has becomes ours. This is an infinite righteousness, that swallows up all sins in a moment. . . . The second kind of righteousness is our *proper righteousness.*"[25] Notice here that Luther was making use of the singular I and you, not the plural, when he speaks of this transfer; it can be spoken of doctrinally in generic terms, but for Luther it actually happens only concretely to you or to me, not to a class of humans.

The third pair of polarity statements is found in his lectures on Galatians[26] from the earliest public exposition of his evangelical theology in the Heidelberg Disputation conducted with his Augustinian monastic brothers the year following the posting of the theses. Here he distinguishes for them this righteousness of faith as being either an *active* or a *passive* righteousness.[27] These are Luther's own words in his exposition of 1 Corinthians 2:7: "The kind of righteousness that comes forth from us, is not the [*active*] righteousness of the Christian; we do not *become* righteous thereby; the righteousness of the Christian is the exact opposite: *passive* righteousness, which we can only receive, about which we do nothing but only suffer it, for, one works in us, namely God. This is not understood by the world. It is

---

24. Luther cited in Dillenberger, *Martin Luther,* 503.

25. Luther cited in Dillenberger, *Martin Luther,* 86–89.

26. The lectures on Galatians first appeared in 1519, with the definitive commentary appearing in 1531. See Dillenberger, *Martin Luther,* 102.

27. Luther cited in Dillenberger, *Martin Luther.*

hidden in secret."[28] Our only option in receiving this gift is to do so passively, precisely because it is a mystery I cannot comprehend, only believe. Note also, "hidden in secret" suggests influence from Luther's early encounters with the German mystical theology (the *Theologia Deutsch*), which taught that almighty God receives me as I am, to become a participant in the mystery of his holiness, becoming a sacrifice for my sins. Listen to Luther's own words in his exposition of Paul's statement—"We speak the mystery of the wisdom of God" (1 Cor 2:7): "That . . . what Christ does on the cross is through faith efficacious for me in my sinful condition."[29]

Luther's belief that this polarity condition would persist for every person of faith, even unto the close of mortal life, gave rise to his most recognized formulation of the Christian's existence: it is *simul iustus et peccator*. He explains this in his preface to Romans: "Faith does not free us from our sins to the extent we can relax into laziness and self-assurance, as if sin no longer exists; it does, but on account of the faith that battles with it, it is not held to our condemnation. Throughout our whole lives we shall be fully employed with our own selves, controlling its members til they obey not the passions, but the spirit."[30] In brief, the person of faith remains exercised by this dialectic, which is a source of freedom for faithfulness to the Word of the cross, our triune faith in which we are baptized. These polarity statements explicate the meaning of his first proposition, that to be a Christian person is to live as a "free lord over all, subject to none, through faith."

The second proposition of Luther's definition of a Christian, that *we are to be servants to all, for Christ's sake*, is, he declares, the "preferable" role of the Christian, insofar as here, more than in his freedom from works righteousness, a person realizes the purpose of his or her life as a human *coram Deo* (or as theological man): It is when faith becomes active in love toward the neighbor and all creatures encountered anywhere in the world, with no exceptions. The most sacred step taken by the person of faith is when that individual reaches out to the least of God's creatures in the realization that there he or she is most wondrously embracing the Lord himself.[31] Luther writes in the *Freedom of a Christian* that the "first born in the Old Testament

---

28. Luther, *Luther Works*, 26:4–12. Cf. Thesis 27 of the Heidelberg Disputation: "The work of Christ shall be called an active work, and ours that which is worked."

29. Bayer, *Martin Luther's Theology*, 330, reflecting the language of article 12 of the Augsburg Confession: "The first part of repentance is the literal terrors stricken into the conscience through the acknowledgement of sin" (Schaff, *Creeds of Christendom*, 3:14).

30. Luther cited in Dillenberger, *Martin Luther*, 29.

31. He writes, "Each one should become as it were a Christ to the other that we may be Christ's to one another and Christ may be the same in all, that is, that we may be truly Christians" (Luther cited in Dillenberger, *Martin Luther*, 78).

was a priest and lord over the others, as type of Christ." This lordship is related to priesthood and is not for dominion but for service of others. We are called to a royal priesthood "to declare the deeds of Him who has called you out of darkness and into His glorious light" (1 Pet 2:9).[32]

Reading this second proposition, an inversion of the first, Luther introduces the reader to the key issue of how these polar propositions are interfaced and conjoined to provide the theological grounding for the new humanity in Christ. This new humanity is actualized by what Miroslav Volf calls a *love exchange* between Christ's righteousness and my unrighteousness, initiated and actualized through his atoning death on the cross, conveyed to you and to me by faith in God's promise (Rom 1:17).[33] Since, in Luther's view, divine mystery is not susceptible to rational explanation, his quest for clarity in faith was assisted instead by appeal to metaphor. Accordingly, he offers three examples in the *Freedom of a Christian*.[34]

First, a *blacksmith's forge*: This metaphor is selected to heighten the wonder surrounding the point of interface that actualizes this exchange. The point where what is unreachable by the commandments of the law is made through faith, is also where "the Word of God rules in the soul."[35] For Luther, this is "just as the heated iron glows like fire because of the union of the fire with it, so the Word imparts its qualities to the soul."[36] Then it is clear the Christian is "he who has all his needs met, with faith." On this point, Luther observes, "if [only] a touch of Christ healed [others], how much more will this tender spiritual touch, this absorbing of the Word, communicate to the soul all things that belong to the Word?"[37]

Second, a *wedding*: Here the relationship of Savior with sinner, which occurs in the cross, is conceptualized through the bridal imagery.[38] In that union, the believing soul can boast of what Christ has (e.g., my sin) *as though* it were his own, and also it is where the soul possesses what Christ has as *his* own. We are invited to compare these two realities and see just who is benefitting more in this relationship:

---

32. Luther cited in Dillenberger, *Martin Luther*, 62–63.

33. Volf, *Free of Charge*.

34. The text for this exposition is found in Dillenberger, *Martin Luther*, 73.

35. Luther cited in Bayer, *Martin Luther's Theology*, 60.

36. Luther cited in Dillenberger, *Martin Luther*, 60.

37. Dillenberger, *Martin Luther*, 58.

38. The soteriological reality being conveyed here is expressed quite differently in the Eastern Orthodox perspective as the joining of the uncreated with the created, or of incorruptibility with corruptibility, described as *theosis*.

Christ is full of grace, life, and salvation. The soul [that is, you or I] is full of sins, death and damnation. Now let faith come between these two, and then sins, death and damnation will be Christ's! While grace, life, and salvation will be ours [the soul's]![39] Christ is God and man in one Person; his righteousness, life and salvation are eternal and omnipotent. Then, by the wedding ring of faith, He shares in the sins, death, and pains of hell which are his bride's! And so, in the face of sin's temptation, death, and hell, I can say, "If I have sinned, yet my Christ, in whom I believe, has not sinned, and all his is mine and all mine is his! (see Song 2:16: 'My beloved is mine, and I am his')."[40]

As explained by Jörg Baur,

In Christ God and the human being exist no longer so that one stands over against the other . . . but that they communicate with one another. . . . The work of Christ in proclamation, acts of healing and miracles, in suffering, cross, resurrection, ascension, and the expectation of his arrival in an epiphany, is not the achievement of an isolated super subject, but is the concrete explication of his communicative nature in dismantling what is old in the rebellious world of sin, law, [devil,] and death. This transfer of the human ground of existence into Christ and into the triune God [is] *sola verba* (solely by the Word of His promise) . . . who takes away from the person who had up to this point . . . [been] grounded in the self, and thus awakens faith as the fulfillment of what [brings us to] life that is directed totally outward.[41]

This paradox, which comprises both the mystery of our salvation and the heart of Luther's theological anthropology, can never be explained by finite human logic, but, for Luther, it is best grasped simply by that poetic metaphor, the blessed wedding exchange. He likens it to a king exchanging

39. Here, Luther speaks of this intimate fellowship with Christ as the *fröhliche Wechsel* or the *blessed exchange* as in a wedding union, between Christ and the soul, like a king trading his robes for the rags of a beggar to bear his painful life for him.

40. See citation in Dillenberger, *Martin Luther*, 33. Luther continues, "While . . . Christians are lords over all things, in that nothing or no one can harm us, and all things serve us in attaining salvation; nevertheless, this does not mean that every Christian is to have control by physical power over others, a madness with which some churchmen are afflicted! . . . Such power belongs only to rulers. But our experience shows that [we real] Christians are subjected to all, and that the more Christian a man is, the more evils, sufferings, and deaths they must endure" (Luther cited in Dillenberger, *Martin Luther*, 62–63).

41. Baur cited in Bayer, *Martin Luther's Theology*, 236–37.

his royal garments for a beggar's tattered garb, which actually consisted of your and my sins, which the King bore on Calvary.[42] Luther later recalls his ecstasy from that moment of illumination when he records in his *Tischreden* (*Tabletalk*) that "I felt that I was truly born again and to have gone through open doors into paradise."[43] He would later direct his students, that if they wanted to understand where his theology is based, they must go to the time of his struggle with *Anfechtung,* which takes him to the cross.[44]

There is also a third metaphor, *a fountain.* Here Luther finds a vehicle to articulate how faith becomes active in love and so to fulfill the command of God. To this point in his treatise, Luther has been presenting that grace, which he asserts as "our inner man has in Christ," whereby we become lords not serfs, free from the dread of sin, death, and the devil. But this is merely half of the picture he is portraying of theological man in the full Christian sense. Now, the best is yet to come. The other half is as follows: Luther's theological man stands legally free from works for salvation. Nevertheless, (1) because we are also called as priests to be priests as well as kings with Christ in a royal priesthood (1 Pet 1), and (2) in light of the immense love that is radiant and contagious in one's life by virtue of Christ's presence within and for that one as their life in Christ, I, like our Lord, am a real servant active in works of all kinds, Henceforth, my life in Christ who intensely loves me spontaneously overflows in what Luther calls an ecstatic love (*quellende Liebe*) for my neighbor.[45] The highest expression of the person of faith then becomes that one who is solely occupied in the joyful service of God, as an expression of Christ's unconstrained love.[46]

42. Luther's exposition of Eph 5:32 (Luther, *Luther's Works,* 31:351). Luther also relates this phrase to Hos 2:19–20 in Luther, *Luthers Werke,* 7:55 (Bayer, *Martin Luther's Theology,* 226).

43. Luther cited in Bainton, *Here I Stand,* 283. See Luther, *Luthers Werke,* 4777.

44. Luther asserted that his theology begins with his *Anfechtung*en. See Bainton, *Here I Stand,* 49.

45. Luther cited in Dillenberger, *Martin Luther,* 75.

46. Although Luther does not address sanctification in the explicit way of Wesley, I see it as an implicit cause of the Reformation in the context of the indulgences controversy. *Contra* the Roman view of meritorious/sacerdotal grace, Luther describes the main function of Christian life as the "*quellende Liebe*" (overflow of love) toward neighbor, as found in the Galatians commentary. It is the overflow of faith (in the Word promising my justification, based on the theology of the cross). This ecstatic "hands-on" love is enabled by the love of Christ flowing through me on behalf of the other. Once freed from the curse of the law, the believer lives by a dimension of incarnational love of neighbor, through the Holy Spirit, which far exceeds the duty to which one had been obligated through outward obedience to the law's commands. This new life in Christ in implicit in Thesis One of the *Ninety-Five Theses*: "When our Lord and Master Jesus Christ said, repent, He called for the entire life of believers to be one of penitence.

Here is a tip: If you want to remember these features of what constitutes the person of faith in relation to Christ's work on the cross, the one we have called theological man, note that Luther has appealed to three metaphors, to catch our attention: They are (1) a blacksmith's forge, (2) a wedding nuptial, and (3) a fountain: iron and fire, a blessed exchange, and faith overflowing in ecstatic love.

Luther describes this mystery at the heart of theological man, as discerning the light of the cross, in these terms from the "Freedom of a Christian":

> Each one should become as it were a Christ to the other that we may be Christ's to one another, and Christ may be the same in all, that is, that we may be truly Christians. . . . A Christian lives not in himself, but in Christ and in his neighbor. Otherwise, he is not a Christian. He lives in God through faith, in his neighbor, through love. By faith he is caught up beyond himself unto God. By love, he descends beneath himself into his neighbor, yet he always remains in God and in His love.[47]

In this same treatise, Luther also presents this discussion of theological man in the language of the *imago Dei* (i.e., the meaning of being a human created in the image of God). This term signifies the human person living according to these two propositions for being a Christian: the inner man (or the free lord) and the outer man (the dutiful servant). Hear his words: "The inner man by faith is created in the image of God, he is joyful and happy because of Christ in whom so many benefits are conferred upon him, and therefore it is his one occupation [in the outer man] to serve God joyfully and without thought of gain, in love that is not constrained."[48] In terms of anthropology, Luther is saying, "The image of God consists of the ability that has been distributed to the human being to re-spond" to God's speech.[49] The inference from this understanding of imago Dei is that "the individual is the representative of God responsible for carrying out his mandates on earth."[50] In actuality, this responsibility to act in accordance with the image of God is thwarted by the human capacity for unfaithfulness to God, resulting in

---

The Scriptural call to repentance is a call to live our whole lives as disciples of Christ, conforming everything we do to his holiness" (Luther cited in Dillenberger, *Martin Luther*, 490).

47. Luther cited in Dillenberger, *Martin Luther*, 76, 80.
48. Dillenberger, *Martin Luther*, 67.
49. Bayer, *Martin Luther's Theology*, 157.
50. Bayer, *Martin Luther's Theology*, 159.

glorifying in one's self instead on continuing in the image of God, and thus to misuse what was promised to him, in the use of reason and language.[51] Unlike the *via moderna*, for whom the meaning of man begins and ends with the centrality of the knowing self and its setting in the world, for Luther it is the opposite. Each of the focal points he introduces directs us to view our human nature as becoming actualized *coram Deo* only in light of the biblical witness concerning Christ's atonement. It is a witness directing us to revelation and not to anthropology *per se* as our beginning and end points, in understanding theological man, unlike the anthropomorphic shift we find in modernity.

THE LARGER IMPLICATIONS OF HUMANITY BEFORE THE CROSS

Since we now have located Luther's doctrine of man in the context of his times, *contra* modernity, we may pose this question: What are the main takeaways that engage the larger implications of his view of humanity in light of the cross in view in the larger cultural context?

First, this portrayal of Luther's theological man is not a formal or systematic definition of the *imago Dei,* as found in Aquinas or Calvin, but an existence concretely grounded *in the promise of God, which comes from the preaching of Christ.* Luther's discussion of that new man who is imaged in the cross is not one addressed to humanity as a general term. It is always specific to each one who takes responsibility for hearing, i.e., for faith. *This presence of God in humanity and in all creatures is only acknowledged by humans amid the dialectic of unfaith and faith,* or God *unpreached* and God *preached.* The promise, which constitutes humanity *coram Deo* ("This is my beloved Son; hear Him" [Mark 9:7b])[52] is available only for those who hear in such a way that they do not remain deaf.

Luther finds sanction for linking our humanness to the act of preaching in his sermon on Jesus' healing of the deaf and dumb man (Mark 7:31–37). This text declares, "The *whole earth* is filled with speaking, but the entire world is deaf!"[53] Working from that base, he sets forth the opposing observations that God "consigned all persons to disobedience so that which

---

51. This discussion is found in Luther's treatise, *Disputatio de homine,* cited in Bayer, *Martin Luther's Theology,* 155–57.

52. Author's translation from Luther, *Das Neue Testament*: "Das ist mein lieber Sohn: den sollt ihr hören."

53. This statement is based on Luther's translation of Mark 9:7a: "Und sie wünderten sich über die Maßen und sprachen."

was promised, given through faith of Jesus Christ, might be given only to those who believe" (Gal 3:22), and that is how faith comes to us.

Second, the inference from this speech, that "the whole earth is filled with speaking," is that creation finds its meaning only in the light of *justification*. What does it mean for Luther to say that *our creation ex nihilo is viewed through the lens of the doctrine of justification*? It is to say that humans are not created for self-realization (as, for instance, in Marx's idea of man the worker). We are created by God as a "speech act," a "dialogue between the God who speaks and the creatures who answer," and God alone is the source of all that we are and can be.[54] Luther asserts in the *Smalkald Articles*, "One cannot go soft or give way on this article, for then heaven and earth would fall," signifying that, apart from the article on justification, "the world is nothing but death and darkness."[55] The essence of our humanness is to exist in faithfulness to God's address to creation expressed in the declaration, "I am the Lord your God" (Exod 10:2). In brief, God comes "among and in all of His creatures" who, in creation and also in the new creation in Christ, declares that our lives are no more nor less than categorical *gifts*.[56] In the larger scheme, justification for Luther is not just one feature in soteriology. It expresses God as unconditional love and humans who exist in response to that love. We read in his "Small Catechism," "I believe that God has created me together with all that exists."[57] To say that our existence is grounded in the gospel is more than just saying our salvation depends on pardon through Christ; it is to declare that our very lives as humans is wholly gift: the gift of our Lord Jesus Christ, in His atoning death on Calvary.

The outcome is a distinctive way of representing what Luther meant in his discussion of redeemed humanity. To say that you and I exist as justified persons in God's sight is his way of saying, in contemporary genre, that, to be called human in the *imago Dei* means, above all, *an undeserved existence*. Such a humanity stands as the ultimate contradiction to the self-made man of modernity. We find this definition of the human in his *Disputation Concerning Man* (1536) where he defines a human as "that being who is justified

---

54. Bayer, *Martin Luther's Theology*, 101. Here, he also notes that recent Luther research has focused on the link between creation and justification, in light of the theme of *promissio* (God's promise, or gift, to all in creation). The anthropological implications of this are explored in Gehlen, *Anthropologische Forschung*, cited in Bayer, *Martin Luther's Theology*, 101.

55. For the article on justification, see Schaff, *Creeds*, 114–21; Bayer, *Martin Luther's Theology*, 98.

56. Luther cited in Bayer, *Martin Luther's Theology*, 105.

57. Luther cited in Lull, *Martin Luther's Basic Theological Writings*, 322.

by faith alone (sola fide), which is to say, by God alone."[58] In making this assertion, Luther is referring not only to the point in one's life when the gift of pardon for sin is received by faith; it means also and more basically, that the very existence of a human is bound up in the declaration that "he can be justified only by faith." That is, to hear and receive that promise is not an addition to being human; rather, the most fundamental meaning of what faith is lies in acknowledging the gift that is human life.[59]

A word of caution: to emphasize justification as the basis for human-ness is not, for Luther, an argument for universalism (or universal salvation) because our justification in Christ does not thereby do away with the re-quirements of the law, including its curse and the wrath of God with regard to the day of judgment. As Bayer explains, the law "even still now brings eternal death, even after Christ."[60] Further, "the judgment of God is not simply behind us because of Christ's cross; all of us go against him through life and death. . . . [Ultimately,] one can speak of justification only as that of the sinner who is really lost and condemned, related to a world that is radi-cally sinful, and set within the framework of the last judgment."[61]

Third, by locating the theology of the cross as the ground for the person of faith, this theological man, Luther counters the *Catholic peniten-tial structure of sacramental grace*. His concern was that the appeal to this structure pointed toward a self-referenced theology of glory. His theological anthropology was expressed over against that prevailing *view of redeemed man*, whereby the accrual of righteousness through an enduring program of meritorious works also signified growth in holiness or sanctification with no substantial difference between the two: to become holy in God's sight was no different from becoming righteous through compliance with his law.[62] Instead, for Luther, our righteousness (read our divine acceptance in

---

58. Luther, *Luthers Werke*, 39:176; Bayer, *Martin Luther's Theology*, 100.

59. Permit me a reflective moment on what Luther is saying here: It is from this base in the atonement that we may profitably read passages, such as, "I will do whatever you ask in my name" (John 14:13). Read in the context of Luther's theological man, this surely means, as Chambers asserted, "The one who abides in Jesus is the will of God" because that one's apparently free choices are his joining in the eternal intercession of Christ. It is from that vantage point that Luther's response to Kant would be, "I will do my duty, but not for duty's sake," but because God is directing my circumstances, even in the smallest choices in my daily life, and that is so because at the very point of my obedience, the grace of God is mine through the atonement. See Chambers, *My Utmost*, 116.

60. Breuer cited in Bayer, *Martin Luther's Theology*, 330.

61. Bayer, *Martin Luther's Theology*, 330.

62. The active righteousness achieved by the penitent and confirmed by the absolu-tion of the church then becomes both the achievement of sanctification and also one's

love through the cross of Christ) hinges on the critical distinction of alien versus proper righteousness, involving Christ, yourself, and myself (as sinner), resulting in freedom from guilt as the gift of grace and unleashing us to unapologetic service (read love) unto our neighbors.

Fourth, Luther also factors in the *role of Satan* in fashioning theological man. Luther does not think those who struggle with demonic forces are for that reason sub-Christian. He notes how David in the Psalms complains about all sorts of enemies contending with him, especially in his meditations. Luther writes, "As soon as the Word of God permeates you, the devil will seek to afflict you so as to make you a real doctor [theologian] and will teach you by his temptations to seek the Word of God and to love it."[63] This theme also comes into play when he speaks of Christ as the ground for our new humanity through his atoning act of bearing our sins with their curse. He does so by this line of reasoning: Our mortal enemy does not object if we profess the general assertion that Christ died on the cross as Son of God for human salvation. However, if I declare that Christ the Son of God has died for *my* sins (not just for humanity in general), and if you confess that he has died for *your* sins, our enemy cannot stand these declarations. Why is that? It is because such a declaration strips Satan of his very grip over our lives, and that is what the enemy of our souls most desperately seeks. It is to master us who have been created in God's image because in that act of subjugation, Satan also triumphs over God himself.[64] The flip side of that devious strategy is the most drastic role reversal in all the universe: The righteous One becomes unrighteous before his heavenly Father for our sakes. Only through this bold and gracious act does the curse that was placed on Adam who followed the tempter's snare become decisively broken, and only through this atoning work of Christ can we find ourselves cut free from that curse upon the old humanity to become recipients of the gift of the cross.

Fifth, Luther thinks outside the box when the "logic" of the cross leads him to reject the longstanding Roman view of grace from being a substance sacramentally infused within us (called *sacrificium*). He does this

---

meritorious ascent toward fulfillment of the righteousness of God through the guidance of the church and participation in its sacramental grace.

63. Luther cited in Bayer, *Martin Luther's Theology*, 36.

64. On Satan, see Althaus, *Theology*. As a corollary, we dare not think of Jesus in his obedience unto death as an innocent Christ who dies for us unrighteous persons; no, it is for Luther the reverse: The One who created this world in all its splendor and he who placed the stars in the heavens that the shepherds followed to see him as a child in the manger becomes the curse of God for you and for me, to break the curse that came upon our first parent through the wiles of the serpent.

by redefining grace in terms of the new dignity of relationship we sustain with our Creator (called *beneficium*), which grounds our new humanity in Christ.[65] Here we also distinguish between *impute* and *impart*. For Luther, Christ's righteousness is imputed to me so that I may have fellowship with the Father. It is not an impartation of deity that would elevate me above general humanity. Nevertheless, there is also a sense in which the promise of this imputed grace *is* also imparted, albeit "without any merit or worthiness in me . . . which I receive first of all when I hear it, in order to be empowered after hearing it."[66] This gifting to speak after hearing God's promise entails the use of language, and here we are reminded of the ancient Greek term for word, *logos*, which suggests a comprehending reason, requiring language for its expression.[67]

Sixth, in all that has been said about Luther's understanding of who we are as human beings, based on his own struggle to the point of spiritual illumination, we have proposed that, despite his connections to late medieval nominalism, which Weaver excoriated as the culprit behind the dilemma of modern man, Luther was not in the final analysis a modern man. We have declared *the outlook of modernity* to stand as the polar antithesis to Luther's discovery. From our vantage point, we can identify the interest of modern man in declaring his freedom not *in* Christ, but rather a freedom *from* the necessity of ever again having to construct his theology on the basis of revelation of a God who acts to break through into this vaunted world. This view of man in modernity came into high expression with the Enlightenment and with Immanuel Kant, in particular. For Kant, God was being marginalized as a noumenal presupposition, posited to allow for the fact that man is a creature of duty, a deontological being who invariably lives in his best moments with a sense of obligation defined by the categorical imperative. To say, "I can, therefore I must" be dutiful toward my fellow

---

65. Luther states, "The words grace and gift differ inasmuch as the true meaning of grace is the kindness and favor [*beneficium*] which God bears toward us of His own choice, and through which He is willing to give us Christ, and to pour the Holy Spirit and His blessings upon us" (Luther cited in Dillenberger, *Martin Luther*, 22–23).

66. Observation of Bayer, *Martin Luther's Theology*, 157, in response to Luther's statement in his "Preface to the Psalter" (1528) that there is "no more powerful nor a more noble work for human beings than to speak, especially since the ability to speak is that which most clearly distinguishes the human being from other animals" (Luther, *Luther's Works*, 35:254).

67. See discussion in Bayer, *Martin Luther's Theology*, 155–62. For Luther's definition of *imago Dei*, see Luther, *Luther's Works*, 34:139–40, esp. thesis 32. He also discusses *imago Dei* with reference to Gen 1:26–28, saying, "Be fruitful and increase in number, wherein the command to produce a righteous humanity is given" (Luther cited in Bayer, *Martin Luther's Theology*, 157).

man is in itself the highest expression of morality, said Kant. In his mind, we can now wipe the slate clean of any dogma we call explicitly Christian. To declare that man is a creature, governed by moral obligation, is, for Kant, the very thing that ought now displace what Kant regarded as the archaic reliance of the church on the ancient traditions concerning the man from Galilee. Once Kant swept aside the authority of biblical revelation, there was little stopping the modernist/postmodernist era from ultimately giving way to the triumph of a self-referenced nihilism and its cohorts of despotism that invariably accompany it.

Such demons can only flourish when there is a void of authentic Christianity due to complacent congregations, which may be an antinomian perversion of the Reformation emphasis on freedom in Christ. Closely related is the pathology that comes from a misuse of his phrase "*simul iustus et peccator.*" Bonhoeffer called it the tendency toward cheap grace: it is to so focus on the inevitability of *peccator* that we completely miss what it means to be *iustus* (i.e., persons imputed with the righteousness of Christ). In Bonhoeffer's terms, we may say, "Well, then, let the Christian live like the rest of the world, let him model himself on the world's standards in every sphere of life, and not presumptuously aspire to live a different life under grace from his old life under sin."[68]

THE THEOLOGY OF THE CROSS AFTER LUTHER: THE WITNESS OF JOHANN ADAM STEINMETZ AND THE CONTINENTAL ROOTS OF THE WESLEYAN TRADITION

Having considered Luther's theology of the cross in light of his theological anthropology, it is our intent to demonstrate how this theme appeared anew in the context of religious revival in the early modern era.

Two centuries after Luther published his "Freedom of a Christian," the theology of the cross was refitted to provide a foundation for a new view of humanity as redeemed, within a Pentecost context. This development also represented the earliest occurrence of revival within Protestant Christianity. The understanding of humanity as redeemed in the context of a Pentecost interpretation of revival in the early modern era is to provide linkage between Luther and Wesley on this central theme from the Reformation, a move facilitated by my locating and translating a series of Pentecost addresses by a prominent Lutheran pastor and spiritual director, Johann Adam Steinmetz (1689–1762). They were delivered in the wake of

68. Bonhoeffer, "Cheap Grace," 349.

his service as chief preacher of the earliest Protestant revival, which occurred in his congregation at Teschen during the decade of the 1720s, with its roots in the children's revival.

At this point, concise explanation of Steinmetz's handling of the key themes of theology of cross, Pentecost, and kingdom are presented to demonstrate the linkage between the theology of the cross in Luther and Wesley, via the mode of Lutheran Pietist revivalism. A full treatment of these themes from Steinmetz may be accessed in the present author's pending publication of Steinmetz's *Pentecost Addresses*.[69]

As a preliminary point, our intent here is to explicate the relationship between Luther's theology of the cross with early modern global awakenings of evangelical Christianity, first occurring under preaching labeled as *Pentecost Addresses* in the first quarter of the eighteenth century. This document appears as probably the first expression of an evangelical message of salvation based on justifying and sanctifying grace, which appeared in a revival context. Through Steinmetz, a Lutheran pastor and spiritual director in Silesia, the mantle of that theological legacy passed to Christian David, leading missional preacher of the Moravians, and from him it was conveyed to the Wesley brothers, John and Charles, where the two-stage order of salvation originating in Steinmetz was reconfigured into its classical expression as Wesleyan theology.

Wesley studies, particularly as represented by Laurence Wood,[70] has now traced the source for Wesley's twofold understanding of soteriology, based on justifying and sanctifying grace, to the influence of the Moravian Christian David, whom Wesley seriously engaged on this subject during his visit to Herrnhut after his Aldersgate conversion (May 24, 1738). Since the source for David's enunciation of that understanding of grace has not previously been identified, it is the intent of this discussion, to explain how David came to his position on grace through the influence of a modified Lutheran theology of the cross by Steinmetz, the lead preacher in the first awakening in Protestant tradition, which was the revival among Lutherans in Catholic Silesia from 1707 to 1730.

This continental connection for the Wesleys would suggest that what is later known as Wesleyan theology had its pre-Wesleyan roots in the latter stage of Lutheran Pietism in German-speaking Europe. It was the era when Pietism as a renewal movement in continental Europe was transitioning into revivalism. That transition would occur in areas of political and cultural instability, with the breakdown of the older Protestant (e.g., Lutheran)

---

69. O'Malley, *Children at Prayer*.

70. Wood, *Pentecost*.

order under the weight of an aggressive Catholic Counter Reformation, advancing from its Hapsburg imperial base in Vienna.

Steinmetz was a recognized scholar and pastor in German Lutheranism who was influenced by the Pietist movement based at the Universities of Leipzig (his alma mater) and Halle (its logistical and intellectual center under the direction of August Hermann Francke, an early associate of Philip Jacob Spener, the founder of Pietism in Lutheranism). After the Silesian revival under Steinmetz's leadership was officially halted by Hapsburg Catholic imperial intervention, its center spread by 1730 from Silesia into four surrounding nations and ultimately throughout Western Europe into Greenland, India, and then North America.[71] It was the first expression of a globalized evangelical Christianity to emanate from post-Reformation Europe, and Methodism would become its most dominant expression, beginning in the second half of the eighteenth century and beyond.

Historical Context

Before developing the "grid," a historical context for the "middle" era between Luther and the Wesleys awaits its introduction. Perhaps one reason for the eclipse of Luther's biblical narrative of Christ in the Age of Reason, which enabled the rise of modernity, was the tendency of Protestant Orthodox theologians to acquiesce rather than to challenge robustly the cultural hegemony of that age with a compelling presentation of the legacy of the Reformation, grounded as it was in the recovery of biblical authority (*sola Scriptura*) and the theology of the cross.

Two shifts occurred in the era of Lutheran orthodoxy (1550–1650), which roughly represented the century following the death of Luther in 1546 and came immediately prior to the Enlightenment, as well as to evangelical Pietism.[72] One was Melanchthon's shift from pulpit to classroom as the focal point for theological education.[73] He sanctioned this shift by his concept of the two kinds of theological knowledge: that which is discovered existentially in the context of preaching and that which is learned discursively through cognition, particularly of the Aristotelian, deductive kind.

71. Steinmetz himself charted the growth of this globalized evangelical Christianity through his influential chronicle covering the era from 1730 through 1760. It has recently been published in an edited format under its original title, *Die "Sammlung."*

72. The height of Pietism spans the half-century from the publication of Spener's *Pia Desideria* (1675).

73. Phillip Melanchthon was Luther's successor and author of the official confession of Protestantism, the *Augsburg Confession* (1530). Protestant Orthodoxy is traced from his systematic treatment of Luther's theology in his *Loci Communes*.

Realigning faith from *fiducia* (trust) to mental assent, as the vehicle for grasping the theology of the cross, strips the latter of its life-changing quality (e.g., the human person is more than cognition). Further, a cognitive rendition of *iustitia crucis* is, in itself, often devoid of the vital witness of the Holy Spirit.

Second, as theological methodology shifted to accommodate a polemical age, theological education focused on doctrinal apologetics to the detriment of pastoral relevance and viability. That was the critique of the clergy and the state of theological education in Spener's *Pia Desideria* of 1675.[74] However, the recovery of Luther's doctrine of the theology of the cross would come from other quarters than Spener. It occurred in the context of the first awakening or revival within Protestant Christianity.

The turbulent seventeenth century ran its course before this recovery event occurred. Further, revival happened spontaneously and unexpectedly, not from the ranks of the schoolmen or the clergy in the centers of academia. It came, instead, in the aftermath of the Counter-Reformation struggle to recapture the Lutheran nation of Silesia, and, in that land desolated by war, it would occur among a group of orphaned children surviving in the hills who, struggling for survival, threw themselves wholly into a spontaneous and protracted season of daily prayer, singing, and prophesying as watchmen of the Lord's coming. And reports for the era indicate the Spirit of the living God did come with such demonstration of power that it resulted in the launching of a revival that, in time, swept through central Europe and reached the shores of England with John Wesley as its vehicle.

Within that context of spiritual awakening, the theology of the cross made its appearance in a new setting. In the decade of the 1720s, we identify the important Catholic-dominated city of Teschen in Upper Silesia. The preacher was a Silesian friend and former student colleague of August Hermann Francke, director of the great Halle reform project in Germany. However, Francke had never seen revival; his focus was on the renewal of a decadent Christendom. Revival happened where the remaining vestiges of a Protestant Christendom had been swept away by the Hapsburgs when their long-term military onslaught, allied to Jesuit religious interests, ran its course through the tumultuous seventeenth century. When revival, or, in the original German, awakening (*Erweckung*), came, it appeared as a God-event, breaking through into that society, through the voices of the children of the combatants and their victims.

---

74. See Spener, *Pia Desideria*, 39–80.

Here is a note on the man of the hour in this moment of potential spiritual breakthrough. Steinmetz was a Silesian by birth.[75] After almost a century of military-enforced recatholicization of Lutheran Silesia by Hapsburg forces from Vienna, a ray of hope for the future appeared in the bush country where Protestants had taken refuge. This hope came in the form of the aforementioned children's revival, which unfolded along the following lines. Bands of orphaned children, who had been scavengering for food in the Silesian hills, spontaneously began fervent prayer, plus the joyous singing of hymns and even prophecy. Their message announced a coming restoration of the *evangelisch* (or Protestant) community, done within a devout and orderly manner. There were no adults involved in their worship, and it was all done out of doors with increasing numbers of children from the ages of 5 to about 12 being added to their group daily. Passersby at first regarded them as delusional while others took pity on them, and then there were some Pietists, with a fervent inward faith, who began to affirm them as authentic, almost angelic, voices, functioning as channels of the Holy Spirit's encouragement for the remnant of a beleaguered Protestant refugee community.[76]

Swensson reports that when their numbers reached a critical mass, the children emerged in the thousands, from the hills, making their way throughout the scores of towns and cities of Silesia in just five days.[77] Apparently even the Catholic authorities, bent on repressing all Protestant worship, stood aside. They had won the silent admiration of the Protestant community in an oppressive environment.

The date for the onset of this children's awakening was an eight-month period between 1707 and 1708. Then, in 1708, a large Swedish Lutheran army, led by King Charles XII, arrived unexpectedly in Silesia on the heels of defeating Polish and Russian armies allied to the Hapsburgs. Thousands of Swedish soldiers were now conducting prayer and hymn-singing exercises

75. Silesia was then a German-speaking nation that was part of the Hapsburg Catholic dynasty based in Vienna. After siding with the Lutheran Reformation in the sixteenth century, it was overtaken in the context of the Thirty Years' War by the Hapsburgs, who began a coercive program of recatholicization that continued into the early eighteenth century. Bordered by Poland, Bohemia/Moravia, Saxony, and Poland, it had large Protestant minorities from these bordering nations who were refugees and the Counter Reformation recatholicization efforts of the Hapsburgs. The destruction of hundreds of Lutheran churches, with the exile of their pastors and families, and the total upheaval of parish life left the Protestants an underground movement. Preaching was done in the bush of the hill areas.

76. For an in-depth study of this movement, see Swensson, *Kinderbeten*.

77. Swensson, *Kinderbeten*, 72. Here he is citing the account of Petersen, *Die Macht der Kinder*, 4.

in their encampments. Later historians, skeptical of the motivations of the children, concluded they were merely copying the exercises of the Swedish soldiers. However, Swensson has documented that they had preceded the Swedes by eight months, and the children were proceeding with no outside or adult intervention.

Locating these developments within a geopolitical context, note that King Charles XII put forth an ultimatum to the Emperor in Vienna, Joseph I, that his forces were to stand back and restore the lost rights to Protestant worship that had been established at the end of the Thirty Years' War in the Peace of Westphalia.[78] Unexpectedly, the Emperor accepted these terms, choosing to avert further hostilities at a time when he was engaged in warfare on multiple fronts. The Protestants saw this concession as confirmation of the prophecies of the children who had spoken of God's coming intervention in their situation.[79]

The largest of the refugee congregations established through this arrangement, the Grace Church in Teschen was a congregation of 70,000 refugee Protestants in a Catholic sector of Silesia. This congregation regularly gathered in an encampment for worship.[80] By 1719, Steinmetz was moved up the chain from a smaller parish to be appointed to this large parish, along with associates appointed to preach in the multiple languages represented among the refugees in residence there.[81] In this Pentecost-like context, amid the gathering of the nations, the children's revival was rejuvenated and broke forth as an awakening that encompassed this large community.

A refugee from Moravia, Christian David, later a prominent leader in Zinzendorf's Herrnhut community, visited Steinmetz's church in Teschen. There he was impacted by this surging awakening and was confirmed in his faith by Steinmetz.[82] Through the latter's influence, the revival spread to

78. There were to be 125 Lutheran churches restored, and six church plants, called Jesus churches, in the traditional Catholic areas of Silesia, which now included a large former-Protestant refugee community.

79. At the Altranstädt Convention, where the two warring sides met, August Hermann Francke, the Pietist leader from Halle University in Germany, entered the negotiations on behalf of the Protestant refugees, offering to raise funds to construct and resource the emergency Grace churches, in the interest of preventing the elimination of a Protestant presence in all the peripheral nations represented by the refugee community in Silesia. See Swensson, *Kinderbeten*, 29–31.

80. Zinzendorf reported there were 40,000 Germans and 30,000 Poles in this refugee congregation. See Nelson, *Christian David*.

81. These languages were high German, Czech, Slovak, Polish, and the Moravian and Bohemian dialects of German.

82. The awakening at Teschen continued under Steinmetz's leadership as senior pastor until 1730, when the Catholic authorities reasserted their aggressive posture,

neighboring lands, including Moravia, Bohemia, and Poland, and, in 1727, it arrived at Herrnhut, Germany, where David was its chief advocate.

A decade later, John Wesley visited Herrnhut, fresh from his evangelical conversion at Aldersgate, a Moravian society in London. Here he was profoundly influenced by the preaching of David, which reflected the latter's change of heart after encountering the Silesian revival under Steinmetz.[83] In his journal entry of August 8, 1738, Wesley addresses this event as follows: "Four times I enjoyed the blessing of hearing him [David] preach . . . and every time he chose the very subject which I should have desired had I spoken to him before. . . . He described the state of those who are 'weak in faith,' who have received forgiveness through the blood of Christ but have not received the indwelling of the Holy Ghost."[84] David also noted, "Many are children of God and heirs of the promise [by virtue of the cross of Christ] long before . . . they are comforted by the abiding witness of the Holy Spirit."[85] Wesley then reported David's exposition regarding "the state the apostles were in from our Lord's death (and indeed some time before) till the descent of the Holy Ghost at the day of Pentecost." David then continued, "They then had faith . . . yet they were not properly converted; and they were not delivered from the spirit of fear; they had not new hearts, neither had they received 'the gift of the Holy Ghost.'"[86] With the arrival of the day of Pentecost, these promises, he noted, were fulfilled.

With this background, we proceed to our comparative task.

---

closing down the revival at this Protestant refugee community. David's trip to Teschen occurred most likely in 1717. Steinmetz's ministry at Teschen ended abruptly in 1730 when a Catholic tribunal charged him with illicit proselytizing of Protestants in a Catholic land. It is reported in David's memoir that, to no avail, he personally intervened on Steinmetz's behalf in "notarized instrument" sent from Herrnhut to the "imperial father confessor in Vienna." See Nelson, *Christian David*. David also reports in his autobiographical account, received by John Wesley, that he went to Steinmetz again in 1722, at Zinzendorf's behest, to gain clarity on the universality of the atonement. This prompted a three day conference with the Moravian leaders at Zinzendorf's personal estate to review the entire saving "economy" of God in Christ, as a basis for the Moravian ministry of evangelism. See Wesley, *Journal and Diaries I*, 273–74.

83. Wood, *Pentecost*, develops this encounter more fully from the Wesleyan side.

84. Wesley, *Journal and Diaries II*, 270.

85. Wesley, *Journal and Diaries II*, 270.

86. Wesley, *Journal and Diaries II*, 271.

A Theological Grid for Comparing Luther and the Wesleys on Cross and Kingdom with Reference to Johann Adam Steinmetz and Christian David as Their Primary Connecting Links

These four historical figures are here compared in terms of their respective ways of expressing the following doctrinal themes: (1) the sinner and the need for the cross, (2) Pentecost and sanctification in light of the cross, and (3) the coming kingdom. The areas of continuity and discontinuity among our four comparative voices on the cross and the kingdom follow.

The Sinner and the Cross

For Luther, the theology of the cross (*theologia crucis*) stands over against the theology of glory (*theologia gloria*). The former locates where faith meets God in his redemptive love in Christ while the latter denotes the triumphal, self-justifying ways the flesh behaves toward God out of a sense of superiority even to God himself: "We Christians are *not* to become 'theologians of glory,' which calls the bad good and the good bad,' but rather 'theologians of the cross, who say what a thing is.'"[87] Luther is typically dialectical here. The cross represents both law and gospel: "The law does indeed terrify me more dreadfully when I hear that Christ, God's Son, had to bear it for me than it does when it is only proclaimed to me with threatenings apart from Christ and apart from this great anguish of the Son of God."[88]

The cross calls Christ to suffer both innocently and unrighteously at the same time by bearing our sins in agape love; it calls us as believers to suffer unrighteously yet joyously not as punishment for sins but by the devil and the world since they are our enemy for the sake of the Word and our faith.[89]

The action of saving grace is focused upon the point of Christ's paschal sacrifice in which Savior and sinner intersect in the cross, which Luther calls the "blessed exchange" (*fröhliche Wechsel*).[90] Christ's righteousness is graciously exchanged for our sin (a life marked by unfaithfulness to the Word): He becomes the sinner and we become, by imputation, the righteous ones, by faith, meaning through trust (*fiducia*) in the promise of grace.

Steinmetz relies on the biblical history of redemption through Father, Son, and Holy Spirit as found in the Augsburg Confession of the Lutheran

---

87. Luther cited in Dillenberger, *Martin Luther*, 503.

88. Luther, *Luthers Werke*, 41:190–91.

89. Luther, *Luthers Werke*, 52:794.

90. Dillenberger, *Martin Luther*, 61.

Church, but his emphasis is upon encountering the crucified and resurrected Christ in the present, via proclamation, sacraments, and mystical encounter. He also laments the misuse of the redemptive work of Christ by the host of cultural Christians whom he calls "mouth" Christians only, who have never encountered Him as Living Lord, inwardly and personally, by faith. He insists that personal access to the work of Christ on the cross comes through the inward sealing of the Holy Spirit, who bears witness to the efficacy of the shed blood of Christ for salvation.[91]

For David, Christ's atoning work is the "word of reconciliation" whereby we are reconciled to God not by our works but solely by the shedding of his blood: "The right foundation is not your contrition, not your righteousness. . . . It is nothing of your own, nothing that is wrought *in you* by the Holy Spirit; but it is something *without you*, viz. the righteousness and blood of Christ."[92] Like Steinmetz, his access to Christ is not historically in the events of Calvary or in one's contrition based upon those events (even when inspired by the Holy Spirit); rather, it is inward, through the present working of the Holy Spirit. Also like Steinmetz, David distinguishes between what we first attempted by our own works and what was "wholly and solely by the blood of Christ."[93] He states that "your contrition" and "your grief" after hearing of Christ's atoning death are all "works of the selfsame Spirit"; nevertheless, "this is not the foundation. . . . All of this is nothing to our justification." In words that Luther would affirm, he adds, "Nay it may hinder it, if you build anything upon it." True faith is nothing within wrought in you by the Holy Ghost, but it is something without you, namely, the righteousness and the blood of Christ."[94]

John Wesley's personal faith in the saving work of Christ was born in his Aldersgate discovery, based on the reading of Luther's preface to Romans in an English Moravian meeting. He there acknowledged Christ as the sole basis for his being made righteous before the Father, through Christ's offering the oblation of himself for the sin of the entire world.[95] Christ's death on the cross is the foundation in righteousness for both justification and

---

91. Steinmetz, *Der Versiegelung*, 1.3a:10.

92. Nelson, *Christian David*, 272.

93. "The person who builds even a trifle on his own work has no sealing through the Holly Spirit, and the entire ground of his hope does not rest on the merits of Christ. . . . The correct sealing and assurance, which comes through the Holy Spirit . . . may clearly be understood as standing on the blood and merit of Jesus Christ, so that a person who comes before that cross may know, see and recognize that he is himself a sinner worthy of condemnation" (Steinmetz, *Versiegelung*, 1.3b:12, c:12–13).

94. Wesley, *Journal and Diaries I*, 272.

95. Collins, *Theology*, 101.

sanctification.[96] As Cell notes, Christ's atoning death on the cross became a "burning issue" for him only after Aldersgate.[97]

Concurrent with John's Aldersgate discovery and trip to Herrnhut, Charles Wesley preached a sermon on "The Threefold State," which affirmed his belief in conversion by one and not by multiple states of faith, called being "made partakers of the divine nature . . . and all holiness."[98] This is a position he would later alter through influence upon John from David and Steinmetz before him.

Pentecost and Sanctification in Relation to the Cross

Pentecost for Luther is a liturgical event in the church calendar but it is not associated with an *ordo salutis* grounded in the theology of the cross, which this study has examined.

In Steinmetz we encounter the first occasion in the revival traditions of Protestantism to distinguish justifying from sanctifying grace, understood as Pentecostal sealing and enabling. He derives these two stages of grace from the theology of the cross. He writes as a Lutheran pastor theologian who finds opportunity, occasioned by the revival, to give renewed attention to Luther's *theologia crucis*. His context is an emergency (or missional) congregation launching its life and mission under the sway of a rising awakening among the masses of Protestant refugees in Silesia.

In the preface to his addresses, Steinmetz identifies Christ's redemptive work on the cross as the core soteriological theme for interpreting the meaning and intent of the awakening in Silesia, which was ignited by the children's revival. He states that this theme can be outwardly known by "theoretical reason" (e.g., as it was then interpreted by Lutheran orthodoxy and in its confessions) or by "godly wisdom." The latter phrase denotes wisdom immediately conveyed by the Holy Spirit to authentic worshippers of the crucified Jesus, which is distinct from that which is deduced through Aristotelian logic in the academy (the preferred mode of Lutheran orthodoxy).

Basic to this task, Steinmetz shifts ground zero for understanding the evangelical experience of salvation to a point beyond the biblical narrative of Calvary, where it was in Luther, to the narrative of Pentecost (Acts 2).

96. Wesley and Kinghorn, "Plain Account," 8.

97. George Croft Cell, *The Rediscovery of Wesley* (New York: Henry Holt and Co., 1934), 300, cited in Collins, *Scripture Way*, 80.

98. Wesley, *Sermons of Charles Wesley*, 139–40. Wood notes this conflation of justification and sanctification came under the influence of the English Moravians who differed from Christian David on this point. See Wood, *Pentecost*, 57.

Only those who become assured of the promise of the gospel, in relation to the cross, occurring through the sealing of believers by the Holy Spirit on Pentecost, may be called real Christians, or the children of God.[99] This reading of Scripture is what he calls the result of godly (e.g., pneumatic) wisdom as opposed to the "natural reason" used by most orthodox or scholastic Protestants.[100] The sealing is what connects Pentecost with the cross because only through the Holy Spirit's indwelling ministry can the blood of Jesus be applied to the inner lives of the children of God.[101]

In his first Pentecost address, Steinmetz explains why the sealing that happened at Pentecost is urgently necessary for assurance of salvation. Unlike Luther, he says the gift of salvation by Christ's righteousness is not passively received in the face of the cross; instead, it is to be urgently sought by overcoming one's inattentiveness to what the cross means, "which is the prerequisite for access to the sealing through the Holy Spirit."[102] However, once the Holy Spirit convinces one of corruption and a state of damnation (through the ministry of the law), one's sense of godlessness has only been compounded. At this point, Steinmetz counsels, do not give up: "You have already won the first victory. There the Holy Spirit has already conquered the evil thoughts which wanted to bind you, that you should now believe."[103] It is the work of the Spirit for preparing the heart to receive the sealing that is then to follow.

Also unlike Luther, for whom freedom from bondage comes when a person confesses that all his or her sin is transferred by Christ onto himself in his atoning death on the cross, for Steinmetz, once the first victory (conviction of sin) is won by the Holy Spirit, we are encouraged to appeal to the Spirit's anointing to enable the "poor sinner" to "triumph" over "those remaining things" in the matchless blood of Christ until, following the lead of Jacob's wrestling with the angel,[104] we pray, "I will hold on until You bless me, as an overcomer who receives the crown, the seal of the Holy Spirit

---

99. Steinmetz, *Versiegelung*, 36–42.

100. Note that "Protestant" is our term for Steinmetz's *evangelisch*, which is synonymous with Lutheran. The former term reflects the political reality in the Holy Roman Empire of Germany that adherents to the Augsburg Confession is the only legal non-Roman religion available to a prince of the realm (recall that the religious choice is for the prince of each principality and not for the people, based on the Peace of Augsburg of 1555).

101. For more information, see Steinmetz, *Versiegelung*.

102. Steinmetz, *Versiegelung*, 29.

103. Steinmetz, *Versiegelung*, 29.

104. Cf. Jacob wrestling with the angel (Gen 32:22–31). Steinmetz, *Versiegelung*, 29.

Himself, the gem of blessedness and of the holy ones, not from the merit of works, but as a pure gift of grace."[105]

The focus has shifted with Steinmetz from overcoming unfaithfulness (as Luther) to ungodliness, suggesting the sanctifying quality of Pentecostal grace in which the forgiven sinner is sealed. Here the Holy Spirit, in the context of Pentecost, is guiding the seeker back to Calvary so that the benefit of being cleansed by the shed blood of Christ may now be appropriated to grant personal assurance of the forgiveness of sins and also to receive the indwelling within the heart unto *Seligkeit*, which is translated as blessedness or sanctification.[106]

In his second Pentecost address, Steinmetz pressed further to declare that the Holy Spirit works not only through signs of his presence; the very Person of the Holy Spirit may serve as the chief seal imprinted within the heart of the believer,[107] along with other "ancillary" seals that usually accompany the Holy Spirit. These include the words of Scripture read and proclaimed, the sacraments (and especially the eucharist, but also baptism), and the immediate sensations of the Holy Spirit whereby he communes with the believer directly, in prayer, dreams, and prophecies.[108] To be assured that the sealing is salvific and not temporal, he emphasizes that God brings persons to faith among his works of sealing through the Holy Spirit for those who are without guile, a childlike quality.

Viewed together, these works of sealing comprise an outpouring of the Holy Spirit. Such assurance also represents a response to Christ's work of conversion from sin to grace.[109] The focal point of that work is a personal identity with the shed blood of Jesus.

105. Steinmetz, *Versiegelung*, 29.

106. Steinmetz discusses blessedness/sanctification (*Seligkeit*) as the consequence of sealing in the blood of Christ unto forgiveness and righteousness by faith in his first Pentecost Address: "With the Spirit there now grows such a grounded, persevering, heaven focused assurance . . . that with it, one may be a child of God. Then, in an instant, a person may stand in a condition in which she will unfailingly become blessed [blessed is from Selig, a term that includes beatification and the highest level of holiness before the Lord]. The entire heart of God is now open with all the treasures and blessings of salvation with have been attained by our Savior Jesus. And who can explain everything which flows for the blessed from the sealing through the Holy Spirit" (Steinmetz, *Der Versiegelung*, 1.3a:10; 1.4:15).

107. This reference to the immediate or direct sealing of the Holy Spirit reflects the Silesian spirituality, which is based in the theology of Caspar Schwenkfeld, the spiritual reformer who disagreed with Luther about whether one may suspend use of the Lord's Supper to focus on Christ's inward presence in the Spirit directly. The Schwenkfelders continue as a denomination in Pennsylvania to the present time.

108. Steinmetz, *Der Versiegelung*, 46–49.

109. Speaking pastorally to those who have not found personal salvation, Steinmetz

Reflecting the influence of Steinmetz, his mentor in the faith, David, writes to him in 1741, saying, "Now, my dear old father and brother, this is what I can report to you of the Brethren. But what should I say about myself, how I stand with the Lamb?"[110] Steinmetz was alone among the Silesian leaders who remained steadfast in friendship with the mercurial David, even after the latter had chosen not to follow Steinmetz's sage advice not to dispatch refugees from Silesia until there was a safe place for them across the border.

On the matter of personal salvation in Christ, it nevertheless appears David did follow his mentor's model. Like Luther, both are grounded in the cross. David declares, "There is no connection between God and the ungodly . . . [because] they are altogether separate from each other. . . . There is nothing in the ungodly to join them to God. . . . [Hence, the] right foundation . . . [is to] go straight to Christ with all your ungodliness."[111]

David also shares Steinmetz's precedent in breaking from Luther by moving to a two-stage view of grace. For Luther, the theology of the cross locates the sinner precisely at the cross before the crucified Lamb of God by whose obedience unto death the Father is enabled to be propitiated so that the Holy Spirit can now assure that Christ is carrying one's sin for which that person alone deserved eternal death. At that moment, Christ, then clothed in our vile sins, is facing his Father and not wooing those who are the intended beneficiaries of his atoning death to respond in faith. They are bowed by *Anfechtung* under the accusatory ministry of the law (Rom 7:5–25) for which only the death of Christ is the redemptive remedy as validated by the promise of the Word of God (Rom 7:9–25).

By comparison, David, following Steinmetz, resets the point where personal salvation through Jesus Christ occurs to a place beyond Calvary, where the focus had remained with Luther, to the disciples at Pentecost.

---

advises not to conclude that God has cut himself off from you if you have been seeking the sealing of the Holy Spirit and nothing can be discerned of his presence in your "inner soul": "Hold on! If you will only focus on discerning your God, and not your own [experiences], He will come, before you even understand it yourself, within a moment, when you are hearing, reading, or observing the Word, even when you are only slightly thinking about all of this. By a word of proclamation, a use of the holy Lord's Supper, or other means, your Jesus will unexpectedly come and apply this seal [of the Holy Spirit] to your soul, whereby your poor heart may profit both in time and in eternity. Do not abandon your confidence. Hasten only to weep and to pray to your God, and to your Savior" (Steinmetz, *Der Versiegelung*, ii, 3, 49).

110. Christian David in a letter to Steinmetz, July 1741 (Nelson, *Christian David*, 55).

111. Christian David, fourth Pentecost sermon preached before John Wesley at Herrnhut, as reported by Wesley, *Journal and Diaries I*, 270.

The scene shifts to the manifestation of the Holy Spirit with anointing upon those who had been waiting, "weak in faith."[112] The disciples had believed the message of the cross yet remained incapacitated until the appearance of the Holy Spirit at Pentecost where they are at last empowered as apostles with the Holy Spirit cleansing and anointing their hearts to become at that moment fully assured that they are the children of God.

The Pentecost event validates Calvary, where they first became heirs of the promise, in an external event observed but which the disciples had not yet inwardly appropriated. David distinguishes between the "intermediate state" experienced after Calvary and before Pentecost, which is described by Paul in Rom 7, which signifies "they had not yet received a new, clean heart," nor "the indwelling of the Holy Spirit," which would render them "pure in heart from all self and sin."[113]

David's fourth sermon, which Wesley transcribed in his journal, speaks of the "ground" of our faith from which this gift of Pentecostal grace proceeds. Here he speaks in the language of Steinmetz's version of the theology of the cross. The atoning work of Christ is designated as the "word of reconciliation" whereby "we are reconciled to God, not by our own works, but wholly and solely by the blood of Christ." Over against the dominant theme of Pietists in the Halle/Francke context, for whom conversion begins with a "penitential struggle" (*Busskampf*), preceding the "breakthrough" (*Durchbruch*) of grace, for David, "the right foundation for conversion is, not your contrition, not your righteousness," but rather, "it is nothing of your own, nothing that is wrought *in you* by the Holy Ghost; but it is something *without you*, viz., the righteousness and the blood of Christ."[114]

David teaches this doctrine in his letters from the Moravian mission field as indicated in his letter from Lithuania in July 1741 where he writes, "The Lamb of God is our witness at what cost we have been purchased and how much the Savior loves souls. . . . As many of us as walk in the light will have our feet covered with dust cleansed (sealed) with the blood of Jesus."[115] That is, the cross leads to sanctification, and *Christus pro nobis* becomes *Christus in nobis*—Christ for us/Christ in us.[116]

---

112. Christian David said Calvary was the place of encounter with Christ for those who were "weak in faith." See Wesley, *Journal and Diaries I*, 270.

113. Wesley, *Journal and Diaries I*, 270.

114. John Wesley's account of Steinmetz's ideas. See Wesley, *Journal and Diaries I*, 272.

115. Nelson, *Christian David*, 52–53.

116. Christian David confesses in his memoir to Wesley of struggling with a proper balance between "Christ for us" (the theology of the cross), and "Christ in us" (the theology of Pentecost). The latter is to confirm the former, but the tendency he faced

After encounters with David, John Wesley learned to distinguish between a first state of justifying grace and a second state embodying the assurance of faith and the grace of sanctification as Christian perfection.[117] In response to hearing David preach this message on Pentecost and sanctification on four occasions at Herrnhut, including extended conversation that followed, Wesley expressed his agreement with David on the basic distinction between the disciples' experience of justifying faith at Calvary where they were only "weak in faith" and the "full assurance of faith" at Pentecost.[118]

After his encounter with David in 1738, Wesley introduced terminology reflecting the theme of Pentecost in his ministry, including "the baptism of the Holy Spirit," and, after a remarkable holiness revival that swept England and Ireland in 1760, he began speaking of this revival as an event resembling Pentecost with as many persons being sanctified as were being justified.[119] Consequently, Charles Wesley and John Fletcher began using the language of the baptism of the Spirit as an expression for Christian perfection, under John's influence. This was the fullness of salvation that was then and remains now available in the preaching of the gospel. Here is reflected his instruction from David that it was at Pentecost that the apostles became "fully assured, by the Holy Spirit then received, of their reconciliation to God by [Christ's] blood."[120] The brothers differed in their emphasis on whether the experience of holiness unto perfection was primarily instantaneous in a crisis moment (John) or gradual (Charles, for whom the new birth is reserved to describe the culmination of that process).[121]

John's conversations with David, as reported by John, convinced Charles Wesley to change to two stages of faith rather than one.[122] Reflecting his new outlook, Charles wrote in his journal in October 1738 that "although I have not yet that joy in the Holy Spirit, nor that love of God shed abroad in my heart, nor the full assurance of faith, nor the proper witness of the Holy Spirit with my Spirit that I am a child of God. . . . I nevertheless trust that I have a measure of faith and am 'accepted in the beloved.'"[123]

---

was an overemphasis upon the one and then the other. See Wesley, *Journal and Diaries II*, 279.

117. Wesley, *Journal and Diaries I*, 272.

118. Wesley gives a comprehensive report of his encounter with Christian David in Wesley, *Journal and Diaries II*, 270.

119. Wesley, "Short History," 473; Wood, *Pentecost*, 120.

120. Wesley et al., *Manuscript Journal*, 1:122.

121. The view of Tyson, *Charles Wesley*, 219; Wood, *Pentecost*, 121.

122. Wesley, *Letters*, 25:554.

123. Wesley, *Journal and Diaries II*, 19.

After John related the details of his visit with David to his brother Charles, we find Charles using the theme of the Holy Spirit's sealing in the blood of Christ as indicative of sanctification. In his hymn, "Sinners, Lift Up Your Hearts," verses two to four include all the themes of the promise coming from the cross, the kingdom, defeat of Satan, the gift of the Spirit, the cleansing blood, and wholly sanctifying by sealing unto the day of judgment:

> Sinners, lift up your hearts
> The Promise to receive!
> Jesus himself imparts
> He comes to man to live
> The Holy Ghost to man is given;
> Rejoice in God sent down from heaven.
> Jesus is glorified,
> And gives the Comforter,
> His Spirit, to reside
> In all his members here.
> The Holy Ghost to man is given;
> Rejoice in God sent down from heaven.
> To make an end of sin,
> And Satan's work destroy,
> He brings his kingdom in,
> Peace, righteousness, and joy;
> The Holy Ghost to man is given:
> Rejoice in God sent down from heaven.
> The cleansing blood to apply,
> The heavenly life display,
> And wholly sanctify,
> And seal us to that day,
> The Holy Ghost to man is given:
> Rejoice in God sent down from heaven![124]

Wood notes that the language of sealing comes from the theology of confirmation in the Anglican theologian Jeremy Taylor.[125] It also derives from the language of David, conveyed to John Wesley and then to his brother Charles, and this language of *Versiegelung* (sealing) comes to David directly

---

124. Wesley cited in Wood, *Pentecost*, 62.
125. Wood, *Pentecost*, 49.

from Steinmetz whose *Pentecost Addresses* make liberal use of this theme, for the first time in the context of revival.[126]

The Coming Kingdom

Given Luther's stance opposing revolutionary spiritualists such as Thomas Muntzer, Luther adopted a conservative affirmation of the legitimacy of the existing offices of imperial government,[127] which he joined to an apocalyptic view of an imminent day of divine judgment.[128] In another sense, the kingdom has already arrived in the heart of the penitent who has trusted in the promise of Calvary. In the death of Christ the "wonderful exchange" has already occurred between Christ and the penitent sinner.

In Steinmetz's *Pentecost Addresses*, he has Luther speaking anew, in the context of revival, with the evangelical admonition, "Tell Him, 'Thou, whose eyes are as a flame of fire searching my heart . . . I plead nothing else.'" Rather than being self-serving by saying, "I am humble," be honest, say, "I am ungodly"; therefore, "bring me to Him who justifies the ungodly, Let Thy blood be the propitiation for me."[129]

Representing the oppressed Protestant state church in Silesia, Steinmetz was in the forefront of supporting revival as the intent of the Spirit in bringing *Erweckung* (awakening) to humanity in history, thereby overcoming the restrictive religious policies of a fading though oppressive *corpus Christianum* (or body of Christendom). At the same time, his intent was to work through and not contrary to the existing political order. Hence, he cautioned David against relocating religious refugees from Catholic Silesia to Germany as violation of sovereign borders.

Overall, Steinmetz was influenced by Spener's hope for a coming "better time for the church" as expressed in the wake of the Thirty Years' War. When the *Parousia* of Christ did not happen in 1700 as expected, his life of ministry in the new century was guided by a new vision of the future, set in place by the children's revival and its consequences, which looked to the coming of the kingdom of God among those in covenant with Christ on earth (who were those sealed by the Holy Spirit). He labored three decades

126. See discussion of Steinmetz and David in this section.

127. As referenced in Rom 13, government is ordained by God to be believed for conscience's sake.

128. This position wreaked havoc in the Peasants War (1524–25) with Muntzer's conviction that the Holy Spirit was directing him to raise up the peasants in holy war against an oppressive state, believing this course would hasten the judgment day for a reprobate state.

129. Wesley, *Journal and Diaries II*, 272.

in this vain to collect the materials for a documentation of the building of the kingdom of God on earth through the extension of *Erweckung* (revival). More than anyone in his generation, Steinmetz documents a network of path breakers in his lifetime who were heralding the spread of the kingdom through the ministry of the Holy Spirit, tapping persons globally for the kingdom.[130]

There is an analogous relation between the personal and the corporate dimensions of this discussion. There is the Holy Spirit's building of that new order, at the personal level, within the redeemed of the Lord through the inward sealing of the Holy Spirit as God's response to the cross. Simultaneously, the empirics of this demographic feature opens the door to visualizing an expanding, critical mass of converts to Christ through the Pentecostal sealing of the Holy Spirit, which would corroborate Spener's hope for a more glorious age of the church in the near future. It is an optimistic vision for the short-term, the inverse of Luther's apocalyptic *Angst*.

Following Steinmetz's lead, David locates Pietist revivalism at its foundation in Luther's theology of the cross.[131] But then he adds this statement: "Tell Him [Christ], whose eyes are as a flame of fire searching my heart, [You] see that I am ungodly. . . . I plead nothing else, let Thy blood be the propitiation for me."[132] In this statement, the scene shifts for David from Calvary and also from the scene of Pentecost to Christ's returning in judgment. David's words about Christ's eyes being as "a flame of fire searching my heart," is not depicting Christ from the position of his death at Calvary, nor is it the event of the Spirit's coming at Pentecost; rather, it is a direct reference to Rev 19:11–12: "And I saw heaven opened; and behold, a white horse, and He who sat upon it is called Faithful and True, and in righteousness he judges and wages war, and His eyes are a flame of fire, and upon His head are many diadems, and He has a name written upon Him which no one knows except Himself." David's theme is still the theology of the cross, but here focus has shifted from Calvary, as well as from Pentecost, where the assurance of the forgiveness of sins is rendered efficacious in the sealing of the Holy Spirit. It has reached the apocalyptic moment of Christ appearing in final judgment. The latter is a second place where the theology of the cross is being altered by David. Our righteousness through the

---

130. At the same time, his intent was to work through and not contrary to the existing political order. Hence, he cautioned Christian David against relocating religious refugees from Catholic Silesia to Germany as a violation of sovereign borders.

131. Recall that all of these voices—David, Francke, and Steinmetz—are officially Pietists who are also Lutheran as is Zinzendorf, as indicated in his intent to maintain Herrnhut's alignment with the parish of Berthelsdorf.

132. Wesley, *Journal and Diaries II*, 272.

imputation of Christ's work on the cross has been relocated to the locus of its implementation, at Pentecost, and also, by anticipation, to the *Parousia* when Christ's kingdom will be established upon earth through his divine judgment.

For David, these three themes of justification located in the theology of the cross at Calvary, in Pentecost sanctification and, at last, in the final judgment, find points of analogy in Steinmetz, by whom David was confirmed in the faith. David's memoirs reflect these themes as appearing after, and not before, his decisive meeting with Steinmetz.[133]

An obvious point of continuity between John Wesley and the two-stage view of grace found in the German Moravians is found in his statement of the purpose for joining the first Methodist class, which convened in Bristol during the revival there in 1739. The three rules for class members were

---

133. There are two possibilities of dating David's decisive encounter with Steinmetz: his Memoir first mentions encountering Steinmetz as a young refugee from Moravia, residing for five years from 1717 in Görlitz on the German/Silesian border. There, under influence from the preaching of Johann Christian Schwedler, a coworker with Steinmetz in the Silesian awakening, he experienced his first awakening to evangelical faith and also met Steinmetz. The second encounter is mentioned some years later (1725) when he was directed by Zinzendorf to leave Herrnhut to consult with Steinmetz, then immersed in revival at Teschen. David had been thrown off balance by the prominent preaching of a Calvinist estate manager hired by Zinzendorf at Herrnhut, who was leading some Herrnhuters to question their salvation. David talked "fully" with Steinmetz on the "head," whether Christ died for all. "I did so, and God fully convinced me of that important truth." He continues, "Not long after, the Count desired that we might all meet together, and consider these things thoroughly. We met accordingly at his house, and parted not for three days. We opened the Scriptures, and considered the account which is given therein of the whole economy of God with man, from the creation to the consummation of all things And by the blessing of God we came all to one mind" (Wesley, *Journal and Diaries II*, 275). It seems inevitable that such comprehensive discussion of the economy of God and man, in the wake of David's meeting with Steinmetz, would of necessity have included the matter of the cross and the sealing with the Holy Spirit at Pentecost, which was the main area of Steinmetz's theology which David began to emulate in his extant letters and sermons after that date, especially the four sermons Wesley heard from him at Herrnhut in 1738). Further, document providing the narrative of his theological conversation with Steinmetz was what John Wesley transcribed and was omitted by Zinzendorf in his memoirs of Christian David. David reported that he and Zinzendorf found agreement on these doctrinal matters at their three-day conference in 1725, although Zinzendorf omitted mention of this in his memoirs on David and also defended a one-stage position in his conversations with John Wesley at London in 1741. This inconsistency in Zinzendorf is not unusual, since he was operating not as a trained theologian but as a community organizer, who could adapt his message to fit the context. These arguments represent the case for regarding Steinmetz as the main theological source for David's two-stage view of saving grace.

framed by the head question: "Do you wish to be freed from your sin and to flee the wrath to come?"[134]

However, John also found space for going beyond apocalyptic judgment to a better state of the church in the future in light of the renewal of Pentecost as the driving theme of the Methodist revival in England and beyond. He gave substance to that hope in his later sermon on "The General Spread of the Gospel," which envisions a "grand Pentecost" that will become global.[135]

He was returning to a theme found in his early letter to his elder brother Samuel (fall 1738) when John confided, "I now enjoy by His free mercy, [although] the seal of the Spirit, the love of God shed abroad in my heart, and producing joy in the Holy Spirit. . . . This witness of the Spirit I have not, but I patiently wait for it."[136]

Charles Wesley made more use of the biblical typology which relates the personal work of the cross to the passover and exodus of Israel, while the work of Pentecost is related to their entry to Canaan, where the promises of God were fulfilled in the indwelling Spirit. In this context the theme of the sealing by the Holy Spirit, prominent in Steinmetz and David, finds its place in a "concealed" mode, which is only fully "revealed" in Pentecost. These verses from Charles embody this typological theme:

> The covenant old in types concealed
> Now in the gospel is revealed
> The gospel covenant has took place
> And saves us not by works but grace,
> The Lord his Spirit's seal supplies
> His people all to circumcise,
> And when our sins and us He parts
> Cuts off the foreskin of our hearts.[137]

---

134. United Methodist Church, *Book of Discipline*, 51.

135. See Wesley, "General Spread of the Gospel."

136. Wesley, *Letters*, 25:575–78.

137. Wesley cited in Wood, *Pentecost*, 68. If the etymology of this motif were explored, it is probably to be found in the symbolic prophetic school of biblical typology found in Reformed Pietism, especially with the systematic theologian Johannes Cocceius (d. 1669) and the federal school, with ties to Cambridge Puritanism and also German Reformed Pietism through Lampe and Otterbein. See O'Malley, *Pilgrimage*.

In Charles's typology, Canaan is the "sanctuary," "the abode," and "the kingdom," all signifying the perfect love for God, which is the mark of the revival initiated by the coming of the Spirit in Pentecost.[138]

Hence, a parallel trajectory appears between the stirrings of revival in central Europe and among the Methodists in Britain in the early modern era. There was the kingdom theme of the Silesian revival whose purpose, beginning with the children, Steinmetz called the "Building of the Kingdom of God on Earth," and that was matched by the homilies and hymns of the Wesleys on behalf of the "grand Pentecost," which was coming from the "General Spread of the Gospel" on earth.[139]

CONCLUSION

The recovery of the Reformation theme of Luther's theology of the cross is enhanced by the discovery that this theme became the foundation from which developed the first theology of Pentecost to appear in the context of revival, within the history of Protestantism. By locating the Pentecost addresses presented by the preacher of that revival, Steinmetz, the theological content that informed that historic revival can now be understood and read in the light of Luther's original doctrine of the cross. The findings of this study have also made evident the similarities between Steinmetz's addresses and the theology of David who transmitted the themes of the cross and Pentecost from Steinmetz to John Wesley and, through him, to his brother Charles and to the larger world of the Methodist revival.

138. Wesley cited in Wood, *Pentecost*, 75.

139. See the title of Steinmetz's account of the Silesian revival and its global extension (as well as Charles Wesley's hymn) in Wood, *Pentecost*, 75. See also Wesley, "General Spread of the Gospel."

PART 2

Enduring Themes of a Twenty-First-Century Theology of the Cross and Kingdom

5

Sovereignly Good
Soteriological Singularity

THE PRIOR PRESENTATION AND analysis should point toward possible trajectories and major themes of a biblical, sound, and germane twenty-first-century theology of the cross. Many of the trajectories in Table 4 have already been articulated or suggested.

Table 4. Cross and Kingdom Leitmotifs

Sovereignly good soteriological singularity
Sovereignly good epistemological singularity
Contra theology of glory and self-glorification
Integrative, conjunctive, theological anchor for cross and kingdom
Kenotic cruciform kingdom holiness
Cruciform liberation and kingdom approximation
Cross and kingdom eschatology and doxology

Perhaps the singular nature of salvation through the cross, putting aside debates concerning theological determinism, unites biblical and orthodox Christians from a variety of traditions influenced by the Reformation. Hence, this chapter should be concise. Luther correctly identified at least five *solas* of the Reformation[1]:

---

1. Luther had it right concerning the five *solas* when the five are properly defined and contextualized, as words are always part of a complex semantic tapestry and context. See Huggins, *Living Justification*, 32.

1. *Sola scriptura*
2. *Sola fide*
3. *Sola gratia*
4. *Solus Christus*, and
5. *Soli Deo gloria*

This list served as five pillars for a *theologia crucis* that viewed the cross as a soteriological singularity.

Whether the *cross alone* should be viewed as a sixth pillar of the Reformation or simply viewed as emerging from the five need not be resolved here. Luther properly contended that the Christ-event was a divinely determined soteriological singularity. Chapter 3 has already nuanced this discussion. That Christ through the cross is the only salvific hope for humanity is central to the Protestant tradition. That God determined such is also not in question though the nature, reason, and logic or order of the determination or decrees is much debated.

Hence, an indisputable core of a biblical theology of the cross must be that the cross is a soteriological singularity: "And there is salvation in no one else; for there is no other name under heaven that has been given among men by which we must be saved" (Acts 4:12). And we are saved through Christ because of the divinely determined singularity of the cross. Also note in the following Scripture passage that the cross is viewed both as part of a Christ-event in the time of the apostles as well as part of the eschatological restoration of all things.

> But the things which God announced beforehand by the mouth of all the prophets, that His Christ would suffer, He has thus fulfilled. Therefore repent and return, so that your sins may be wiped away, in order that times of refreshing may come from the presence of the Lord; and that He may send Jesus, the Christ appointed for you, whom heaven must receive until the period of restoration of all things about which God spoke by the mouth of His holy prophets from ancient time. (Acts 3:18–21)

Any alternative to a salvation through Christ alone that is based on the cross alone amounts to a presumptuous theology of glory.

Luther often framed this soteriological singularity within a comprehensive and theologically deterministic context. Attempting to determine whether Luther was an ironclad determinist, or a sublapsarian, or a hard-to-define pre-Calvinist and vintage Lutheran, as noted in chapter 2, misses the point of this work. Luther clearly jumps, via a seeming non sequitur, from this singularity (*contra* works righteousness), that the Christ of the cross alone saves, to a broader deterministic framework that animates his entire theology of the cross. This determinism spawns his questionable pastoral advice and application of the theology of the cross to his suffering and dying mother. Yet this deterministic debate goes beyond the purpose of this present work.

The orthodox consensus of a divinely determined soteriological singularity need not embrace theological determinism or the five points of Calvinism or universalism, and certainly not religious pluralism, for that matter. This singularity, relative to the theology of the cross, speaks more to soteriological exclusivity, salvation by grace alone in Christ, and overflowing love for sinners who find God through Christ and the cross alone. Some critics will argue that unless the entire soteriological schema is grounded in deterministic decrees with a certain order, that our salvation collapses, but that debate is left to other venues. Some will argue that this soteriological singularity is most compatible with either exclusivism or inclusivism, but the resolution of that debate also falls beyond the range of this book. In terms of assumptions, I would argue that an unlimited atonement neither requires inclusivism nor is irreconcilable with exclusivism.

Hence, the emphasis of this work is that the salvific event of the cross is certainly singular and determined by God and lies at the core of soteriology, but this singularity can and has been framed in both deterministic and non-deterministic fashions.

If the cross is for us and for all, then the "cross reveals the heart of God. It does not change God, it discloses what he has been from 'before the foundation of the world'" (Eph 1:3–7). This glorious singularity, "the way the truth and the life," is revealed in "the cross of Christ, where 'love and faithfulness meet together; righteousness and peace kiss each other'" (Ps 85:10).[2]

---

2. Wiley, *Christian Theology*, 2:285–86.

6

Sovereignly Good
Epistemological Singularity

A REVEALED SINGULARITY

LUTHER RIGHTLY AFFIRMED THAT the cross-centered *via* or *ordo salutis* is an epistemological singularity, and this epistemological singularity is the exclusive and divinely determined revelation of how we are to be saved. Yet Barth and Brian and the apostle Paul are correct that a biblical mystery, and this mystery in particular, that was once hidden is now revealed—"which is Christ in you, the hope of glory" (Col 1:27). The *Deus absconditus* must be contextualized within the full revelation of Christ and the universal preaching and teaching of the gospel.

Hence, the veil shrouding Christ as savior, as Paul clearly states in 2 Cor 3:15 (NIV) is perceptual or phenomenological, not ontological, and can be removed when and if "anyone turns to the Lord." *Theologia crucis* affirms that God can be known savingly, by sinners, only through the cross. God is not known in a salvific sense, by sinners, because they are unsaved sinners and the veil has not yet been removed. Presumably unfallen angels and humanity before the fall were capable of knowing much about God. It would be theologically risky, if not crazed, to suggest that humanity had to sin and Christ had to die for sinners in order for any creatures to know anything about God. Hence, the cross is an epistemological singularity for sinners, not because we affirm an unknowable or untouchable God. God did not introduce a new attribute or collection of attributes on the cross; God revealed who he already was via the cross. The cross reflects the heart of God, but the nature of God is shrouded because of humanity's fallen condition. As noted in chapter 5, the cross of Christ is "where 'love and faithfulness meet together; righteousness and peace kiss each other.'"[1]

This epistemological distinction between saving knowledge and general knowledge of God, or between the phenomenological reality of the sinner and the actual ontological status of the knowledge of God by creatures created in God's image, is absolutely critical to this discussion, apologetics, evangelism, and the mission of the church. The perceived "scandal" or "folly" of the cross is not authentic "wisdom" but authentic folly. The true scandal is the rejection of this sovereignly good and eternal gift "where love and faithfulness meet together; righteousness and peace kiss each other."[2] The *Deus absconditus* properly describes the following, which includes but is not limited to: the perceptual, phenomenological, and experiential reality of fallen humanity in an inverted world, especially cultures and individuals in moral and spiritual decay; the ontological fallen nature of the world that God so loved; and, the existential angst of Christ on the forsaken cross or the believer bewildered by unrelenting suffering and persecution. God is often most clearly revealed where *we* suspect he is not—with an emphasis on *we*. Yet God, God in Christ, and the Scriptures certainly were not surprised by Calvary. Calvary was never hidden in the ontological and epistemological sense of what was actually real and knowable. Indeed, given who God is eternally, the absence of Calvary would be incongruous with the nature of the triune God in view of the fall. The hiddenness of God in the Christ of the cross was because of us and for us, not because of who God was or the actual nature and limits of human knowledge. We need to quit putting the onus on God because we have covered our eyes with a veil, then stubbornly refused to remove the veil, and even spurned the healing touch that would restore our sight. The meek who respond to prevenient grace and mourn over their sins and spiritual poverty are the ones who have the veil removed and proleptically regain eyes to see and ears to hear (Matt 13:16; Mark 4:9; 8:18; Jer 5:21).

A SOTERIOLOGICAL AND PHENOMENOLOGICAL SINGULARITY

As noted in chapter 2, a more careful reading of Luther suggests that even Luther acknowledged that information about God, which could become an

1. Wiley, *Christian Theology*, 2:285–86.
2. Wiley, *Christian Theology*, 2:285–86.

idol or a theology of glory, was possible apart from the revelatory singularity of the cross. It is questionable, however, as to whether non-salvific knowledge of God always leads to an arrogant theology of glory and idolatry or has no apologetic, evangelistic, or preparatory and pre-evangelistic value. It is also questionable as to whether non-salvific knowledge of God can be isolated from salvific knowledge of God. Is not knowledge of God more organic or symbiotic? Did not the cross shine more brightly because the heavens and earth that declare the glory of God (Ps 19:1) turned to darkness and underscored the profundity of the cross? Did not the shrouding of the sun at Calvary underscore the capsized nature of the world? Did not the attributes of God "clearly" revealed ("clearly seen" and "understood" by all) in creation (Rom 1) provide an indispensable epistemological foundation for understanding the message of the cross? Did not the cross take place in creation, in time, in and through history with centuries of advance preparation? Is not a bifurcated knowledge of God ultimately gnostic in nature? Is it not better to speak of the knowledge and wisdom of God in a unified sense with the cross being a soteriological and epistemological singularity *for sinners*?

Perhaps our beloved, explosive, and reactionary Luther, known for polarities, created a false epistemological dilemma. Yet that question is best reserved for the ongoing scholarly discussion. Certainly, many epic Christian leaders from the early church to the present (e.g., C. S. Lewis, Augustine) seem to have navigated partial knowledge about God as a stepping-stone to saving personal knowledge of God. And perhaps partial or preparatory or pre-evangelisitc knowledge of God, which certainly can be an idol, also might, in certain contexts, have an ameliorative civilizational impact, in contrast to a civilization and culture premised entirely upon *absconditus*?

While Luther was targeting certain forms of philosophy, perhaps for Luther the emphasis is too great on philosophy as a chained handmaiden to theology, as opposed to a sanctified and liberated handmaiden. He was doubtless pummeling certain forms of philosophy (e.g., Aristotle, Aquinas, scholasticism, or perspectives he rejected with passion relative to the realism and nominalism debate). Nevertheless, even given these qualifications concerning Luther, his polemic seems targeted at more than Aristotle or Aquinas and poisons the wellspring of the knowledge of God necessary for ethics, civilization, apologetics, pre-evangelism, evangelism, and cooperative social engagement with those outside of the Christian, evangelical, orthodox church.

AN APOLOGETIC SINGULARITY

Perhaps it is almost too convenient for those following an anti-apologetic trajectory of thought, in the name of the theology of the cross, to avoid the loving trench warfare and extreme relational and educational sacrifices requisite for responding to the often legitimate queries of modern and post-modern skeptics. Perhaps it is too easy, and theologically and philosophically inadequate, simply to suggest that the best apologetic is merely to preach the word or preach the cross. Perhaps some have overlooked how many key thinkers have been reached by grace-assisted apologetic ministries (e.g., Francis Collins). Perhaps some fail to recognize the critical importance of the philosophical and apologetic task for encouraging the faithful, not to mention pursuing positive civilizational influence in the academy, law, media, politics, and entertainment. Perhaps some are oblivious to how the sacrificial work of Christian apologists in science, history, philosophy, theology, and film have influenced some to consider the cross and eventually kneel at the foot of the cross. Perhaps some are unaware that I was most dismissive of the gospel when evangelicals pointed to the story of the cross, and when I pressed them for a response they had little or nothing to offer. Not until other evangelicals stepped up to the plate and addressed intellectual obstacles was I willing seriously to research and reconsider Christian origins and the claims of the cross for my life, for time, and for eternity.

Viewing the cross as a soteriological and even an epistemologically soteriological singularity does not necessarily entail the entire dismissal of the apologetic task. One cannot use the uniqueness of Christian soteriology to determine, in advance and without careful analysis, the implications of that singularity for epistemology. For example, the cross may be the only epistemological avenue for saving, personal knowledge of God, but that hardly discounts at least the possibility that someone not in an evangelical or salvific relationship with God—meaning that they are not justified or regenerate—could, by grace, conclude that humanity is radically corrupt and in need of forgiveness and transformation via a personal, loving, transcendent Being. I certainly did, and such knowledge directed me back to the *via dolorosa*.

7

Contra Theology of Glory and Self-Glorification

LUTHER NEEDS LESS INTERPRETATION and filtering relative to his theology of glory, which is actually a critique of false glory. The theology of glory that too easily identifies with sociopolitico-cultural-theological structures, personal agendas, success, and power, whether of the religious or political left or right,[1] certainly may cloak and empower the demonic, even in the church. Gorman summarizes the Pauline contrast between true glory and honor as follows:

> This countercultural, cruciform (holy) love pays special attention to the weaker members of the community . . . and special honor to apostles who exhibit Christ-like power in weakness . . . and it has a counterintuitive commitment to absorbing injustice rather than inflicting it. . . . Such cruciform holiness stands in marked contrast to the dominant Roman cultural values of promoting the self by seeking honor [or glory] and honoring the powerful.[2]

"GLORY" VERSUS GLORY

This work is focusing on theological reflection concerning leitmotifs relative to the prophetic version of the theology of the cross, and hence an extended

1. The left or right as defined by the contemporary American context.

2. Gorman, *Inhabiting the Cruciform God*, 110–11.

analysis of the Scriptural usage of the term glory exceeds our scope. Yet some distinctions concerning glory should prove helpful for advancing a theology of cross and kingdom.

The discussion point thus far primarily has been Luther's negative understanding and critique of the theology of glory. This work argues that integrating cross, kingdom, and glory allows for all three terms to be utilized biblically, and appropriately, in positive as well as prophetic or negative senses. The realistic but ultimately optimistic theology of the kingdom rescues the theology of glory from only being used as a negative critique. The theology of the kingdom rescues the theology of glory from a one-sided and almost inherently contrary critique of church, state, culture, and civilization. Even a cursory analysis of biblical texts reveals that Old and New Testament terms translated as glory have different meanings depending upon the context. Luther referenced Exodus 33 (see chapter 2 of this work) yet he emphasized the New Testament *sola* soteriological orientation. Hence, the majority of the references in Table 5 are derived from the New Testament in order to respond to Luther's one-sided and negative framing of the theology of glory.

Table 5. Scripture and Glory

Reference	Emphasis
Exod 33:18 (*kabad/kabod/kabed*)	God's glory is overwhelming
Ps 106:20 (*kabad/kabod/kabed*)	Israelite idolaters during the Exodus exchanged true glory for false idolatrous glory
Isa 6:3 (*kabad/kabod/kabed*)	The earth is full of God's glory.
Hos 4:7 (*kabad/kabod/kabed*)	God will remove the glory of idolatrous Israel and replace it with shame.
Matt 6:29 (δόξα)	Solomon's glory is acknowledged but the glory of God's creation is even greater.
Luke 2 (δόξα)	God's glory surrounds the angelic visitors and God is glorified for sending the Messiah.
Luke 9:26 (δόξα)	Christ will return in his glory, the Father's glory, and the glory of the angels.
John 8:50 (δόξα)	The Son does not seek his own glory but the glory of the Father.
Synoptic Gospels and John (δόξα) (e.g., John 12:23; Luke 24:26)	Christ's death and resurrection are central manifestations of God's glory.
Rom 3:23 (δόξα)	All humans fall short of the glory of God.

2 Cor 4:17 (δόξα)	Temporary, earthly affliction and suffering will result in "an eternal weight of glory far beyond all comparison."
Phil 3:21 (δόξα)	The resurrected bodies of believers will be transformed "into conformity with the body of His glory."
Heb 2:7 (δόξα) (also see Ps 8:5–6)	The Messiah has been crowned with "glory and honor."
1 Pet 5:4 (δόξα)	Believers will receive "the unfading crown of glory."
Rev (δόξα) (e.g., 19:1)	God repeatedly is given glory for his eschatological victory.

Numerous other biblical passages reference glory than these illustrative verses, and a detailed analysis will be left to the exegetical experts, yet what is clear is that the term translated to glory (often meaning honor) in English

- Has multiple nuances,

- Is nuanced by the context,

- Can refer to God or Christ,

- Can refer to God's glory in the creation,

- Can refer to false, human, and idolatrous glory

- Can properly and positively refer to the glory of the Solomonic kingdom, though much less glorious than God or God's creation,

- Can refer to God's presence in our space-time continuum or to his complete, transcendent, and eschatological glory currently unapproachable by fallen humanity (Exod 33),

- Can refer to God's holy standard of righteousness,

- Can refer to a future glorious reward and experience for believers,

- Can refer to the nature of the resurrection body of Christ and believers, and

- Can refer to the glorious presence and glorious victory of final eschatological victory.

Raymond B. Dillard provides and assists by distinguishing between two senses of the glory of humanity:

> The Bible *does speak of the glory of mankind and of the individual in two different ways, one positive and the other negative.*[3] The word in the OT usually translated as "glory" can also be translated as "wealth, honor, status" as the context may demand (Gen 31:1; 45:13; Num 24:11; 1 Sam 2:8). Men and women strive for wealth and honor as their glory in the world. God gives them this status (1 Kgs 3:13; 1 Chr 29:12; Pss 21:5; 84:11; Prov 3:16; 8:18), but he can also take it away (2 Chr 26:18; Job 19:9). On the whole, however, the attitude of the Bible toward the glory achieved by humankind is transitory, and "you can't take it with you" (Ps 49:16–17). All flesh is like grass that withers (Isa 40:6), a vapor that vanishes (Jas 4:13–16). Pride in appearance and boasting come from evil motives; faith in the glorious Lord discounts human glory (Jas 2:1–4); pride should not be in appearance but in a pure heart (2 Cor 5:12). All the glory of Solomon could not compare with that of a flower (Matt 6:29). The glory of nations can be toppled in a moment (Isa 10:16; 16:14; 17:4; 21:16; Jer 48:18; Ezek 31:18; Hos 4:17); the glory of all the kingdoms of the earth could not tempt Christ to forsake the law of God (Matt 4:8–9). Rather than seek self-glorification (Luke 14:10–11; John 12:43; Rom 2:7–8), all people should give praise to God (1 Cor 1:29–31; Eph 2:9). Pretensions to the glory of God bring only death (Acts 12:23).[4]

Luther rightly criticized a malignant theology of glory. To what degree he properly applied this insight to all the nuances of the theology of glory, and how he related it to the theology of the cross, is the subject of much of the current discussion. Luther was aware of the positive meaning and usage of glory, but he tended to apply it in an almost exclusive fashion to God or heaven. The argument of this work is that there are other important nuances of glory, which are scriptural and grounded in sound theology, especially in relationship to eschatological, already/not-yet, and approximative theology. This work affirms a positive and true glory that applies to this current age and life, and the next, that is a fulfillment of the Abrahamic blessing to all nations, and which typically emerges in a fallen world *via dolorosa*.

3. Emphasis added to highlight that Scripture nuances glory as both a positive and negative construct. So should we.

4. Dillard, "Glory," 870–73. Note: Scriptural abbreviations have been conformed to publisher style guidelines.

FALSE GLORY VERSUS ESCHATOLOGICAL GLORY

Hence, glory can be used as a positive as well as a negative construct. Luther's theology of glory as well as others have often emphasized the negative construct; hence, this discussion is illuminated by distinguishing between false or corrupt glory and real glory. This distinction is absolutely critical.

Much of the confusion concerning the theology of glory may be attributed to the failure to distinguish between these different nuances in Scripture and even in theological reflection on glory. As will be argued in chapters 9–12, authentic or proleptic or eschatological approximations, by grace alone, in church and civilization of the in-breaking kingdom should not be confused with pseudo-glory. A theology of glory that is only a negative construct is deleterious to the kingdom work of the church in God's world. The Christian influenced abolition of slavery in England and the overturning of apartheid, though not an abolition of all slavery or racial discrimination for all time, were authentically glorious advances that should be celebrated. Real glory is already and not yet. Real glory is eschatologically rooted. False glory is certainly evident, pervasive, and already, but false glory is also ultimately vanquished. It lacks eschatological reality, ultimacy, and finality. False glory was crucified on the cross, thus revealing true glory, but the not yet of authentic glory remains prior to the new creation. False glory is already but ultimately "not." False glory is eschatologically transient and ephemeral.

BIBLICAL GLORY

Biblical and historical narratives may illustrate these points (see Table 6). While the biblical term for glory is typically used in relationship to God, though not exclusively relative to Luther's concern, the concepts of false glory versus real but approximative glory may provide some clarity. For example, the endless list of evil judges and kings (Jer 22) who relished in their power, wealth, possession, and status, which certainly illustrates Luther's unfavorable conception of the theology of glory, are not viewed as possessing true, proleptic, or eschatological glory (or power, for that matter). The prophet Jeremiah rhetorically asks, "Does having a lot of cedar in your house make you a great king?" (Jer 22:15). While the term "glory" is not used in this text, the biblical author goes on to contrast true glory (i.e., doing "what is right and fair") with such false glory. Other biblical and historical narratives reinforce this point:

Table 6. Pseudo versus Proleptic Glory

False Glory (Luther's "Theology of Glory")	Approximative, Proleptic or Partial Glory
Murderous and scheming brothers of Joseph	Joseph (admirable, Christlike, but imperfect leader during a glorious era in the history of Egypt and Israel)
Saul's pathological obsession with glory and power	David (flawed but a better approximation of the Messianic kingdom than Saul)
Evil kings	Solomon (most imperfect yet certain aspects of his rule certainly are viewed as more glorious than other kings, including culture, architecture, and wisdom)
Herod and Pilate	John the Baptist and Jesus (proleptic glory)
Pope Leo X	Luther (also imperfect, but a glorious Reformation that was reformed but ever being reformed under Scripture)
Hitler at the Nuremburg rally	Bonhoeffer in prison
The *British Raj*, the Brahmin/Brahman caste	Gandhi and Mother Theresa[5]

Luther was ever passionate and vigilant concerning identifying the false glory of his day in the church and state, illustrated in the left column of Table 6. It is not a reach to suggest that Luther might have concerns about ecclesial pseudo-glory today.

CONTEMPORARY GLORY

I am increasingly alarmed how, even in the church, numerical and fiscal success amidst our pragmatic culture is simplistically identified with God's blessing and approval or the blessings of Providence. Christian leaders have made stunning statements, suggesting that large church or educational enrollment growth and positive financial reports evidence or prove kingdom advance and divine blessing and sanction. In light of Scripture the assumption of approval for such pragmatic outcomes may or may not be the case. In some cases, such claims of blessing may be utilized to baptize the quest

---

5. This is not to say, consistent with religious pluralism, that Gandhi should be classified as an orthodox evangelical Christian. This is to say, and see chapter 3 concerning prevenient grace, that elements of his life and teaching better reflected true glory than abuses of power.

for personal glory. Orthodox, evangelical Christians should be as attentive, if not more attentive, as postmodernists to verbal religious spin in Christian organizations that highlights sometimes superficial measures of success and obscures foundational pathologies. It is all too easy to use spiritual language to cover up or baptize false glory and pathology.

Some "success" may actually be an erroneous theology of glory that celebrates superficial rather than actual kingdom advance and approximation. For example, a fruit-bearing church of twelve that truly experiences Christlikeness at the deepest and most profound and missional level—and therefore is shamed or persecuted—may well be a better representation of the kingdom than a church of twelve thousand that superficially comports with Scripture. Twelve may be preferable to twelve thousand members in some contexts. The small church is not necessarily more kingdom-centric than the large church, and may simply be failing, but it is possible that a small church is more glorious than a mega-church. Numerical growth might be a fruit of the kingdom (Acts 2), but larger numbers of followers do not always evidence divine blessing of biblical fidelity (consider Rom 1; 1 Kgs 19; or the Unification Church growth in the twentieth century and the massive Marriage Blessing services). Consider the biblical definition of the *success* of the heroes of the faith in Hebrews 11, which implies that there are certainly two types of "glory," and the biblical way typically involves cruciform sacrifice. A church may actually decline due to faithfulness to the gospel. Many turned away and quit following Jesus. Jesus, the cornerstone of the church, was crucified as his followers fled and hid, and Peter was likely crucified upside down in an upside down world.

CONTEMPORARY ECCLESIAL GLORY

Ecclesial emphases on growth and seeker sensitivity need to be filtered by the theology of the cross and the theology of glory. The description "seeker-sensitive" may in some cases be nothing more than a euphemism for consumerist and accommodationist outreach. Are churches increasingly growing via this subtle or overt sales pitch—"Come as you are—stay as you are"? Today, it is hard to resist the conclusion that some of the statements made by leaders of religious numerical and fiscal successes, even when qualified with gratitude, border on a self-congratulatory theology of glory. Sometimes God actually may be more at work in the hidden church of the twelve or struggling and persecuted Christian organizations.

Luther, hardly a non-sacramentalist who identified with the emergence of vibrant congregational worship and singing, spared no words on images of an unbiblical theology of glory inside of the church:

> Alas, the word "service of God" has nowadays taken on so strange a meaning and usage that whoever hears it thinks not of these works of God, but rather of the ringing of bells, the wood and stone of churches, the incense pot, the flicker of candles, the mumbling in the churches, the gold, silver, and precious stones in the vestments of the choirboys and celebrants, of chalices and monstrances, of organs and images, processions and church-going, and, most of all, the babbling of lips and the rattling of rosaries. This, alas, is what the service of God means now. Of such service God knows nothing at all, while we know nothing of this. . . . Unless we learn and experience these works of God, there will be no service of God, no Israel, no grace, no mercy, no God, though we kill ourselves with singing and ringing in the churches and drag into them all the goods in all the world. God has not commanded any of these things: undoubtedly, therefore, He takes no pleasure in them.[6]

Those today who only view Luther's rant as a critique of high church worship or sacramentalism and fail to apply this to possible theologies of glory in our midst and in our worship may not fully grasp the meaning of the theology of the cross, the theology of glory, or where such false "glory" manifests itself in the present century.

One possible application of Luther's view today, noted in chapter 1, is that if your church seems more like Starbucks, a movie theatre, or a rock concert than a church, it probably is. Luther continues, "There is today in the churches a great ringing of bells, blowing of trumpets, singing, shouting and intoning, yet I fear precious little worship of God, who wants to be worshipped in spirit and truth, as He says in John 4:24."[7]

Kadai argues that the "real praise," according to Luther, "is God's own work which He performs in the believer; it is joyful suffering."[8] Perhaps Luther and Kadai are engaging in a false dichotomy by suggesting that real praise always involves suffering, or the assumption that all suffering is determined. Regardless, surely the possibility that a pseudo-theology of glory has invaded the church, including the evangelical church, merits consideration.

---

6. Luther, *Sermon*, 350.

7. Luther, *Sermon*, 325.

8. Kadai, "Luther's Theology," 188.

In the contemporary American context, the false unqualified gospel of success, emotional happiness, wealth, and health promises certainly reflect elements of the theology of glory. Christ is the primary exemplar of faith and obedience, yet his success led to the cross. Paul and Peter became fallible paragons of Christ to the Gentiles and Jews (1 Cor 11:1). Paul was likely beheaded and Peter was likely crucified upside-down. James, the brother of Jesus, modeled exemplary faith and obedience, and his journey led to execution by stoning or being cast from a building and beaten. Stephen's amazing faith (Acts 7) and obedience led to death by stoning with Saul's blessing but not before Stephen recounted the consistent and ceaseless persecution of the prophets in Israel. Such persecution of the prophets certainly reflects a false theology of glory by the persecutors and a genuine theology of the cross by the persecuted.

Luther spent much of his life in distress and hiding. The early Methodists faced constant ridicule and abuse. Mother Theresa spent her life of relative poverty amidst disease. Middle Eastern Christians today are regularly marginalized, raped, abused, burned, oppressed, beheaded, and drowned. One wonders what biblical and historical evidence is lacking to demonstrate that great faith—or doing everything right to use cotemporary idiom—often culminates in a cross.

This is not to say that faith, biblical principles, and obedience have no relevance to individual, community, or civilizational flourishing. Scripture is replete with such references (e.g., Ps 33; Prov 3; 14), but these references, as noted in chapter 1, are clearly qualified and contextual. The same exemplary apostle who promised the peace that passes all understanding (Phil 4:7) also rehearsed a detailed enumeration of his persecutions, beatings, sufferings, abasement, and sleepless nights (2 Cor 11). Paul then added, "Apart from such external things, there is the daily pressure on me of concern for all the churches" (2 Cor 11:28).

In an evil context, biblical faith and obedience typically lead to scorn, ridicule, persecution, or worse. One may well end up in the gulag or the concentration camp for living and speaking the truth in love. Perhaps this is increasingly so in the formerly Christian-influenced West, which again points to the urgent contemporary relevance of a biblical understanding of glory, cross, and kingdom.

In a context where biblical principles have some or significant influence, a genuinely biblical evangelist that would be persecuted in other contexts may be well received and have endless opportunities for flourishing, freedom, and kingdom influence. Even John Wesley, as noted in chapter 1, observed how he had once been a scandal and object of ridicule in England but later in life was treated with dignity and respect—almost as a celebrity.

The problem emerges when the understandably desired outcome of human flourishing drives, dominates, or norms theology and produces an idolatrous theology of glory, including self-absorbed ecstatic praise and worship or the gospel of health, happiness, and wealth, or even culturally escapist and disengaged quests for personal peace and prosperity. The evangelical church needs to be disabused of the notion that obedience always, and in each and every individual case, brings this-worldly blessings. The reality is that if you obey you often pay the price, and if you lead in kingdom advance in a fallen cultural context, you often bleed. In my journey it has often been the case that the greater the obedience and Christlikeness, the greater the pain. In an evil context, the truism that no good deed goes unpunished is often painfully evident.

This argument will be advanced in more detail in chapter 9 and subsequent chapters, but a genuine theology of the cross certainly drives kingdom advance and makes possible human and civilizational flourishing. Yet legitimate advance occurs only when the biblical kingdom has absolute priority. If the kingdom is not placed first, above false glory, then we, to borrow from images articulated by Luther, too easily confuse the backside of the devil with God's glory.

8

Integrative and Conjunctive Theological Anchor

SCRIPTURAL PLENUM

THEOLOGIES OF THE CROSS that view the soteriological singularity of the cross as central to orthodox, evangelical, biblical theology, and the analogy of faith, certainly have it right. Yet even with Luther, this singularity, while centered in the cross, is also inclusive of the *plenum* of the Christ-event. The Christ-event includes the incarnation, life, teaching, death, resurrection, the ascension of Christ, and the sending of the Spirit by the triune Christ at Pentecost (John 14:6). A biblical theology of the cross does not exist in a vacuum and certainly not apart from triune theology and triune resurrection. Indeed, the entirety or *plenum* of Christian theology (i.e., creation, anthropology, theology proper, triune theology, hamartiology, soteriology, Christology, pneumatology, ecclesiology, and eschatology) is tethered to the theology of the cross.

CROSS AND RESURRECTION

Many observers have noted that some expressions of Christianity emphasize the cross more than the resurrection or vice versa. This is often viewed as an Eastern versus Western Christianity issue, but perhaps that oversimplifies global variations. In any event, congruence with Scripture requires that the cross and resurrection be integrated and presented as per scriptural emphases. For example, in 1 Cor 15 Paul integrates Christ's death on the cross with the following: soteriology, the official gospel or evangel handed down and received, justification by faith alone, the burial, the bodily resurrection, the resurrection appearances, and personal eschatology. And Paul does all this within less than twenty verses. In Rom 6 Paul integrates the cross with spiritual and likely physical baptism, the identification of the believer with Christ in death, burial and resurrection, and actual sanctification or holiness—all within less than ten verses. The theology of the cross must integrate and be integrated with the whole of Scripture and theology.

KINGDOM

The cross and resurrection are unequivocally the central soteriological historical events or acts of God in history. The Christ-event is the soteriological singularity. Yet for Christ, the didactic framework for his entire ministry and teaching was the initiated and already-but-not-yet kingdom of God. This conclusion is evidenced by the whole structure, content, parabolic material, and tenor of the synoptic gospels: the synoptics' summary of John the Baptist's ministry as "repent for the kingdom of heaven is at hand" (Matt 3:2) and Luke's summary of Paul's Mediterranean ministry as "preaching the kingdom of God" (Acts 28:31). Hence, the incarnation, birth, life, incarnational teaching, death, resurrection, and Pentecost *are* the central Christ-event. The in-breaking kingdom rule of God is the central theological framework for that event.

The scope of this book is not sufficient to make the entire case, but I would affirm that, especially in view of the prior discussion, more clarity, balance, depth, coherence, and theological integration might be brought to theologies of the cross via a unification of the theology of the cross with the theology of the already-not-yet kingdom. Hence, the title of this book suggests a theology of cross *and* kingdom. The theology of the cross can be presented and utilized as a critique of the theology of glory, or, better yet, it can also be a central piece of a robust theology of kingdom advance that discards false glory and seeks to mediate proleptic glory. The cross births real glory already. The way of the cross brings the future into the present and crucifies false glory. The cross is the way to the kingdom. The kingdom issues forth from the cross.

Oscar Cullmann refers to this tension between presentist and futurist views of the kingdom of God as reflective of genuine biblical teaching on the kingdom of God, where there is a more than evident paradox between the present and future kingdom as "already, but not yet."[1]

Cullmann recognizes the already aspect of New Testament teaching on the kingdom. For New Testament believers, the "characteristic thing" of "this present period" is that "the 'world' has already been drawn into the redemptive process," the kingdom has decisively invaded the present world order.[2] Note the contrast here on kingdom teaching with teaching and preaching that tends to locate Satan's defeat, social betterment, and the kingdom itself solely in the future.

In marked contrast to this excessive and despairing futurism, Cullmann synthesizes the future and present aspects of the kingdom. He explains, "The situation in redemptive history of the present, which lies between Christ's resurrection and *Parousia*, is a complex one; it is determined by the noteworthy tension between past and future, between 'already fulfilled' and 'not yet fulfilled.' The world is already ruled by Christ, and yet its present 'form' is passing away (1 Cor 7:31)."[3] Cullmann's theses that the world has been drawn into the redemptive process, that the kingdom has decisively invaded the present, and that Christ's reign already has in some sense been established are strikingly pregnant with relevance to our discussion. His recognition that the consummation is yet future guards against pre-*Parousia* utopianism, utopian triumphalism, colonial triumphalism, anti-colonialist utopianism, anti-Western utopianism, and all false theologies of glory. Some false theologies of glory take the posture of cultural accommodation (e.g., classical liberal theology). Some theologies of false glory claim to be countercultural and in alignment with compassionate social justice while drifting into yet another accommodationist and utopian theology of glory that manipulates, oppresses, or creates debilitating or manipulative dependency on liberators in the name of mercy and compassion. Cullmann's framework is a helpful corrective to the assumptions guiding all such distortions.

Cullmann's outlook, which corresponds very well with biblical data and both positive and negative historical realities, is given its classic illustration by the analogy of the relation between D-Day (June 6, 1944) and V-E

---

1. Cullmann, *Salvation*, 15, 165–85. Cullmann's emphasis on the importance of this tensions has, as is well known in scholarship, been affirmed by countless other scholars and popularizers (e.g., Henry, Ladd, Beasley-Murray, Stassen, Gushee, Hauerwas, and Campolo).

2. Cullmann, *Christ and Time*, 212.

3. Cullmann, *Christ and Time*, 212.

Day (May 8, 1945).[4] He depicts this concept of the kingdom in a vivid and memorable fashion:

> The decisive battle has already been won. But the war continues until a certain, though not as yet definite, Victory Day when the weapons will at last be still. The decisive battle would be Christ's death and resurrection, and Victory Day, his *Parousia*. Between the two lies a short but *important* span of time already indicating a fulfilment and an anticipation of peace, in which, however, the greatest watchfulness is demanded. Yet it is from the decisive battle now won and the Victory Day yet to be achieved that this span of time gets its meaning and its demands. If this interval of time is given greater and greater extension there will, of course, be consequences that must be described in detail, But the *constant* factor is from the outset the presence of this tension. This means that I see the general foundation for the whole New Testament in a salvation-historical orientation.[5]

> Just as the "Victory Day" does in fact present *something new* in contrast to the decisive battle already fought at some point or other of the war, just so the end which is still to come also brings something new. To be sure, this new thing that the "Victory Day" brings is based entirely upon that decisive battle, and would be absolutely impossible without it. Thus we make for the future precisely the same confirmation as we did for the past. It is a unique occurrence; it has its meaning for redemptive history in itself; but on the other hand it is nevertheless founded upon that one unique event at the mid point.[6]

A powerful averment of the biblical doctrine of creation exists in Cullmann's interpretation of the biblical teaching on the kingdom. The Christ-event, including the cross, the incarnation, resurrection, ascension, and Pentecost, is in time and in the creation and pro-creation. Consistent with Cullmann's thesis, in the New Testament, the resurrection, in contrast to Greek speculation, is historical and physical and paves the way for the eschatological

---

4. The objection by some Christians to any military references whatsoever in writing or preaching seems misguided, especially as related to the discussion in this chapter. Scripture is, as well-known, replete with positive military references in both the Old and New Testaments. Nevertheless, even if the objection has legitimacy, the point of Cullmann's analogy is to illuminate the relationship between an initiatory event and its consummation rather than to glory in war.

5. Cullmann, *Salvation in History*, 44.

6. Cullmann, *Christ and Time*, 141.

consummation of and in this world. Resurrection is inherently eschatological and pro-creation.

Cullmann observes that the world is "drawn into the redemptive process" as the result of the Christ-event at the "center" or "midpoint" of the Christian view of time.[7] The cross includes, as Wright notes, how individual Christians get to heaven but also how heaven gets to earth via the revolution of the cross.[8]

The Christ-event is, profoundly so, a theological and eschatological singularity. The *Parousia* is not yet, but the cross and resurrection mean that already "Christ rules as Lord over all things on heaven and on earth!"[9] The "not yet" will occur on earth and in time and will transform the created order. Cullmann denounces the Platonic polarization of time and eternity,[10] a polarization that still persists in theology,[11] and a polarization that may explain some of Luther's extreme (and amillennial) polarities relative to the theology of glory and the theology of the cross. This concept cannot be overemphasized: A proper biblical theology of the cross is fundamentally eschatological.

Narcissistic and imperialistic theologies of glory should not be identified with the potentially non-utopian but ameliorative ecclesial, cultural, and civilizational impact, even glory, of the already dimension of the cross and kingdom. Such ameliorative impact is premised upon and made possible only by and through Christ's cross and all those who follow in his steps on the *via dolorosa*. Theologians need to be very discriminating and as attentive to the positive fallout from the Christ-event as they are to the negative fallout from pretentious theologies of glory. Theologians of the cross also need to be most discriminating and as attentive to the possibilities of authentic cruciform kingdom advance and holiness as they are to the realities of non-cruciform pseudo-righteousness and pseudo-glory.

---

7. Cullmann, *Christ and Time*, 211–12.

8. See chapter 11.

9. Cullmann, *Christ and Time*, 211.

10. Cullmann, *Christ and Time*, 62.

11. Cullmann, *Christ and Time*, 213.

9

Kenotic Cruciform Kingdom Holiness

My children, with whom I am again in labor until Christ is formed in you.

—GAL 4:19

For, I think, God has exhibited us apostles last of all, as men condemned to death;
because we have become a spectacle to the world, both to angels and to men.
We are fools for Christ's sake, but you are prudent in Christ; we are weak,
but you are strong; you are distinguished, but we are without honor.
To this present hour we are both hungry and thirsty, and are poorly clothed,
and are roughly treated, and are homeless; and we toil,
working with our own hands; when we are reviled, we bless;
when we are persecuted, we endure; when we are slandered, we try to conciliate;
we have become as the scum of the world, the dregs of all things, even until now.

—1 COR 4:8–13

We are afflicted in every way, but not crushed, perplexed, but not despairing,
persecuted, but not forsaken; struck down, but not destroyed; always carrying about in the body the dying of Jesus, so that the life of Jesus may also be
manifest in our body. For we who live are constantly being delivered over to

death for Jesus's sake, so that the life of Jesus also may be manifested in our
mortal flesh. So death works in us, but life in you.

—2 Cor 4:8–12

Therefore we do not lose heart, but though our outer man is decaying,
yet our inner man is being renewed day by day. For momentary,
light affliction is producing for us an eternal weight of glory far beyond all
    comparison,
while we look not at the things which are seen, but at the things which
    are not seen;
for the things which are seen are temporal, but the things which are not seen are
    eternal.

—2 Cor 4:16–18

Through the cross and the triune resurrection, ascension, and sending
of the Spirit, the already-not-yet kingdom decisively envelops the present
age. The triune reality and work of the Spirit is the bridge between cross,
resurrection, and kingdom advance. The symbol of the cross hovering over
the world that God so loved ever proclaims that the world is upside-down,
and, in one sense, even after the victory of the Christ-event, the world will
remain on the balance upside-down prior to Christ's return. Only in a world
where its inhabitants share in spiritual vertigo is the Agent of creation and
Redeemer crucified. In such a world his followers continue to be shamed,
oppressed, and crucified: "He was in the world, and the world was made
through Him, and the world did not know Him" (John 21:10).

D-DAY AS FOUNDATIONAL

Jesus did everything right, and he was crucified by the religious establishment, assisted by the political establishment of an oppressor. Yet that very
crucifixion was D-Day in the advance of the kingdom rule of God. The
cross is kingdom-salvific, not merely individually salvific as important as
individual salvation is (e.g., the lost sheep, Luke 15) for the epic kingdom
Christ-event.

The cross is the ultimate expression of authentic kingdom holiness and overflowing love: "Greater love has no one than this, that one lay down his life for his friends" (John 15:13). That holy love lies at the heart of "Father, forgive them; for they do not know what they are doing." (Luke 23:34). Hence, the cruciform sacrificial suffering and holiness of Christ brings salvation and serves as the D-Day of kingdom advance. Similarly, in the Petrine literature believers are called, not in a meritorious fashion, to share in Christ's holy suffering amidst a pagan society:

> For you have been called for this purpose, since Christ also suffered for you, leaving you an example for you to follow in His steps, who committed no sin, nor was any deceit found in His mouth; and while being reviled, He did not revile in return; while suffering, He uttered no threats, but kept entrusting *Himself* to Him who judges righteously; and He Himself bore our sins in His body on the cross, so that we might die to sin and live to righteousness; for by His wounds you were healed. (1 Pet 2:21–24)

SUFFERING AS EXPECTED

In an inverted kingdom, Christ is crucified. In an upside-down kingdom, evil may prosper, the wrong individual is promoted, and the wrong person becomes president or the leader of a corporation, country, church, or denomination. The illegitimate theology of glory often rules. In a cancerous kingdom, the innocent increasingly suffer or are persecuted. In a dark world darkness is rewarded and often for lengthy terms. Hitler came to power in 1933 and ruled for over a decade. Stalin's rule endured even longer. Rome and China's tyranny endured through decades or centuries. Many prayed for deliverance from these genocidal tyrants, yet deliverance and justice were delayed and ultimately true justice and deliverance are only fulfilled in the *eschaton.* Drug dealers and pornographers often accumulate millions, and not all are held accountable in the short-term.

The innocent person is struck down by an intoxicated driver. An eighteen-year-old writhes in pain on a battlefield that leads to the liberation of a concentration camp. Thousands are brutalized, suffer, and die as slave labor in every era of history and in every region of the globe. Those forced into slave labor for the 1945 Messerschmitt jet project that sought to thwart the liberation of Europe and empty the death camps prayed for deliverance but often found death. Sin and disease and cancer rage unchecked at times. Some prayers for deliverance simply are not granted in this life. Suffering and ultimate deliverance are to be expected. Indeed, according to the whole of Scripture, it is often an upside-down religious environment that crucifies those who are truly righteous and members of the genuine Abrahamic line of promise. Abraham's real children are often the persecuted and crucified. The religiously and politically powerful are often of their father, "the devil" (John 8:44).

The Way (Acts 22:4), or the Christian movement, launched with eyes wide open in the shadow of the cross. Their Christ had been crucified. The followers of the Way, as per Scripture and early church history, almost joyfully stepped into *via dolorosa.*

KINGDOM ADVANCE AS EXPECTED

A proper biblical framework cannot fully respond to the existential and emotional realities of suffering, especially in a pastoral sense, but the already/not yet kingdom does suggest that suffering is to be expected in this present age. Injustice should be countered, and at times can be meliorated, but it is also to be expected until the fullness of the new creation. Slavery and apartheid were abolished in England and Africa, and these victories were real and to be applauded. Nevertheless, human trafficking and slavery exist in many parts of the globe to this very day.

Utopianism is animating and energizing for a season; harnessing utopian eschatological visions has repeatedly harnessed world-changing passion. Eschatology is the fuel of change. Yet utopianism is ultimately disillusioning, as reality and the dream usually are quite distant. Hopeful future-visions must be framed in dialog with the cross.

Fatalism and escapism are self-fulfilling and equally disillusioning for this present age and life. Endless unfulfilled and overly pessimistic projections, including predictions of the end, ultimately lead some to set aside the essential eschatological impulse for a better future now. For others, the fatalistic narrative is entrenched, regardless of the historical evidence, and becomes a self-fulfilling prophecy. Such self-fulfilling prophecies can send brothers and sisters in Christ to the cross because civilization is allowed to putrefy. Imagine if Wesley's followers had given up on "The General Spread of the Gospel" and abandoned abolitionism. Eschatology fuels action or inaction. Hence, the proper framing of eschatology as absolutely essential to the mission of the church is the eschatological fuel that endures for the duration.

Via the already kingdom, the darkness is sometimes partially and proleptically rolled back. The lame walk, the dumb speak, the slaves are liberated, and the alcoholic is holistically saved. Yet that kingdom advance is typically via those living out the theology of the cross, not the presumptuous theology of glory.

HISTORY AS "CRUCIPLASTIC"

History is fluid and kingdom advance is "cruciplastic." History is fluid and somewhat indeterminate, and the church partially writes the future pages of history, often *via dolorosa*. Sacrificial and cruciform holiness, in the shadow of the cross and the dawning of the *Parousia* and in a broken and largely upside-down world, is the seed of a better future already for civilizations, communities, churches, families, and individuals.

God is sovereignly good (see chapter 3) and providentially sustains and guides all things within the context of a humanity capable of receiving or resisting grace, and even that very receptivity is only possible because of a grace that awakens the hardened heart. Within that theological framework, it can be said that history and genuine kingdom advance is cruciplastic. Simply put, ecclesial and civilizational progress is possible, but typically no real moral or spiritual progress is possible without traversing the way of the cross. Why? The answer is, very simply, theological anthropology. Fallen human nature and sinful culture oppose the kingdom of God. Hence, we must maintain an already-not-yet cross and kingdom symbiosis to comprehend and engage in kingdom work rightly. The cross, even the cross that believers take up and bear, is typically the primary means for advancing the kingdom. Sacrifice precedes kingdom advance.

CRUCIFORM SUFFERING AS SCRIPTURAL

The entire narrative of Scripture, from the story of Abel to the heavenly martyrs of Revelation, portrays an upside-down world where the righteous suffer for being righteous. At the center of this narrative is the cross. Abel did what was right and was murdered. Righteous Joseph was thrown into a pit and later falsely accused and then thrown in prison. True prophets were opposed and often martyred. Unrighteous kings and religious leaders abused power and people. John the Baptist was beheaded. The apostles were executed or exiled. Peter was likely crucified upside-down in an upside-down world. Paul was beheaded. The righteous in Revelation, those refusing to pledge allegiance to darkness, are executed. Hebrews 11 views the heroes of faith as righteous "strangers and exiles" who "died in faith, without receiving the promises" while incarnating a proleptic vision (Heb 11:13) that propelled them forward, through persecution, to the not yet city of God. This proleptic example became the norm for the faithful in subsequent centuries and throughout history who partially turned an upside-down world right side up. And at the center of this great reversal is the cross of Christ.

Hence, the whole of Scripture irrefutably views cruciform suffering as central to authentic faith and kingdom advance. Nevertheless, the Pauline literature is especially helpful in reinforcing, clarifying, and applying this core biblical imperative. In 2 Cor 11–12, Paul recapitulates his kingdom journey:

> Are they servants of Christ?—I speak as if insane—I more so; in far more labors, in far more imprisonments, beaten times without number, often in danger of death. Five times I received from the Jews thirty-nine lashes. Three times I was beaten with rods, once I was stoned, three times I was shipwrecked, a night and a day I have spent in the deep. I have been on frequent journeys, in dangers from rivers, dangers from robbers, dangers from my countrymen, dangers from the Gentiles, dangers in the city, dangers in the wilderness, dangers on the sea, dangers among false brethren; I have been in labor and hardship, through many sleepless nights, in hunger and thirst, often without food, in cold and exposure. Apart from such external things, there is the daily pressure on me of concern for all the churches. Who is weak without my being weak? Who is led into sin without my intense concern? If I have to boast, I will boast of what pertains to my weakness. The God and Father of the Lord Jesus, He who is blessed forever, knows that I am not lying. (2 Cor 11:23–31)

Cruciform kingdom advance and proleptic living converge in Paul's theology of cross and glory. Note that Paul was tempted to some form of glory or self-exaltation:

> Because of the surpassing greatness of the revelations, for this reason, to keep me from exalting myself, there was given me a thorn in the flesh, a messenger of Satan to torment me—to keep me from exalting myself! . . . And He has said to me, "My grace is sufficient for you, for power is perfected in weakness." Most gladly, therefore, I will rather boast about my weaknesses, so that the power of Christ may dwell in me. Therefore I am well content with weaknesses, with insults, with distresses, with persecutions, with difficulties, for Christ's sake; for when I am weak, then I am strong. . . . I will most gladly spend and be expended for your souls. If I love you more, am I to be loved less? (2 Cor 12:7, 9–10, 15)

Weakness is not an afterthought or an accident in the Christian life: "For indeed He was crucified because of weakness, yet He lives because of the power of God. For we also are weak in Him, yet we will live with Him because of the power of God directed toward you" (2 Cor 13:4). Paul continues: "Now I rejoice in my sufferings for your sake, and in my flesh I do my share on behalf of His body, which is the church, in filling up what is lacking in Christ's afflictions" (Col 1:24).

Cruciform suffering advances the kingdom and creates a context for Christlike formation, personal holiness, and social holiness, not that these two types of holiness can be severed. Paul summarizes the thrust of his ministry as follows: "My children, with whom I am again in labor until Christ is formed in you" (Gal 4:19). And Paul models cruciform Christlikeness and affirms that there simply is no life without death:

> For, I think, God has exhibited us apostles last of all, as men condemned to death; because we have become a spectacle to the world, both to angels and to men. We are fools for Christ's sake, but you are prudent in Christ; we are weak, but you are strong; you are distinguished, but we are without honor. To this present hour we are both hungry and thirsty, and are poorly clothed, and are roughly treated, and are homeless; and we toil, working with our own hands; when we are reviled, we bless; when we are persecuted, we endure; when we are slandered, we try to conciliate; we have become as the scum of the world, the dregs of all things, even until now. (1 Cor 4:8–13)

> We are afflicted in every way, but not crushed, perplexed, but not despairing, persecuted, but not forsaken; struck down, but not destroyed; always carrying about in the body the dying of Jesus, so that the life of Jesus may also be manifest in our body. For we who live are constantly being delivered over to death for Jesus's sake, so that the life of Jesus also may be manifested in our mortal flesh. So death works in us, but life in you. (2 Cor 4:8–12)

Eschatology is the fuel and vision of the future that drives and frames cruciform kingdom advance and holiness: "Therefore we do not lose heart, but though our outer man is decaying, yet our inner man is being renewed day by day. For momentary, light affliction is producing for us an eternal weight of glory far beyond all comparison, while we look not at the things which are seen, but at the things which are not seen; for the things which are seen are temporal, but the things which are not seen are eternal" (2 Cor 4:16–18).

In Colossians Paul directly unites his understanding of cruciform mission with the desired holiness or Christlikeness outcome of that mission: "He has now reconciled you in His fleshly body through death, in order to present you before Him holy and blameless and beyond reproach—if indeed you continue in the faith firmly established and steadfast, and not moved away from the hope of the gospel that you have heard, which was proclaimed in all creation under heaven, and of which I, Paul, was made a minister" (Col 1:22–23). Paul's kingdom mission and theology of the cross naturally entails the following: "It is he whom we proclaim, warning everyone and teaching everyone in all wisdom, so that we may present everyone mature in Christ. For this I toil and struggle with all the energy that he powerfully inspires within me" (Col 1:28–29, NRSV).

For Paul, the theology of the cross requires sacrifice or cross-bearing (Matt 16:24) by the followers of the cross and is missionally targeted toward what Wesley referred to as the "great salvation," meaning far more than the merely getting to heaven,[1] "so that you may become blameless and pure, 'children of God without fault in a warped and crooked generation.' Then you will shine among them like stars in the sky" (Phil 2:15). Luther naturally devoted much of his life to forever defeating works righteousness, but the cross is also integral to proclaiming and actualizing a gospel of both alien and actual righteousness. As noted in chapter 4, this expanded understanding of the *theologia crucis* accompanied and perhaps propelled the pietist and Weselyan revivals that emphasized saving grace, sanctifying grace, and kingdom advance.

Because we are fallen, we surprisingly find the kenotic Alpha and Omega in the cross, but that cross is the D-Day propelling kingdom progress toward V-Day and already delivering the possibilities of grace such that believers may be complete and blameless in Christ in this life. And believers are honored to suffer with Christ in proclaiming and sharing this great salvation. Hence, Paul in Philippians affirms that he is in prison "for the greater progress of the gospel" (Phil 1:12) and that because of his imprisonment "the cause of Christ has become well known" (Phil 1:13). His cruciform kingdom suffering has motivated others toward cruciform kingdom service. These servants of Christ, operating "out of love" (Phil 1:16), and now "trusting in the Lord for [because of] my imprisonment, have far more courage to speak the word of God without fear" (Phil 1:14). Paul concludes, "Christ will even now, as always, be exalted in my body, whether by life or by death" (Phil 1:20). Paul then encourages the Philippians to continue in the way of cruciform kingdom holiness: "For to you it has been granted for Christ's

---

1. Wesley, "Salvation," 129.

sake, not only to believe in Him, but also to suffer for His sake, experiencing the same conflict which you saw in me, and now hear to be in me" (Phil 1:29–30).

Paul is also explicit that divine deliverance from suffering and martyrdom is already-not-yet. In other words, God does sometimes deliver from the snare of the fowler and the deadly pestilence (Ps 91:3) in this present age (already), but sometimes deliverance is only in the next age or final *eschaton*. For Paul, on the most important level it really does not matter: "But the Lord stood with me and strengthened me, so that through me the proclamation might be fully accomplished, and that all the Gentiles might hear; and I was rescued out of the lion's mouth. The Lord will rescue me from every evil deed, and will bring me safely to His heavenly kingdom; to Him be the glory forever and ever. Amen" (2 Tim 4:17–18).

KINGDOM ADVANCE AS KENOTIC CRUCIFORM HOLINESS

Hence, this kenotic (Phil 2), or self-emptying, cruciform kingdom holiness theology views the sacrificial offering of Christ as the primary reason for the incarnation and self-emptying—to die on a cross and actualize the cosmic D-Day which lies in the shadow and dawning of Victory Day. The cross is also the clearest manifestation of Christ's divinity and overflowing love, which should have incalculable implications for ecclesiology, mission, and formation in the life of the cruciform believer. Paul clearly views his own suffering as an expression and a model (to believers) of such cruciform kingdom holy advance: "But even if I am being poured out as a drink offering upon the sacrifice and service of your faith, I rejoice and share my joy with you all" (Phil 2:17).

The implication of the theology of the cross for what is loosely referred to as spiritual formation, Christian formation, or Christian holiness is significant. The redeployment of Cullmann's analogy, D-Day—especially the cross and the way of the cross—may better frame, reflect, and actualize authentic, incarnational Christlikeness and kingdom advance than popular means and images of Christian piety. In view of this incarnational theology of the cross much of what we count as spirituality, piety, spiritual growth, and Christlikeness seems rather Docetic or at least disengaged from the crucible of reality where faith is actually formed, nurtured, and displayed.

Attempts to grow in Christ and encounter God, often by retreats, meditation, sacramental experiences, ecstatic worship, and spiritual growth programs certainly can have value but should not ignore the kenotic and cruciform theology of the cross. By way of illustration, the analogies for authentic Christian or spiritual formation processes and fruit should sometimes look more like the journey of Justin Martyr, the Vietnamese and Chinese martyrs, Felipe Sonsong, Jim Elliot, the Nag Hammadi martyrs, the Coptic martyrs, the sacrifices of the young heroes on the beaches of Normandy, the incarnational heroic actions of Schindler or the ten Booms, or the carrying of and caring for the diseased by Mother Theresa than many of our contemporary manifestations of so-called Christian or New Age spirituality.

While it is important not to confuse a theology of suffering and pain with a theology of the cross,[2] my spouse and I, as noted earlier in this work, have often been surprised in recent years with how God seems unexpectedly and palpably present during the suffering of loved ones in the halls and rooms of hospitals and care facilities. The hospital experience, as noted in chapter 1, while including joys such as new birth and saving lives, also includes endless beeping monitors, constant interruptions, hopeless pain, the sense of abandonment, sleep deprivation, loss of critical information between shifts, endless cries for help echoing down the hallways, struggled breathing, costly medical mistakes, and many gasps and tears. Perhaps the hospital, at times, is a more realistic metaphor for kingdom living than contemporary alternatives such as the emotional feel of a rock concert or the adrenaline high of a retreat. Hospital suffering is not necessarily Christian persecution or suffering for the kingdom per se. Yet the theology of cross and kingdom frames, makes sense of, and provides a framework for utilizing all such experiences for kingdom advance. The cross and kingdom frames why we experience so much suffering in a fallen world prior to Christ's return, and why not all are delivered just yet. And the cross and kingdom points the way through suffering to the certain and better future both already and not yet.

I reluctantly must confess that God has often and unexpectedly shown up in amazing ways in experiences of weakness and suffering that challenge prevalent assumptions of success. As one who has reveled in and enjoyed some measure of accomplishment in music, sports, interpersonal relationships, and academics and typically enjoyed the very good health of self and family members, this new theological hermeneutic is a significant eye-opener. Genuine success by grace in things such as sports or music, if ethically achieved, is not to be condemned. Yet the theology of the cross underscores that an inverted world often rewards false success and punishes

---

2. Theodicy, the purpose of suffering, God's relationship to and involvement in suffering. See the following works for an introduction: Lewis, *Problem*; Kreeft, *Making Sense*; Rice, *Suffering*; numerous works by Nouwen.

authentic kingdom success. The righteous suffer. This new vantage point also creates more empathy for those who seem to be struggling just to get through the day. I remember speaking in Texas once about the many facets of holistic and balanced Christian development (physical, social, intellectual, and spiritual). My American audience was most appreciative. A friend from Mexico, however, while affirming the main points, sent me a note pointing out that "my people are just trying to figure out how to survive each day."

This theology and eschatology of the cross and kingdom has sparked much more compassion for: those who are seemingly oppressed by endless medical challenges; those who truly try hard at work, school, or at the office but so often fail; those single parents who wrestle day and night with seemingly overwhelming challenges and limited resources; those who are plagued by chemical imbalances and emotional distress; and those who truly sacrifice all to follow Christ in hostile environments. The theology of cross and kingdom allows us to affirm appropriate success of some while also acknowledging the heartbreaking challenges of others in our midst.

As noted, the suggestion that God either is in weakness or in strength is a false dichotomy—he is in both when properly defined, but if we only know him in strength and success we may be in need of Luther's chastisements concerning the theology of glory. And if we only know God in success, health, wealth, and strength, we may not know God at all if Luther is fairly handling the Word of God. I did not expect to find more real and enduring spiritual growth in a hospital or assisted living facility than a well-planned spiritual retreat or conference, but that has often been my experience. The personal experience of suffering and pain by believers, or the journey through the pain and suffering of loved ones, is not necessarily, or strictly speaking, suffering for kingdom advance. And these life crises should be viewed less as divinely determined and more as divinely and providentially redeemed. Such experiences, however, seem to remove the veil of denial and superficial spirituality. When a loved one is in seemingly endless agony with no relief, or forever leaving us and the present earthly realm, pseudo-faith, pseudo-spirituality, and pseudo-piety evaporate. Suffering and pain move us from consumerist spirituality toward the profound reality of the cross. Suffering seems to jar or shock us into the realm of actuality, and ultimately only makes sense within the context of a theology of cross and kingdom. Pain is the reality check plumb line of genuine piety. Growth emanating from such *kairos* events also tends to play out over months or years, as opposed to a weekend retreat, and deeply tests and touches our core character. Retreats and powerful worship experiences, if biblically framed, may prepare us for these shadowy nights of struggle, but only the crucible of walking through the dark passageway itself delivers us from the bondage of denial. And, in contrast to our emoticon culture, let us be clear: Authentic and lasting growth does not always feel good.

As an aside, while the status of so-called near death experiences (NDEs) is still debated,[3] these, often hospital-based, experiences typically share in life-changing perceptions of encounters with God in the midst of unparalleled suffering. NDEs also commonly document radical lifestyle changes that seem greatly to exceed the response to other human experiences. Whatever one thinks about NDEs (perceived or real), the reality of suffering and death seemingly can foster reality, passion, and commitment in one's spiritual journey.

Somewhat *contra* Luther's emphasis on the contrast between the cross and reason, what often emerges out of the shadows and confusion of the hospital, or the concentration camp for that matter, is the confident and crystal clear assurance (by grace) that the triune God in Christ makes perfect sense. While at bedside holding the hand of a loved one slipping into eternity, the legion rational objections to the triune Christ are seemingly crucified by the wisdom and theology of the cross. The only proper response I could muster to such painful yet hopeful reality was "Wow!"

When my 108-year-old grandmother was in her last days, my wife and I were desperately trying to get from Nashville through a snowstorm to be at her side. She was my buddy in many ways, as well as the last real spiritual matriarch for our family. We simply could not make it, but the one relative who was present for her passing and homecoming reported being absolutely overwhelmed by the presence of the Holy One. If I got this right, this relative affirmed that this deathbed experience was one of the most significant experiences of God's presence ever encountered.

It is important to reaffirm that suffering is not always directly connected to kingdom advance. The line is clear and straight relative to persecution of the Gospel. Yet one does not have to be a theological determinist to recognize providentially that God is willing to "pitch His tent" (John 1:14) in the midst of every moment of pain and shame and journey with his children through the valley of death (Ps 23:4). When entrusted via a profound faith to the faithful hands of the Creator, not one tear or moment of pain and suffering will ever be wasted by the loving hands of the Potter who forms us and graciously allows every second to matter for all eternity. Suffering is often the springboard to authentic kingdom advance. Suffering is a window to cruciform, proleptic kingdom advance. *The blood of the martyrs and the*

---

3. See Habermas, *Beyond Death*; Marsh, *Out-of-Body*.

suffering of the faithful often sow the seeds of spiritual, individual, community, and civilizational freedom and flourishing.

This already-not-yet conceptualization of kenotic suffering, blessing, and holiness is an essential theological framework for biblical hermeneutics. Proper biblical interpretation certainly includes immersion into the hermeneutical circle of specific biblical texts and passages and the original languages and context. Yet equally if not more important, however, is the theological framework that both emerges from the text and explains the text.

Following godly principles (Proverbs) certainly can bring blessings to nations and individuals in the already, especially *if* the civilizational and cultural context is receptive and nurturing. Godly living can also bring martyrdom in a dark or demonic context. Doing everything right may lead to human flourishing and kingdom approximations, or it may very well land one in a concentration camp or hanging from a cross or tree. Yet eschatological or not-yet blessing (Matt 5) is more than an assured and proleptic already—it is the true future.

The false theology of glory is not to be confused with cruciform kingdom approximation and genuine blessings in this life. As noted in this chapter, the abolition of slavery was a Christian-influenced approximative advance. All genuine *already* blessings are ultimately grounded in the certainty of the not yet, not the fluidity of a fallen world.

It is also critical to view Paul's sacrificial kingdom mission as more than plucking souls from the fire. As noted, Paul summarized the broader scope of this mission with utter and urgent clarity: "My children, with whom I am again in labor until Christ is formed in you" (Gal 4:19). Cruciform kingdom mission seeks to bring people to Christ and in conformity with Christ's character. This dynamic and activist conformity is then the key to civilizational impact.

We suffer because our world is fallen; we sacrificially suffer for others; we suffer to advance the kingdom; we suffer because sacrifice is an expression of kingdom holiness and love; and, as Luther noted, suffering can bring us increasingly into actual holy conformity with Christ and directly engaged in cruciform kingdom advance. Kenotic, cruciform kingdom suffering is not a Scriptural afterthought: "My God, my God, why have you forsaken me? Far from my deliverance are the words of my groaning" (Ps 22:1).

Kenotic, cruciform kingdom suffering,[4] according to Scripture,[5] is the proper framing of a robust biblical theology of the cross and kingdom that at least includes these key points and emphases:

- Christ's kenotic suffering and sacrifice for the sins and salvation of the world and the initiation of the kingdom;

- Christ's kenotic incarnation, life, teaching, crucifixion, suffering, burial, resurrection, ascension, and Pentecost as the theological D-Day that grounds cruciform personal and social holiness;

- Kenotic cruciform suffering by believers as Christocentric and kingdom-centric;

- Cruciform suffering by believers for the testing and establishing of genuine faith;

- Kenotic cruciform suffering by believers to bring the gospel of salvation to the lost;

- Kenotic cruciform suffering by believers to model and bring the great salvation or actual holiness to all;

- Suffering as discipline for and purification of believers (Heb 12); and,

- Cruciform suffering as a basis for eschatological reward (Matt 5:12)—"Rejoice and be glad, for your reward in heaven is great; for in the same way they persecuted the prophets who were before you."

Authentic kingdom advance in an upside-down world is through the way of the cross and via those who are increasingly "being transformed [often via the way of the cross] into the same image from glory to glory, just as from the Lord, the Spirit" (2 Cor 3:18). This theology of the cross will only escalate in relevance as Judeo-Christian civilizational influence wanes. It is uncertain to what degree the famous story of the monk Telemachus is historically accurate, but his story, where he sacrificially challenged and helped to end the brutal gladiatorial games in ancient Rome, may increasingly become our story. To sum,

- No cross, no kingdom;

- No cross, no kingdom approximation;

- No cross, false glory;

---

4. As mentioned a number of times previously, such suffering is non-meritorious for believers relative to their justification before God, though certainly reflective of their relationship to God and the orientation of their heart.

5. Also see the appendix.

- Cross before genuine kingdom;

- False kingdom, false glory;

- Cross and kingdom before genuine glory;

- Transformed from glory to glory *via dolorosa*; and,

- Cross and kingdom advance the glorious new creation.

CRUCIFORM KINGDOM HOLINESS AS "CRUCIPRAXY" AND "CRUCIPATHY"

This dedicated march to already/not yet glory, then, issues forth in "crucipraxy," which flows from an overflowing heart of love shaped by "crucipathy." We identify with the kingdom advance of D-Day, and the suffering and forsakenness of D-Day. We take up our cross daily. The overflowing love of D-Day and "Father forgive them" (Luke 23:34), spoken from the vantage point of the cross, necessitates pathos for Christ's mission and passion. Crucipathy sparks pathos for all suffering and for all who are suffering. From incarnationally sharing the dark nights of hospital rooms or hospice to actual martyrdom for the kingdom, we are the people of the cross that defines a fallen world. Crucipraxy issues forth from crucipathy for all who are increasingly "being transformed into the same image from glory to glory, just as from the Lord, the Spirit" (2 Cor 3:18).

EXCURSUS: CORPORATE, PROLEPTIC, KENOTIC, CRUCIFORM, AND CRUCIPLASTIC ASPECTS OF THEODICY

While theodicy or the problem of evil is not the focus of this work, the prior chapters have touched on this question, and it is unavoidable when discussing a theology of the cross. Endless books on theodicy are available and have attempted to tackle this challenging question. This present work will certainly not suggest any resolution in a few short paragraphs. Some observations at this juncture, however, are in order.

If this present work is right, countless believers have wrestled with why Scripture (especially the Psalms) seems to promise deliverance and blessing and healing, yet experience suggests almost infinite unanswered prayers and unabated anguish. As noted, when believers read the eschatological promises of the Bible through individualistic and non-eschatological lenses, confusion and disappointment necessarily follows. Such promises and blessings need to be framed within the larger context of a redemptive history that spans millennia and culminates in the new creation. Blessings are the hors d'oeuvres of the future but not the main banquet feast. Over the course of the millennia, some invited to the banquet will experience famine, though the day will come when the heavenly manna or the multiplying loaves of bread will be eternal rather than temporal. Godly principles and behavior do bring blessings, properly defined, in this life, given certain spiritual and cultural contexts. Godly principles and practices also may bring the cross. Nations founded on or pursuing the pillars of the true future may, emphasize may, experience partial blessings of the future. Such nations also may be crushed by evil powers because of following those same principles. Context is king.

Scripture is clear: Not all are healed and not all are delivered in this life, even the heroes of the faith. Hebrews 11 is explicit that the biblical assurances and favor are not all received in this life. Some of the greatest blessings are more spiritual in nature and often emerge in the crucible of the already. The promises of blessing, protection, and healing in this pre-*Parousia* age are framed in a corporate context and are contextual and proleptic. In a context where godliness is honored, individual blessings often abound to the faithful (e.g., within a godly family). In an anti-Christian context, the faithful may well be persecuted or martyred (e.g., within a family or culture militantly opposed to Christianity). Godly principles certainly have value in the pre-*Parousia* era to communities and nations. Strong families are good for civilizations relative to crime, productivity, or even illicit drug usage, but cultures and civilizations are so complex that it is rather challenging to affirm simplistically that nation A will be blessed if such and such a policy or action is implemented.

Blessings, healings, and protection are all partial and anticipatory in nature and rooted in the initiated kingdom rule of God. Some are healed and delivered in anticipation of the new creation, but many, and often most, are not. To blame the lack of healing or blessing on a lack of faith is bad eschatology; it completely misunderstands and confuses biblical eschatology. Such blame is even worse pastoral psychology. I remember talking with a lovely friend once who was enamored with the faith and healing movement. She categorically stated that if she had faith that all sickness, throughout her entire life, could be healed. My immediate question, of course, was whether she would ever physically die. This friend naturally responded that she would live forever. I pressed on this seeming equivocation by asking, "Without first dying?" She of course responded that she would be raptured and never die. This was the 1980s and Hal Lindsey was still most influential with his prediction that within 40 years of 1948 Christ would return. Perreti was waiting in the wings to be the next end-time best seller. With full awareness of my folly, I pressed on: "What if Christ does not return in your lifetime. Will you die?" Once again, sensing the sharp horns of a dilemma, this friend paused, looked perplexed, and then adamantly said, "No!"

This story reflects the cognitive dissonance of those who not only misunderstand faith but also have entirely gone off the royal pathway relative to eschatology. In contrast, already and not yet eschatology, or proleptic eschatology, can absorb the data of seemingly endless unanswered prayers. Our prayers should never be that God must heal or bless because of some kind of faith contract to which he agreed relative to mountain relocation projects, which was of course intended as a hyperbolic metaphor (Matt 21:21). Our prayers should be, "Lord deliver us for the sake of your kingdom and your glory," with a full understanding that the same God who delivered Paul at one point in ministry also allowed Paul to perish at another point in kingdom advance.

Hence, God works through suffering and evil via a cruciform holiness that radiates for time and eternity. And this same cruciform holiness, as noted previously, impacts and influences a cruciplastic, moldable, malleable, or ameliorable world that God so loved. Within this context eschatology is affirmed as the best answer or framework for responding to the challenge of theodicy.

10

Cruciform Liberation
and Kingdom Approximation

SALER

SALER, ATTEMPTING TO BE faithful to Luther and influenced by Moltmann and others, properly articulated how a rejection of a theology of glory and an adoption of a theology of the cross was essential for authentic kingdom increase.[1] This book emphasizes that such advance must be defined as non-utopian and framed within the context of Cullmann's already-not-yet kingdom. In addition, for Saler, such kingdom advance inherently leads to identification with oppression, weakness, suffering, the marginalized, and the finding of the only true God (often) amidst the scandalous and deplorable realms of human existence. For Saler, the theology of the cross is, by nature, liberationist.

CULLMANN AND MOLTMANN

Relative to Saler's and Moltmann's visions, Cullmann's conceptualization of the kingdom guards both against misguided utopian liberation and the status quo.[2] Moltmann argues that, for some, "in adopting this so-called realism dictated by the facts [of reality] we fall victim to the worst of all

1. See chapters 2 and 9.
2. See chapter 9.

utopias—the utopia of the *status quo,* as R. Musil has called this kind of realism."[3] Moltmann illustrates this tension between realism and hope: "It is difficult to wage a revolution without the Bible (Ernst Bloch). It is even more difficult not to bring about a revolution with the Bible."[4] Note that Wright's recent book on the theology of the cross calls for a revolution, for the cross is the day that the new creation revolution began.[5]

Affirmation of the theology of the cross and rejection of the theology of glory is especially relevant to Moltmann's fundamental concern: "Christian theology exists for the purpose not of following after the *Zeitgeist* and bearing its train, but for carrying before it the torch of hope and enkindling the fire of criticism in lazy humanity."[6] The shadow of the cross ever hovers hauntingly and hopefully over an inverted human existence.

Unfortunately, Moltmann's concept of liberation is ultimately framed within a flawed and shrewd utopianism.[7] Cullmann provides an eschatological foundation that properly counterbalances all forms of utopianism and fatalism. This foundation and the issues surrounding utopianism and fatalism will be explored below, but for now it is critical to apply Cullmann's central insight to the theology of the cross, the theology of glory, and the theology of approximation.

CROSS, GLORY, APPROXIMATION

Integrating the theology of the cross with the theology of the already-not-yet-kingdom, including resurrection theology, requires judicious and attentive cultural hermeneutics relative to what constitutes a theology of glory today. Kingdom approximation in the present age—already—should not be confused with a negative understanding of the theology of glory (e.g., Luther's view). This distinction is absolutely critical for this discussion. The Quakers and Methodists contributed to the abolition of slavery via kingdom approximation, often *via dolorosa* (e.g., the decades of ridicule of Wilberforce, a convert to Methodism). The celebration of the emancipation of the slaves via kingdom approximation should not have been viewed as an arrogant theology of glory simply because of influencing law and culture and utilizing the power of law. This civilizational gain should instead be received as an approximative gift of grace. Wesley's abolitionism and Lincoln's

3. Moltmann, *Theology of Hope*, 23.
4. Moltmann, *Theology of Hope*, 6.
5. See chapters 1 and 11.
6. Moltmann, *Experiment Hope*, 46.
7. See chapter 12 for a critique of Moltmann's shrewd utopianism.

abolitionism reflect the unification of a biblical theology of glory *and* a biblical theology of the cross. The oppressed slaves, who identified the hanging tree with the cross, were liberated in a proleptic fashion, and this was truly glorious! In the abolitionist journey, a true theology of the cross and a true theology of glory coincide.

CONTEMPORARY SOCIAL JUSTICE AND GLORY

Unfortunately, as noted in chapter 2, Saler's grand liberationist vision based on the theology of the cross appears to engage in the redundant non sequitur of so many passionate advocates of social justice today, such as the Sojourners movement and magazine. Sojourners calls for faith in action for social justice.[8] Saler and Sojourners seem to confuse the commitment to and passion for justice and liberation that should be shared by all authentic kingdom believers with one of many triumphalist, elitist political ideologies. Yes, such movements claim to be anti-triumphalist and cruciform, when in fact they often resemble a state theology of glory and power-seeking political ideology.

For example, Saler, as noted in chapter 2, affirms that the theology of the cross is incongruent with the "optics of the marketplace."[9] The degree to which the marketplace does or does not approximate the kingdom or advance human flourishing is a fair debate, but what is notably absent from Saler's critique is similar cross-centric queries concerning the optics of Leviathan-like statist claims to advance compassion and justice. The optics of greed in the marketplace are, at times, undeniable, but so are the evil and greedy optics and crushing, or even sometimes genocidal, realities of legion movements claiming to be for justice, for the people, for the have-nots, for the oppressed, or for the working class or proletariat.

Social justice movements are quite capable of incarnating the triumphalistic and manipulative theology of glory and, without even blushing, claiming to speak for God on even the minutia of social and political strategy, policy, and tactics. Social justice is not necessarily socialism, and liberation is not necessarily liberation theology. What if the assumption today that the government is the primary if not sole distributor of justice and relief runs counter to Scripture, biblical ecclesiology, and common sense? Debate and discussion, not an elist and condescending moral decree, are needed. Similarly, assumptions that the best guarantor of justice, prosperity, and human flourishing is decentralized government and free enterprise must be

8. Sojourners, "Who We Are."
9. Saler, *Theologia Crucis*, 82.

debated and not assumed. My journey has seen American evangelical leadership move from one definition of social justice and appropriate governmental entitlements to another, identifying one model with compassionate justice while scandalizing other models. Social justice methods and models should be debated and not assumed.

In any event, Luther rightly challenged what Saler referred to as the politico-theological edifice of power[10] that represented the oppressive theology of glory that crushed those living out the theology of the cross. Saler's application of Luther is helpful concerning such complex edifices. However, at least in the West, a rather unstable formula has emerged relative to power and justice. Those most often proclaiming themselves as the champions and arbiters of social justice and the needs of the oppressed—the media; entertainment; and the legal, political, and educational complex, or edifice—are also those who often possess the most crushing and marginalizing power. And because of this edifice or complex, accountability is often minimal. Is it really necessary to review the fact that powerful twentieth-century movements such as Stalinism claimed that their actions were in the name of social justice and for the people or the working class? Is it really necessary to remind Christians enamored with social justice that this edifice is increasingly claiming, in the name of social justice, that core Christian ethical convictions and conduct are unjust and discriminatory and, perhaps, deserving of social or criminal sanction? Is it really that difficult for American social justice advocates to look across the pond (the Atlantic) and learn from endless governmental acts of oppression against biblical faith in the name of progress, inclusion, toleration, and justice? Virtually every social movement claims that their cause is just, or for the people, or for the oppressed, or for the victimized, or for the humiliated—even the Third Reich made such claims.

The contemporary media, entertainment, legal, political, and educational edifice in the West that self-proclaims its own justice and righteousness and solidarity with the weak may actually be a prime candidate as a contemporary expression for what Luther referred to as the corrupted theology of glory—all the while virtue signaling and masquerading under the cover of identifying with the marginalized and the way of the cross. The social justice claim today has almost become meaningless. Everyone claims this moniker, from the conservative American Center for Law and Justice to the liberal Sojourners organization. Social justice has become a shallow shibboleth used to silence meaningful and rigorous dialog concerning the true nature of social justice.

10. See chapter 2.

Because some of these powerful social justice groups frequently attempt to vaporize any remaining echo of Judeo-Christian influence and Christian religious freedom, while claiming to identify with the weak and marginalized, a sensible, not frantic or militant, discussion of "privilege" is warranted. What is notably absent from such discussions in the Western context is the reality of the politically liberal privileged sitting atop many of the power structures of society. Liberal privilege, at least in the Western context, dominates public education, law, media, and entertainment.[11] Liberal privilege is sometimes so oppressive as to deny the very free speech often associated with classical political liberalism. Classical political liberalism, which staunchly defended free speech and the balance of governmental power, is seemingly becoming a mere echo in Western civilization. Liberalism today is not your grandmother's liberalism. One increasingly wonders if the free speech movement (e.g., University California, Berkeley) was more of a wedge strategy for liberal advocacy as opposed to the more principled free speech and free association movements of fledgling seventeenth- and eighteenth-century republican democratic movements in the West.

Liberal privilege typically dominates politics. As many have pointed out, fighting oppression and poverty is increasingly becoming big business. Contemporary political liberals often seem more like colonial era plantation owners who claim to be benevolent and caring while promoting dependence. Yes, the loudest critics of colonialism today often seem to be fresh incarnations of an ideological neo-colonialism. This irony should be no surprise for those grounded in a theology of the cross fully cognizant of the universal nature of human depravity—depravity that persists even in spite of grace. Generational dependency serves liberal privilege very well. To be fair, many liberals truly seek biblical social justice, though the means of justice are often assumed or flawed.

Indeed, contemporary political liberals and politically liberal Christian social justice advocates may well be, knowingly or unknowingly, the new power class benefiting off of the perennial cycles of generational dependency on liberal advocacy groups and big government: "You are a victim and you need us—forever." Big governments are to be feared as much as or more so than big corporations, since they often have direct and even greater power to wield the sword of the state and have ultimate and direct control of free speech and currency.[12] These governmental optics are also less than desirable and not rooted in a genuine theology of the cross.

11. Contemporary political and ideological liberalism, which is not to be confused with classical liberal political ideology. For representative expressions of the classical model, see Hamilton et al., *Federalist*.

12. Yes, big corporations certainly can influence or buy government favors, but

Not all Western political liberals intentionally or consciously seek to create dependency, but the impact of the movement is just such dependency. Legitimate criticisms of conservative movements have already been articulated by Saler and countless others and have received plenty of press in Western culture, so there is no need to rehearse such arguments here. The contemporary liberal edifice is most powerful and controls most of the centers of power.

Liberal privilege needs to be called out because it is a hidden darkness and reflects a rather seductive form of the theology of glory today, and this darkness is increasingly evident in so-called compassionate and social justice-oriented evangelicalism. In Luther's day those individuals and institutions powerfully parading as especially righteous were, according to Luther, prime examples of a theology of glory most deleterious to biblical faith and biblically influenced culture. Luther's day was not dissimilar to the generation of Christ in first-century Palestine.

Hence, relative to the quest for liberation, a never-ending "*Reformata, Semper Reformanda*"[13] liberation and social justice quest rooted in the cross and sound theological anthropology is needed. The worthy goal must never be uncritically identified with any political or ideological means, all of which fall short of the values of the not-yet kingdom. Discriminations need to be made between models and methods of compassionate social justice. Some are no doubt more effective and biblically influenced than others. Yet peaceful dialog is much preferable to manipulative and tribalistic diatribe as we serve and seek kingdom approximations in the shadow of the Second Coming.

---

unless one is convinced by extreme and even global centralized conspiracy theories, corporations do not have direct access to the entire authority, power, military, law, and weight of Leviathan governments—Eisenhower's concerns about the industrial-military complex notwithstanding. The blood-soaked genocidal landscape of the twentieth century certainly evidences the sin of the theology of glory and the demonic nature of governmental Leviathans.

13. The full intent of this phrase seems to be: Reformed by (Christ and) Scripture yet ever being reformed by (Christ and) Scripture. Scripture is the cradle of Christ.

11

Glorious Cross as Kingdom Eschatology

Hasn't the individualistic question about personal salvation almost completely left us all? Aren't we really under the impression that there are more important things than that question (perhaps not more important than the matter itself, but more important than the question!)? I know it sounds pretty monstrous to say that. But, fundamentally, isn't this in fact biblical? Does the question about saving one's soul appear in the Old Testament at all? Aren't righteousness and the kingdom of God on earth the focus of everything, and isn't it true that Rom 3:34ff is not an individualistic doctrine of salvation, but the culmination of the view that God alone is righteous? It is not with the beyond that we are concerned, but with this world as created and preserved, subjected to laws, reconciled, and restored. What is above this world is, in the gospel, intended to exist for this world; I mean that, not in the anthropocentric sense of liberal, mystic pietistic, ethical theology, but in the biblical sense of the creation and of the incarnation, crucifixion, and resurrection of Jesus Christ.

—DIETRICH BONHOEFFER, MAY 5, 1944.[1]

LUTHER'S THEOLOGY OF THE cross, theology of glory, and the *Deus Absconditus* properly emphasized soteriology and epistemology. These emphases were biblically intuitive in an age of works righteousness and

---

1. Bonhoeffer, *Letters*, 286.

church-state epistemological and soteriological hegemony and corruption. In countering works righteousness, Luther argued for a theology of the cross that stood in stark juxtaposition to the theology of glory. Hence, many of Luther's statements are cross *versus* glory. This is helpful to some degree, but as argued previously, the cross is also glorious and advances the already-not-yet kingdom of God. The positive meaning of both *theologia crucis* and the theology of glory can be hijacked, depart from Scripture, and corrupted. Yet within the context of biblical kingdom eschatology, a sound understanding and definition of cross and glory points to a glorious cross as kingdom eschatology.

Over a half millennium after Luther's theological Copernican revolution, as the evangelical, Christian, cultural, and civilizational consensus fragments amidst an age characterized as post-Christian, post-Christendom, postmodern, post-critical, and ultramoderm,[2] the integration and filtering of Luther's best insights via dialog with the already-not-yet kingdom eschatology is most promising. Utilizing a biblical scholar of the stature of N. T. Wright should prove helpful as a segue to the central eschatological assumption and applications of this work in the next chapter. In particular, Wright serves as a critical transition to the constructive work of the next chapter relative to viewing the cross as especially eschatological in nature and underscoring the centrality of eschatology for the whole of theology and for any theology of cross, kingdom, and glory.

WRIGHT'S REVOLUTION

Wright is helpful at this juncture of church history regarding the cross and the constructive eschatological task. The cover of his recent *The Day the Revolution Began* affirms that the death of Jesus "launched a revolution" because "God had suddenly and dramatically put into operation his plan for the rescue of the world."[3] This is the point of Cullmann's "D-Day" analogy discussed in chapters 9 and 10. "It is finished" is, for Cullmann and Wright, far more than the foundation for the famous evangelical warmed heart (or warm fuzzy) experience recounted by John Wesley:

> In the evening, I went very unwillingly to a Society in Aldersgate-Street, where one was reading Luther's preface to the Epistle to the Romans. About a quarter before nine, while he was describing the change which God works in the heart

2. See chapter 13.
3. Wright, *Day*.

through faith in Christ, I felt my heart strangely warmed. I felt I did trust in Christ; Christ alone, for salvation; and an assurance was given me, that he had taken away *my* sins, even *mine*, and saved *me* from the law of sin and death.[4]

For Wesley, this wonderfully transformative evangelical experience, where "my chains fell off, my heart was free,"[5] was contextualized by a robust theology of the *General Spread of the Gospel* and the *New Creation* and must be viewed in connection to Wesley's heroic cultural and political engagement. Yet, for many, according to Wright, this broader Wesleyan theological orientation is truncated and the personal heart-warming experience is the beginning and end of the application of the cross to theology, ecclesiology, life, mission, and calling. Wesley's rich experience and theology have, in the evangelical movement, sometimes been distorted and truncated. Wright views such a diminution as reducing the death of Jesus to nothing more than a heartwarming means of "God saving me from my 'sin' so that I could 'go to heaven.'" Much could be said concerning the sociopolitical and cultural assumptions and consequences of such a diminished and shallow theology of the cross. Wright's eschatological point is that, if isolated, such a theology of the cross "misconstrues why Jesus had to die, the nature of our sins, and what our mission is in the world today."[6]

To amplify and borrow Cullmann's language, while the cross is our personal D-Day, this warmed-heart experience cannot be separated from the cosmic D-Day of the in-breaking kingdom. Hence, for Wright, while the "personal meaning is not [to be] left behind, the true followers of Jesus "saw it as the day the revolution began."[7]

When the personal and experiential "D-Day" rules the theology of the cross, this "can lead us into a private or even selfish way of seeing things, in which our immediate needs may seem to have been met (our needs for forgiveness in the present and salvation in the future), but without making any difference in the world. Some, indeed, may make a virtue of that irrelevance."[8] Wright does not want to abandon the wonder of the personal D-Day and the miracle of forgiveness, where we can "scarce take it in."[9]

Wright does want us, in praise, hymn, and Eucharist to connect this profound experience, in a participatory fashion, to God's plan to rescue,

4. Wesley, "From the Journal."

5. From his brother Charles Wesley's well-known hymn, "And Can It Be."

6. Wright, *Day*.

7. See Wright, *Day*, 4.

8. Wright, *Day*, 5. Sometimes due to escapist eschatology.

9. From the classic hymn, "How Great Thou Art."

revolutionize and redeem the world. He wants us to experience the "revolutionary power" of the cross. He wants praise, worship, and Eucharist to be missional.[10] Wright wants the cross to be tethered to the resurrection, more in line with the Eastern churches (and Irenaeus's recapitulation theory) who view the cross as a "preamble to the resurrection," with the cross leading to "the real moment" that "is just about to begin."[11]

Before proceeding, it is important to elaborate and emphasize that Wesley's "for me" was contextualized within a firm belief in a dawning new creation and the constructive general spread of the gospel. Wesley's "for me" also countered what Luther viewed as a works-righteousness theology of glory. The death of Christ "for me" should spark the humility of "and can it be . . . infinite and free," that runs from hypocrisy (Matt 7) and runs toward the deconstruction of any self-righteous ideology that oppresses others. In addition, Wesley's view of the unlimited atonement, as with Arminius,[12] was pregnant with all of the Arminian assumptions birthing legion revivalism and social reform movements—Christ died for me was also Christ died for all, all are equal before the cross, and this glorious cross sparked the new creation. One must be careful not to misread or misapply Wright's comments to Wesley.

Wright affirms that Luther and the Reformers were understandably concerned about how to be saved amidst ecclesial and hegemonic works righteousness, which amounted to a theology of glory, but this reaction inadequately synthesized the resurrection and eschatology.[13] Luther's brilliant theology of the cross, and much of Protestantism, suffered. The "Reformers failed to challenge the larger heaven-and-hell frameworks itself" and focused on Romans and Galatians rather than Ephesians, which changed "the entire history of Western Europe."[14] Wright's immersion in the details of Scripture and church history is a helpful corrective today.

The key emphases of this aspect of Wright's staurology are relevant to and reinforce some of the motifs of this book. Our upside-down world often neglects justice and mercy and practices unspeakable evil, but believers may be comforted that the rescue operation is already underway and the outcome is certain:

> When you or I, faced with a major miscarriage of justice or mercy in our world or a major crisis in global politics or in the

10. Wright, *Day*, 13–18.
11. Wright, *Day*, 27.
12. See chapter 3.
13. Wright, *Day*, 28–30.
14. Wright, *Day*, 33.

life of our own community, can praise the God we know in Jesus as the one who has already won the victory over all the powers of evil . . . [and hence] we are able to go to our work, in whatever sphere it is, in a totally different spirit from the one full of fear and frustration that might otherwise accompany us.[15]

While *Christus Victor* can be presented as merely another theory of the atonement, even crude, it also can reflect a more optimistic, cosmic, incarnational, and missional understanding of the cross. The powers of darkness have, already, in one very real sense been vanquished: "It is finished." This connection among cross, resurrection, and victory is essential for Wright:

That is why I argued in *Surprised by Hope* that evangelism needs to be flanked with new-creation work in the realms of justice and beauty. If we are talking about the victory over evil and the launch of new creation, it won't make much sense unless we are working for those very things in lives of the poorest of the poor. If we are talking about Jesus winning the victory over the dark powers and thereby starting the long-awaited revolution, it will be much easier for people to believe it if we are working to show what we mean in art and music, in song and story.[16]

Hence, the "normal" idea of "eschatology" must be abandoned: "If we start with the simple idea of 'going to heaven,' what the New Testament says about the cross won't quite fit, but if we start instead with the new creation, it all makes sense."[17] Wright continues:

And the same is true about the view of *the cross itself*. If we imagine that we can have either half of Galatians 1:4 (the Messiah "gave himself up for our sins, to rescue us from the present evil age") without the other, we will reduce and distort the full meaning. And, finally, this message challenges the usual views of *mission*. Mission, as seen from the New Testament perspective, is neither about "saving souls from heaven" nor about "building the kingdom on earth." It is the Spirit-driven, cross-shaped work of Jesus's followers as they worship the true God and, confronting idols with the news of Jesus's victory, work *for* the signs of his kingdom in human lives and institutions.[18]

---

15. Wright, *Day*, 404.
16. Wright, *Day*, 405.
17. Wright, *Day*, 406.
18. Wright, *Day*, 407.

This cross-shaped work of Christ's followers is referred to as "cruciform mission" by Wright and resonates with the discussion in chapters 9 and 10 concerning cruciform personal and social holiness.

Cruciform holiness is inherently eschatological and includes cruciform mission—and vice versa. Wright helpfully points out "a word of caution," however, concerning suffering: "The idea that 'suffering is good for you, therefore you need to put up with the conditions we are laying on you' . . . [can be] at best callous and patronizing. At worst it is unpardonable and abusive. . . . Life will throw quite enough problems at us without the church adding more while telling us sanctimoniously that it's good for us." Nevertheless, Wright also points out that the cruciform advance of the new creation "is still the means by which the work goes forward."[19] He also queries the church: "Did we really imagine that, while Jesus would win his victory by suffering, self-giving love, we would implement that same victory by arrogant, self-aggrandizing force of arms?"[20]

Wright contends that the actualization of the new creation is via patient, incremental, Christlike love and missional, cruciform suffering: "Love will always suffer." Wright does not expound upon the theology of glory at this point, but probes, "Think of the pomp and the 'glory' of the late medieval church. But the 'victory' will be hollow and will leave all kinds of problems in its wake" if the advance is rushed, militaristic, triumphalistic, or "taken in some other spirit" than that of love.[21] In a telling passage concerning Wright's theology of the cross, he continues,

> Yes, it will mean taking up our own cross. Jesus warned us of exactly that (Mark 8:34–38). It will mean denying ourselves—a phrase we used to hear in hymns and sermons, but for some reason don't hear quite so much today. How remarkable it is that the Western church so easily embraces self-discovery, self-fulfillment, and self-realization as though they were the heart of the "gospel." . . . Yes, following Jesus will mean disappointment, failure, frustration, muddle, misunderstanding, pain and sorrow—and those are just the "first-world [or minority world] problems." As I have already said, some Christians, even while I have been working on this book, have been beheaded for their faith; others have seen their homes bombed, their livelihoods taken away, their health ruined. Their witness is extraordinary, and we in the comfortable West can only ponder the ways in which our own unseen compromises—perhaps because of our

19. Wright, *Day*, 373.
20. Wright, *Day*, 373.
21. Wright, *Day*, 374.

platonic [and escapist] eschatology—have shielded us from the worst things that are happening to our true family only a plane ride away.

These are not simply horrible things that may happen to us despite our belief in the victory of Jesus. They are things that may come, in different ways and at different times, *because* this is how the kingdom comes.[22]

Martin Luther King Jr. reportedly said, "Only in the darkness can you see the stars."[23] Wright seems to be affirming that the kingdom can best be seen and realized in the shadow of the cross.

Wright's formulation of the theology of the cross, then, is eschatological through and through: "*New creation can happen because the power of satan, of Babylon and Pharaoh has been broken.*"[24] Wright concludes,

When the New Testament tells us the meaning of the cross, it gives us not a system, but a story; not a theory [or theory of the atonement], but a meal and an act of humble service; not a celestial mechanism for punishing sin and taking people to heaven, but an earthly story of a human Messiah who embodies and incarnates Israel's God and who unveils his glory in bringing his kingdom to earth as in heaven. The Western church— and we've all gone along with this—has been so concerned with getting to heaven, with sin as the problem blocking the way, and therefore with how to remove sin and its punishment, that it has jumped straight to passages in Paul that can be made to serve that purpose. It has forgotten that the gospels are replete with atonement theology, through and through—only they give it to us not as a neat little system, but as a powerful, sprawling, many-sided, richly revelatory narrative in which we are invited to find ourselves, or rather to lose ourselves and to be found again on the other side. We have gone wading in the shallow and stagnant waters of medieval questions and answers [about how to avoid hell] taking care to put on the right footwear and not lose our balance, when only a few yards away is the vast and dangerous ocean of the gospel story, inviting us to plunge in and let the wild waves of dark glory wash us, wash over us, wash us through and through, and land on the shores of God's new creation.[25]

22. Wright, *Day*, 410.
23. The documentation of this quote has not been located.
24. Wright, *Day*, 414.
25. Wright, *Day*, 416.

Wright's final plea is to "celebrate the revolution that happened once for all when the power of love overcame the love of power. And, in the power of that same love, join in the revolution here and now."[26]

WRIGHT'S REDUCTIONISM

Wright, as many have quipped, is often right and sometimes, perhaps rarely, wrong. Well, to be crystal clear on my intent here, attempting to refine, modify, correct, or enhance a well-established scholar such as Wright also merits caution and pause. Nevertheless, certain observations might be helpful at least to compare and contrast the perspective of this present work with Wright's recent work on the cross. Wright's apparent reductionism and other related concerns revolve around his nearly thoroughgoing eschatological preterism, his utilization of the concept of revolution and grasp of cultural transformation, and his ambiguity and lack of specificity concerning the precise nature of the Parousia.

Wright's general approach to the theology and eschatology of the cross is sound, with brilliant and moving application to individuals and ecclesiological mission. Precisely how much positive change can be mediated prior to Christ's return is, however, essential to a sound and biblical theology that unites cross and kingdom. In a crucial but lengthy passage, he approaches specificity on the critical issue of the nature of change possible prior to Christ's return:

> Let us be clear, too, about the relation between our present work, our present reshaping of our world and the future world that God intends to make. Christians have always found it difficult to understand and articulate this and have regularly distorted the picture in one direction or another. Some have so emphasized the discontinuity between the present world and our work in it on the one hand and the future world that God will make on the other that they suppose God will simply throw the present world in the trash can and leave us in a totally different sphere altogether. There is then really no point in attempting to reshape the present world by the light of Jesus Christ. Armageddon is coming, so who cares about acid rain or third-world debt. That is the way of dualism; it is a radically anticreation viewpoint and hence is challenged head on by (among many other things) John's emphasis on Easter as the first day of the new week, the start of God's new creation.

26. Wright, *Day*, 416.

On the other hand, some have so emphasized the continuity between the present world and the coming new world that they have imagined we can actually build the kingdom of God by our own hard work. I am thinking not just of the old so-called liberal social gospel but also of some aspects of the Calvinist heritage, which in its reaction against perceived dualisms of one sort or another has sometimes played down the radical discontinuity between this world and the next. This is sorely mistaken. When God does what God intends to do, this will be an act of fresh grace, of radical newness. At one level it will be quite unexpected, like a surprise party with guests we never thought we would meet and delicious food we never thought we would taste. But at the same time there will be a rightness about it, a rich continuity with what has gone before so that in the midst of our surprise and delight we will say, "Of course! This is how it had to be, even though we'd never imagined it."[27]

Wright concludes the argument by utilizing the continuity and discontinuity of the resurrection body referenced in 1 Corinthians 15 and affirming the following:

There is a vital and important *continuity* as well as discontinuity between this world and the next which is to be, precisely because the new world has already begun with Easter and Pentecost, and because everything done on the basis of Jesus' resurrection and in the power of the Spirit already belongs to that new world. It is already part of the kingdom-building that God is now setting forward in this new week of new creation.[28]

Nevertheless, a glaring lack of specificity concerning the many key eschatological nuances of the theology of the cross seems conspicuous in his more recent work *The Day the Revolution Began*. This work calls for a revolution, and the work approaches nearly 450 pages. Yet unless I somehow missed such specificity on the limits of this revolution prior to Christ's return, or the precise nature of the ecclesiological, socio-cultural, and political engagement of the revolutionaries in this or other works, including summaries of *The Day the Revolution Began*, then Wright's conceptualization of the revolution is a call to action without appropriate guidance. And I would not be alone in missing that needed specificity and nuancing.[29] My

27. Wright, *Challenge*, 179–80.

28. Wright, *Challenge*, 180.

29. For a sympathetic appraisal of this ambiguity, please see Middleton, *Creation*. For a less sympathetic view by a popular evangelical author and speaker, see Richardson, "N. T. Wright and Eschatology." Here is Richardson's own self-description from

research and analysis focused on Wright's recent publication on the cross, so it remains for other scholars to comprehensively evaluate whether Wright's eschatological ambiguity in *The Day the Revolution Began* truly reflects the entirety of his tremendous scholarly contribution and output.

Relative to *The Day the Revolution Began*, Wright is correct that the cross advances the eschatological kingdom, but does revolutionary language, applied to the present pre-*Parousia* age, sometimes run counter to the very caution in the lengthy quote above and create an unrealistic expectation of permanent and global change possible in this age? Is the revolution global, or local, or limited? Kingdom theology suggests that the revolution must be global in scope, but what exactly does that mean pre-*Parousia*?

The church needs a precise formulation of socio-eschatology in order to have a desperately needed and precise understanding of ecclesiology, mission, and a biblical, appropriate, realistic, and optimistic definition of the proper political and cultural engagement in a "post" world. The humorous quip, "I'm pan-millennial—it will all pan out in the end" is good humor but absolutely cancerous theology. If the church can't clearly define and delineate the scope of the new creation revolution prior to Christ's return, then the church flounders relative to civilizational engagement. Nineteenth-century American evangelical utopianism, twentieth-century American evangelical escapism, and liberation theology, all are indicative and illustrative of imprecise and flawed approaches.

This work offers preliminary suggestions. Can revolutionary language, applied to this age without nuance, foster the very kind of naïve utopianism Wright tries to counter? Does not revolutionary language applied to this age play into the hands of both conservative and liberal triumphalism and imperialism and shroud his nuanced caution? Does revolutionary language foster compassionate social justice movements that improperly speak for God and reflect false glory more so than the cross of Calvary? Is not the lack of specificity, exactitude, and particularity concerning the precise and actual historical nature of Christ's return and the limits of kingdom advance prior to his return necessary to preserve both continuity and discontinuity between this age and the next? Should not eschatology define outcomes and set appropriate limits on programs for biblical justice and kingdom advance? Do not the principles of continuity, common sense, and sound theological anthropology suggest that there will be a transitional phase after Christ's return, something akin to an earthly millennium, which implies appropriate limits on millennial approximations prior to Christ's return?

his blog: "Joel Richardson is a New York Times bestselling author, film-maker, and teacher." See also Richardson, "N. T. Wright's Perversion."

Concerning this last point, is Wright caught on the horns of a dilemma? If he wants to emphasize that after Christ returns the new creation immediately has arrived in all its fullness, then continuity has been lost. If he wants to emphasize and salvage continuity between the current age and the new creation because of how much the kingdom has advanced prior to the *Parousia*, then he is most vulnerable to some form of utopianism or a neo-utopianism and makes Christ's return somewhat superfluous to the vanquishing of evil, underestimating personal and systemic evil. The arguments follow in the remaining chapters, but this pre-*Parousia* world is best described as being capable of being significantly influenced and impacted, but not transformed or revolutionized in any strong sense, prior to Christ's actual, supernatural, historical, trans-historical, and redemptive return.

Biblical theology, framed within a unified kingdom theology, certainly makes such important distinctions concerning the limits of cruciform advance prior to Christ's return. Christ died for our sins, and his death sparked a kingdom initiation, or intrusion, or initiatory restoration. Our death to sin is identified with his death on the cross and the basis for ecclesial kingdom advance. I argue that having some clarity concerning the limits of global kingdom impact prior to Christ's return is just as essential to positive civilizational engagement as the rejection of escapist, Platonic, and individualistic eschatological distortions.

As with Wright's other works and even blogs,[30] ambiguity also seems to remain concerning his understanding of the nature of the return of Christ—though such analysis exceeds the purpose of this work. As many have said, speculating about the furniture of heaven or the temperature of hell is unwise. Likewise, going beyond Scripture and sound biblical interpretation and speculating about the details of the return of Christ, or engaging in reckless biblical literalism, is unwise. Issues such as the temperature of hell, the furniture of heaven, and the type of cloud (if any) to be ridden by the returning Lion aside, Cullmann and many others (e.g., Ladd, Beasley-Murray, Henry) properly and unapologetically emphasized that the new creation cannot be fully realized on earth apart from a supernatural event the magnitude of which equals or exceeds the creation, exodus, and incarnation/resurrection. Wright's revolution is either ill-defined or seems overly hopeful.

The new creation can be approximated prior to Christ's return, often in a fleeting fashion as gains are often lost, but the global holiness of the new creation forever lies beyond the grasp of this pre-*Parousia* age. Kingdom advance is incrementally *already*, but the theologically indispensable *not*

---

30. See, for example, Wright, "NTWrightPage."

yet, prior to the return of Christ, remains and this limit must be viewed as absolutely central to our theology of cross and kingdom.

Wright seems torn between a shrewd utopianism (see chapter 12) and an optimistic (for this present age) amillennialism relative to the possibilities of the present pre-*Parousia* age. To summarize, these are truly normative theological and practical questions: To what degree can the present pre-*Parousia* age be redeemed or restored? To what degree will the post-*Parousia* era have a transitional phase as opposed to a magical moment when all is completely transformed, on every level (individuals, communities, civilization), in an instant? Yes, we shall be changed "in the twinkling of an eye" (1 Cor 15:52), but the clear context of this reference is resurrection immortality—as with the "dead in Christ." Is it rational or scriptural to affirm that the return of Christ is not followed by a transitional phase relative to culture, civilization, creation, and human nature? Is not the specificity of Cullman on the possibilities and limits of pre-*Parousia* kingdom advance more helpful as a framework for cruciform cultural and political engagement?[31] Is not the slavery example referenced many times in this work helpful to providing needed clarity on these questions? Yes, we can and should abolish slavery in one part or even a significant part of the globe prior to Christ's return. Yet new forms of slavery (e.g., human trafficking) will inevitably assert themselves over time. More importantly, the centralized power needed to eradicate completely all slavery globally, in a fallen world prior to Christ's return, virtually ensures the kind of totalitarianism and oppression on an unprecedented global scale that births slavery or an equivalent oppression! Beware of some claims to compassionate social justice.

Additionally, Wright's eschatological preterism (whether full or partial) can be employed relative to many biblical passages, yet does not the whole tenor of Scripture, biblical anthropology, and many specific sections of Scripture clearly concur that the already kingdom will only approximate the future prior to the *Parousia*? Does a nearly or completely preterist view that is rather optimistic concerning the present pre-*Parousia* age ultimately fall into a dangerous but shrewd utopianism? If there is no significant transitional phase after Christ's return, then either pre-*Parousia* (and nearly) utopian realization is required before Christ returns or a magical in-an-instant transformation of all things is required after Christ returns to move reality to the new creation. The former, in terms of sound theology, historical analysis, and reason, misreads the current possibilities of change. The latter sounds like the very kind of escapist Platonism that Wright abhors.

---

31. See chapters 9 and 10.

Dispensational or literalistic conceptions of the millennium (and rapture) are not required to avoid Wright's dilemma but something analogous to a transitional phase of history after Christ's return seems theologically and rationally needful. This debate is best reserved for another work,[32] yet the avoidance of magical and escapist conceptions of the *Parousia* and the avoidance of shrewd yet nevertheless utopian views of the present age prior to the *Parousia* would seem to assist with a proper understanding of the possibilities and limits of cruciform civilizational impact. Wright seems unclear relative to providing some defined limits to civilizational and cultural melioration prior to the *Parousia*. What are the limits and goals of his revolution? As they say, if you aim at nothing, you are bound to hit it. If you swing for the fence with a broken bat, you will likely fail. If Wright or anyone wants to affirm an optimistic amillennialism that sets clear limits to pre-*Parousia* change and affirms the need for a significant (in length and quality) transitional phase after Christ's return, that sounds a great deal like a non-literalistic, non-dispensational, historic millennialism!

None other than Walter Rauschenbusch made the case for maintaining the kernel in the husk of the oft-distorted millennial eschatology:

> We need a restoration of the millennial hope which the Catholic Church dropped out of eschatology. It was crude in its form but wholly right in its substance. The duration of a thousand years is a guess and immaterial. All efforts to fix "times and seasons" are futile. But the ideal of a social life in which the law of Christ shall prevail, and in which its prevalence shall result in peace, justice and a glorious blossoming of human life, is a Christian ideal. An outlook toward the future in which the "spiritual life" is saved and the economic life is left unsaved is both unchristian and stupid. If men in the past have given a "carnal" colouring of richness to the millennial hope, let us renounce that part, and leave the ideals of luxury and excess to men of the present capitalistic order. Our chief interest in any millennium is the desire for a social order in which the worth and freedom of every least human being will be honoured and protected; in which the brotherhood of man will be expressed in the common possession of the economic resources of society; and in which the spiritual good of humanity will be set high above the private profit interests of all materialistic groups. We hope for such an order for humanity as we hope for heaven for ourselves.[33]

---

32. I will be addressing this question head-on in a forthcoming work, *Approximating the Millennium*.

33. Rauschenbusch, *Theology*, 224.

Setting aside some of Rauschenbusch's socialistic, sentimentalist, moralistic, and utopian tendencies, which is also a debate for another place and time, he masterfully points not toward a magically and instantaneously perfected order, which ultimately seems escapist and Platonic, but toward the longed-for and next transitional phase of human and redemptive history. This work argues that this glorious next phase may be approximated pre-*Parousia* through cruciform kingdom advance and will only be fully realized post-*Parousia* through the actual return of the Lamb who was slain and who returns as the Lion of Judah. This pre-*Parousia* advance also contributes constructively and directly to the post-*Parousia* glorious transitional phase, which ultimately blossoms into the fullness of the new creation:

> The point at which a modified [essential and approximative] . . . millennialism would differ with Rauschenbusch is in his sole dependence upon the developmental model, and his polariza-tion of heaven and earthly hope [since hoping for heaven is hop-ing for ourselves]. Why must the realization of the millennium be either catastrophic or developmental? Could not present millennial approximation and future millennial realization is-sue forth from both process and catastrophe? Could not heaven include the present earth radically transformed? Total reliance on the organic model too easily succumbs to uncritically seeing "the coming Kingdom of God in all ethical and spiritual prog-ress of mankind," as Rauschenbusch puts it. On the other hand, overemphasis on catastrophe undermines world-affirmation, Creation, and Incarnation [not to mention undermining a bib-lical continuity between the present age and the historical phase after Christ's return]. The black or white fallacies of catastrophe or development, crisis or evolution, transcendence or imma-nence, "from above" or "from below," may be less than helpful in the study of eschatology.[34]

Hence, to be clear, cruciform kingdom victories now contribute to kingdom victories in the transitional phase after the return of Christ and the ultimate journey to the new creation. Civilizational and cultural continuity and discontinuity characterize the relationship between the present age and the age subsequent to Christ's return. Yet apart from the return of Christ, such cruciform kingdom advance would not endure and would ultimately falter. For example, the elevation of the status of women is a real gain in some cultures, and Christianity has, at times, played an important role, but without the return of Christ such advances can be fleeting, or only regional

---

34. Matthews, "Approximating," 46–47.

rather than universal. In America, for example, it is arguable that women have been elevated and liberated in some very important ways while simultaneously being increasingly objectified and enslaved in others. Patriarchal and traditional familial structures certainly can be oppressive, but so can the poverty, sociology, and psychology of broken families.[35]

The supernatural intervention of the return of Christ must be radical because even the greatest kingdom advances in the present age fall conspicuously short of the not yet. It is also must be radical because Christ's return will go to the very root of personal, systemic, and global evil. Careful verse-by-verse and chapter-by-chapter biblical hermeneutics and exegesis are critical for the orthodox church, yet a theological hermeneutic of the entire Bible and the entire corpus of Christian theology is also most essential. The whole of Scripture is clear that we should not fool ourselves into thinking that the totality of the present creation, culture, and civilization will be nearly identical to the new creation prior to the *Parousia*. Such a theological error is not new or desirable and has deleterious effects and short-lived successes. Flawed eschatology also leads to disillusionment (e.g., the collapse of postmillennialism in the nineteenth and twentieth centuries). Wright could bring clarity to this discussion, but such specificity has not yet been found in his many writings.

Terms such as *prolepsis*, approximation, influence, and impact applied in a nuanced fashion are much preferable to the term revolution in most historical contexts and certainly preferable when applied to the totality of history and creation prior to Christ's return. Attaching revolution to the purpose of the cross and the mission of the church in this pre-*Parousia* age is largely unwise, as it implies a global revolution and unrealistic outcomes. It also plays into the dangers of utopianism and seems to resurrect the naïveté of the cultural revolutions in the West of the 1950s and 1960s. Unfortunately, many are still stuck in the 60s relative to the true nature and limits of social amelioration and the creation of a new humanity.

Civilizational influence and impact are more biblical goals for the mission of the church than revolution or even transformation. Transformation is a term I have increasingly abandoned in reference to the pre-*Parousia* possibilities of Christian mission. Revolution may be good marketing and is applicable to the not-yet dimension of Christ's work, but this term is too easily identified with movements that naïvely thought they could turn the world right side up by starting over again or by following the latest utopian ideology.

---

35. The impact of broken families certainly is debated in the literature, and it goes beyond the scope of this work to attempt resolution or nuancing, but please see data such as Anderson, "Impact of Family Structure," 378–87.

Revolutionary and liberationist movements, even (and especially) those identifying with the oppressed and marginalized, are more than capable of becoming triumphalist and even demonic. Social justice is easily employed to advance a demonic and utopian Trojan Horse birthing a new form of oppression, or dependence, or entitlement. There is no ideological or theological exemption from the hard and disappointing realities of pre-*Parousia* theological anthropology. In the West the communist revolution, the Cuban revolution, and the French Revolution are all illustrative. In the east the revolution in China is instructive. The common story is like a broken record, but the consequences have been most calamitous: Great evil was identified only to be replaced by revolutionaries who spawned countless other evils. The consequence was sometimes arguably a net loss to civilization even when replacing corrupt dictators.

The cross is a radical statement about human depravity, just as the cross and resurrection are radical statements concerning humanity's true future. Yet the fullness of that future is decidedly not yet prior to Christ's return. Hence, revolutionary movements typically suffer from flawed, messianic, utopian, neo-utopian, and elitist theological anthropology—profound misunderstandings of human nature. Even the American Revolution, intentionally and consciously preserving elements of the past heritage, is better referred to as war of emancipation based on the unresolved "long train of abuses" articulated in the Lockean *Declaration of Independence*. What the American Revolution especially got right, as my spouse often reminds me, was the clear statement limiting the Revolution to pursuing "a more perfect" union rather than a perfect union.

Passionate beliefs and movements for change are essential and move forward via the energy provided by eschatology or future-visions; thus, such movements should have an eschatological flavor. Eschatology can be the rocket fuel of progress. Yet cultural and political revolutions easily exceed the wrongs they seek to right apart from biblical anthropology, staurology, and eschatology. Biblical eschatology provides the impetus and fuel for civilizational improvement, but the formula for the rocket fuel must be just right to avoid both stasis and self-destruction. The revolutionary's Achilles heel is her or his own nature and the fallibility of all human constructed ideologies. That being said, however, there certainly are historical contexts where the term *revolution* might be appropriate (e.g., amidst Stalin's purges) as long as the revolutionaries understand theological anthropology, eschatology, history, and especially that "we have met the enemy, and he [or she] is us."

Wright also seems to be falling into the same theology of glory tendency to masquerade as a compassionate theology of the cross, which was the error of Saler. Liberal political conclusions are apparently self-evidently connected, in Wright's mind, to his new creation and revolutionary cross theology. However, this political to and fro exceeds the purpose of this book, so the references in this chapter to the risks and blindness of the contemporary social justice and self-righteous edifice are more methodological concerns and should suffice for now. This work merely seeks to challenge the method and presumptuousness of such theologically framed political ideology. The choice in the present pre-*Parousia* era is not between heaven and hell. The most fluid reality is that in a fallen world, in view of the cross and initiated kingdom, we may approximate heaven or hell.

Wright honorably notes, concerning his new creation theology of the cross, that he is "not suggesting that nobody has said all this before, only that the point of view I have been putting forward, rooted in the New Testament, is a long way from what most Western Christians, and Western non-Christians for that matter, imagine to be the meaning of the cross."[36] Indeed, the suggested and enhanced specificity and rich nature of such previously articulated themes should be of great assistance as we conclude this present work and will be the subject of the subsequent chapters. Ultimately, however, on the use of revolutionary language and scope of change prior to Christ's return and the simplistic tendency of Wright to align his theology with liberal political fads that are less than solidly grounded in theology, Wright's wrong is theological reductionism.

The already kingdom beachhead delivered a sovereignly good soteriological and salvific epistemological singularity at the very crossroads of history, space, and time. This singularity runs counter to fallen wisdom and corrosive conceptions of glory via kingdom prophetic prolepsis and engenders genuine wisdom and glory. This cross and kingdom eschatology properly and prophetically witnesses to the inverted nature of a fallen world while pointing to the already great reversal of kingdom approximation after D-Day. Such approximation prior to Christ's return is hopeful but realistic, possible but limited, theologically global but often local and transitory. This cross and kingdom eschatology serves as a conjunctive and integrative theological anchor for the whole of biblical and Christian theology. The proclamation and reality of this eschatological cross and proleptic kingdom are advanced by the grace-assisted church and overflowing love via non-meritorious, kenotic, cruciform holiness, often bearing the civilizational fruit of non-universal liberations and kingdom approximations; and the eschatology of the cross and kingdom ultimately birth and inspire rich, triune, passionate, and transformative doxology.[37]

---

36. Wright, *Day*, 407.

37. "Transformative" is appropriate for what can take place in the lives of individual

12

Normative Eschatological Assumptions Framing Cross and Kingdom Theology

As NOTED IN CHAPTER 1, in the late 1980s and early 1990s an eschatological framework for a kingdom-centric theology of the cross was crystallizing in my thought. The contention of this chapter is that this background material underpins and greatly augments a full understanding of a properly framed theology of cross and kingdom. This conceptualization predates but includes some of the emphases in Wright's theology of the cross, as well as his *Surprised by Hope*.[1] Essential explanations of this critical eschatological framework have already been introduced. The argument that follows elaborates and directly connects this framework to an integrated theology of cross and kingdom. What core eschatological assumptions should posture, guide, and drive our theologies of cross and kingdom? The contention here is that a clear understanding of this underlying framework is indispensable. And especially needed is more precision concerning the possible scope of cruciform cultural and civilizational impact and influence prior to the *Parousia*. In view of a theology of cross and kingdom, what is the proper and missional goal of civilizational engagement, influence, and impact for the orthodox, evangelical, Christian church? What are the normative eschato-

---

believers, the church, and church worship. The established change from an abusive alcoholic to a sober caring father through Christ and Christ's church, verifiable over significant time, can reasonably be described as an enduring transformation. The tenuous gains in culture and civilization are better categorized as Christian impact and influence, especially given the multi-complex nature of culture and civilization.

1. Wright, *Surprised by Hope*.

logical assumptions that should guide the apologetic, evangelistic, Christian formation and civilizational mission of God in the world?

In the 1980s eschatology, ever relevant, seemed in some respects to lie at the crossroads of theological and philosophical reflection, not to mention American evangelical cultural and political engagement. The utopian delusions of modernism and classical liberal Christian theology were fragmenting. Postmodernism was becoming a chic buzzword along with the reactionary terms dystopian or dystopianism.[2] Barth and others had seemingly obliterated faulty theological anthropology, the Theology of Hope recentered theology in eschatology and redefined God as cruciform, and the eschatological "Make America Great Again" (Reagan, 1980) vision bore political fruit and was deftly synthesized by American political conservatives with wildly popular "last generation" eschatomania, perhaps with great cognitive dissonance.[3]

Within this late twentieth-century eschatological context, a more refined already-not-yet eschatology, which had actually emerged much earlier in the twentieth century, made additional inroads into the scholarly realm of the American evangelical movement. Even some traditional dispensationalists morphed into progressive dispensationalists under the influence of the already-not-yet consensus. This helpful theological consensus and orientation properly grounds the present discussion and is foundational to the key points of this work, as well as foundational for Wright's new creation and cruciform mission eschatology.[4] An essential component of this perspective and eschatology is a rejection of fatalism.

A NON-FATAL VISION

The already-not-yet eschatology counters, or at least tempers, fatalistic eschatological pessimism. The kingdom is certainly future but also decisively present, which negates less hopeful interactions with the present age. These less hopeful views, which often affirmed they were very hopeful about escape and final victory but not hopeful about the present age prior to Christ's return, seemingly dominated evangelicalism in the late twentieth century.

2. See Lepore, "Golden Age."

3. The term *eschatomania* probably originated with theologian Millard Erickson in the early 1980s. See Erickson, *Christian Theology*, 1152–53.

4. All direct quotations are from primary sources (unless otherwise noted) and documented throughout this work, but for easy and comparative references this chapter also includes material from and modifications of Matthews, "Approximating," 3–4, 13, 33, 39–43, 55, 66, 105, 110–11, 151–52, 211, 217–18, 314–26, 328–29, 332–35, 396–404, 415–19, 431–32, 438–40, 451–52.

Authors such as Hal Lindsey, Tim LaHaye, and Frank Peretti sold books to the tune of multiple millions. The popularity of these works included Perreti's top nonfiction series for an entire decade, with forty million in total sales. The series was described as a "phenomenon" by Barnes and Noble, with fifteen million copies purchased for a single book, rivaling John Gresham during the same time period.[5] Walvoord and Hoehner provided the theological foundation for this fatal vision and represented a key underlying assumption that contrasted with Wright's vision of significant kingdom advance. Walvoord writes, "Instead, things are going to get worse and worse. There will be more oppression, more injustice, more immorality as the age wears on."[6] Hoehner confirms, "I think the whole thing [social melioration] is wrong-headed . . . I just can't buy their basic presupposition that we can do anything significant to change the world. And you can waste an awful lot of time trying [time better spent on evangelism]."[7] This mind-set was most evident in and partially rooted in the nineteenth-century writings of D. L. Moody who viewed the world as a "wrecked vessel." Moody affirmed that the appropriate response to this eschatological reality, just like those going down with the Titanic, was to "save all you can." History was "getting darker and darker." The darkness results from the fact that humanity is repeatedly a "failure" in every dispensation or historical age.[8] Moody's pessimism is critical to the current conversation, for he "did more than anyone else to shape the nature of evangelical revivalism during the second half of the nineteenth century."[9] This fatal vision became the foundation for much of twentieth-century evangelical theology and eschatology.

A SHREWD BUT HOPEFUL VISION

In contrast, the already-not-yet perspective of Cullmann, Wright, and others, while certainly negating utopianism to one degree or another, is also

5. These sales milestones are well-known, but please see representative data from *Publisher's Weekly* or Barnes and Noble: Nelson, "Frank Peretti"; LaHaye and Jenkins, *Left Behind Collection*. See also Kirkpatrick, "Evangelical Sales are Converting Publishers." Sales figures by themselves do not entirely prove but do suggest significant influence, especially "40 million." It is most doubtful that twenty million book purchasers of these works, for example, disagreed entirely with the eschatology of such works.

6. Walvoord, "Why Must Christ Return?," 43. Walvoord was associated with Dallas Theological Seminary.

7. Hoehner, "Christ or Satan," 42–44. Hoehner taught at Dallas Theological Seminary.

8. Moody, "Return," 185.

9. Nash, *Evangelicals*, 52.

much more hopeful concerning the present age. For example, the next phase of redemptive history (phase one of the new creation, or the millennium)[10] could serve as a Christocentric and creation-affirming focus for life in the present between what Cullmann has described as D-Day and V-Day.[11] Identification with the coming King could mean alignment with the realities, character, and values of the next phase of the advancing kingdom. This millennial future, purged of biblical literalism,[12] could serve as the *telos* for the present. Restoration of the present created order in the journey toward the next phase of the new creation could become the central pre-*Parousia* and approximative leitmotif of the followers of the King. Other motifs, such as apologetics, cultural engagement, evangelism, discipleship, and worship would then naturally issue forth from such a refined and balanced kingdom perspective.[13]

This already-not-yet orientation sets both intellectual and praxis-oriented trajectories in motion that are vitally relevant to the church's orientation in the present. Humanity and society can and will be transformed, and the Incarnation event already has unleashed the power or reality, in an initiatory, preparatory, or provisional fashion, of this ultimate transformation. Prior to the ultimate and *Parousia*-dependent transformation, Christian influence or impact is the theologically sound goal. Periods of tribulation are not necessary or inevitable since final transformation is a divinely sanctioned metaphysical ultimate and certainty. The symbol of antichrist, central to many pessimistic eschatologies, rather than serving as a fatalistic prediction might serve as a powerful reminder of the dark power opposing renewal in every age. Awareness of antichrist warns of the dangers of unchecked power, Luther's theology of glory, the vulnerability of naïve utopianism, and the need for wise and concerted efforts at civilizational influence. Future history can record either amelioration or degeneration, and the cruciform church bears grave responsibility for which history will be written or is being written today. Escapist and non-cruciform evangelicalism bears moral responsibility for decline. This historical openness means that every program for progress either could succeed or become an antichrist. Yet a

---

10. See the argument of the prior chapter where agreement and convergence might appear between a modified premillennialism and an amillennialism (like Wright) that can acknowledge a millennium like transition period on the way to the new creation. "Millennium like" means lengthy but not perfected and with widespread rebellion still possible.

11. Cullmann, *Christ and Time*.

12. See the prior chapter.

13. Balanced in the sense of neither utopian nor fatalistic.

church that merely and passively waits for the *Parousia* assures the victory of antichrist or antichrists and the actualization of tribulation.

Christian social praxis must conform to the values and the character of the King and the coming kingdom to truly make a difference. The values and character of the present always stand under the prophetic Damocles's sword of the future. Evil powers already have been judged at the cross and ultimately have no future.

The next phase of the new creation, referred to as the millennium by many evangelicals, purged of dispensational accretions, is a real future on this earth. The new creation envelops rather than obliterates the cosmos, including the history and reality of world history, culture, and civilization. This next phase underscores or affirms the creation and the Incarnation and suggests that the present cosmos, the object of God's intense love, will not be annihilated at the *Parousia* but will be transformed.[14]

This affirmation of this-worldly restoration has mammoth implications for current cultural and civilizational engagement, especially when significant continuity between the present and the millennial age is assumed. Cruciform service now not only has the potential of writing the pages of the future now, but of shaping the very contours of the next phase of cosmic restoration—the transitional phase after Christ's return. A more balanced millennialism, historic premillennialism, defines the next phase of history while being a mega-step toward the new creation as still having the possibility of widespread rebellion. Hence, for historic premillennialists, history is elevated in the glorious millennium, yet that glory will be tainted by one final rebellion. The debates concerning whether this post-*Parousia* transitional period or millennium is a literal thousand years or is symbolic of completion and/or a lengthy interim or how literalistic the final rebellion should be understood are not central considerations to this discussion. The key point is that current history is moving toward transitional millennial-like glory on the way to the fullness and complete glory of the new creation. The *Parousia* will move history and social existence one giant step forward in the process of realizing the ideal of heavenly new creation. The transformations subsequent to the Parousia are consistent with and will build upon already kingdom advances in the present age. Hence, significant continuity

---

14. See this recent dissertation concerning the future of the cosmos, Juza, "New Testament." I had the privilege of receiving a copy of the dissertation presented for the oral dissertation defense. Some of Juza's conclusions align with arguments I put forth some two decades ago and have been frequently articulated by Wright. Unfortunately, the dissertation is almost exclusively focused on specialized issues related to biblical studies.

characterizes the short- and long-term missional programmatic for an organic theology and eschatology of cross and kingdom. The present mission of God contributes to and prepares for but does not actualize the millennial mission and reign of God. Such theological distinctions are indispensable and urgent.

Historic millennialism, as used intentionally, non-literalistically, and rather loosely in this work, seeks to find common ground between non-Dispensational historic premillennialism and what I like to refer to as new earth or new creation amillennialism. Let me explain. *Historic* is used in a very broad sense and is a hybrid of a preterist and futurist biblical hermeneutic. *Historic* also suggests that some prophecy and apocalyptic Scripture may have as its primary referent events that unfold throughout or in various ages of history. Yet significant futurism remains in both Old and New Testament literature. For example, there may be "many antichrists" (1 John 2:18) throughout history and many tribulations throughout history, but the possibility remains of a future era of temporary darkness that is the culmination of all historic antichrists and tribulations. Yet, rather than viewing the future in deterministic terms, all of humanity, especially the church, bears great and grave responsibility for influencing the timing, intensity, and contours of all tribulations.

New earth amillennialism believes that the present earth will be restored/renewed/transformed both by and after the coming of Christ and the saints and acknowledges that the post-*Parousia* transformation will not take place in a magical moment. Wright, as noted, seems to lack specificity, but his view seems close to a new earth neo-millennialism. This new earth neo-millennialism contrasts with traditional amillennnialism, which sees the wheat and tares growing together until Christ returns, destroys evil, annihilates and replaces the cosmos, and magically establishes the new creation.

A total transformation of civilization in a magic moment is ultimately more Platonic than biblical. By way of analogy, American evangelicals also, in contrast to Wesley, seem to view the bodily resurrection and truly final and entire eschatological glorification and sanctification of believers as taking place in just such a magical moment. Therefore, one may become truly saved, yet not fret over carnality, spiritual immaturity, lack of holistic growth (including intellectual, psychological, or interpersonal growth), or fret over civilizational melioration and enhancement, because God will take care of all of that in the future and magic eschatological moment. This strikes me as irrational, non-Hebraic, and eminently unbiblical. Hence, my suggestion is that Scripture and reason dictate that a transitional period after the *Parousia* is needed in order to move believers, time, history, and creation toward the full glory of the new creation.

In my earlier writings, I was comfortable with speaking of a purged, "kernel in the husk," modified, or non-dispensational premillennialism. That case can still be made, but the term *premillennial*, in spite of the work of many balanced, solid, and nuanced premillennial scholars like Ladd or Henry, is difficult to communicate persuasively in view of the high profile of premillennial authors such as Lindsey, LaHaye, Perretti, and an army of traditional dispensational scholars and popularizers. For the broader theological conversation, then, phrases such as a transitional millennial phase or historical millennialism may illumine the pathway and advance the discussion.

Historic or transitional millennialism affirms that the eschatological sections of Scripture likely have application to all of human history, Jewish history, and church history, and the ultimate future. This approach contrasts with Wright's nearly thoroughgoing preterism. Transitional millennialism contends that there is an underlying continuity throughout past, present, and future history and that there is both continuity and discontinuity in already/not yet redemptive history, which is akin to the continuity and discontinuity of the resurrection body of Christ. Christ's return is necessary to move reality via a quantum leap toward the new creation, and there is a necessary transitional phase between the return of Christ and the fullness of the new creation that is analogous to what premillennialists refer to as the millennium.

In this chapter I argue that naïve postmillennialism should be rejected as soundly as escapist, literalistic, dispensational, and fatalistic premillennialism. While contending that shrewd postmillennialism is a great improvement over nineteenth and twentieth-century naïve utopianism, shrewd utopianism still typically drifts from orthodox beliefs in other areas and ultimately fails relative to theological and anthropological assumptions and scripturally sound projections on the limits of civilizational change prior to the *Parousia*. In one sense, though shrewd utopianism is better than naïve utopianism, it also is arguably more dangerous because it is more seductive. Saler and Wright seem to lean toward just such a seductive and shrewd utopianism.

Hence, *heaven, the symbol of the ultimate perfected future, may be, from the human standpoint, the present cosmos transformed.*[15] The next eschatological phase or millennial transitionary period would be understood as a process,[16] and its character should direct, lure, and find approximation in the present.

---

15. This italicized sentence is a direct quote (Matthews, "Approximating," 41).

16. It is important to note that Cullmann's perspective is markedly different from

The twin anticipations of cruciform approximation and millennial consummation in history, when synthesized with premillennialism's awareness of the reality of sin and antichrist, may provide an adequate foundation for a theology of cultural engagement that is prophetic, proleptic, hopeful, and realistic. Such an approach is also more precise than existing options concerning the outcomes and limits of cultural change. It may be able to combine the spirit and creation affirmation of postmillennial activism with the cruciform and realistic awareness of the intransigent nature of sin typical of amillennialism and premillennialism—and with all of these themes integrated under the umbrella of a biblically, theologically, and philosophically sound and empirically based view of the future.

A RELEVANT VISION

Brown notes, "It need not be the case the concern with eschatology leads to irrelevance or to a widening of the gap between Christian faith and social responsibility. In fact, I would urge that it is within the framework of Christian eschatology that social and political concern can be understood most profoundly.[17] Eschatology is the rocket fuel of movements for change, whether for good or ill—with the Great Century of Missions, the City Set on a Hill, the Third Reich (realm or kingdom), the War to End All Wars, "I have a dream," anarchistic dystopianism, or the classless society being examples of such familiar visions in the West. Eschatology rules church, state, and culture. It is most important to note that the kingdom concept is at the core of biblical eschatology and that the kingdom concept is at the core of the

---

traditional dispensational premillennialism and many more Platonic versions of amillennialism. While Cullmann certainly has a futurist element in his view of phase one of the new creation, his view truly separates the gold from the dross and is better characterized as an already-not-yet view of the kingdom. Relative to millennial views, his view would be best classified as a greatly modified premillennialism or even more so an amillennialism that not only emphasizes transformation of this present age, but also implies that continuity remains between the present age and phase one of the new creation (and beyond). Cullmann's key emphases relevant to this study include the significance of the already in-breaking kingdom for current kingdom advance, and the significance of the continuity of history for grounding all current kingdom work in the future restored (rather than abolished) creation. Platonic eschatology tends to make rigid divisions between the present and the future, such as affirming the absolute and total destruction of the current cosmos, viewing heaven as otherworldly, or viewing the *Parousia* and millennium as trans-historical rather than viewing the future through the lens of continuity and fulfillment. For Cullmann, history is history—there are not multiple radically and qualitatively distinct kinds of history. See Cullmann, *Christ and Time*; Juza, "New Testament."

17. Brown, "Eschatological Hope," 146.

Third Reich (realm or kingdom) Nazi heresy. The kingdom concept is the implied core of virtually every civilizational future vision. No wonder the kingdom was the central concept guiding the teaching, life, and ministry of Jesus. The issue is not if one has an eschatology but which one, is it sound, and what are its personal and civilizational consequences.

Stanley Hauerwas has criticized theologians such as Reinhold Niebuhr who are suspicious of eschatology, for in Hauerwas's view "eschatology is the *very basis* for Jesus' ethical teaching" and thus for social activism.[18] If this is true, then Cullmann and others are right in affirming that the cross and resurrection are fundamentally eschatological events.

Rauschenbusch, discussed in the prior chapter, rightly observes that escapist eschatology is actually inconsistent with the essential assumptions of premillennialism and "all the more pathetic because the pre-millennial [sic] scheme is really an outline of the social salvation of the race." He remarks concerning such misconceptions, that, in his day, "no other theological influence so hampers and obstructs the social gospel as that of eschatology."[19]

While the allegations of fatalistic eschatological pessimism have merit relative to some premillennialists, the accusations do point to this eschatology's valuable and deep awareness of the brokenness and ambiguity of human existence. Those suffering from dispensational eschatomania were not terribly surprised by the negatives of the twentieth century—by Auschwitz or Hiroshima or Rwanda. Premillennialism, even in its crude form, points to a human nature and civilization in need of cross and resurrection. Amillennialism always has recognized human fallenness, but twentieth-century events especially brought sad confirmation of premillennialism's deep sensitivity to apocalypse and the power of antichrist—the extremes of cultural depravity and depraved power. We should not be entirely surprised by premillennial fiction selling forty million copies in the late twentieth century, for there is a kernel in the husk of this flawed perspective. When purified of gross premillennial speculation and literalism, this not-yet and apocalyptic paradigm effectively informs the church concerning these past and future anthropological and historical realities. Close attention to this not-yet emphasis might have made unnecessary the following: "Karl Barth in Europe revived the Calvinist picture of human depravity, and Hitler arose to illustrate it."[20] Reinhold Niebuhr might not have had to struggle to remind the church and the world of "the brutal character of human collectives," the

18. Hauerwas and Willimon, *Resident Aliens*, 76–87.

19. Rauschenbusch, *Theology*, 210–11. Rauschenbusch does not embrace premillennialism but notes that it is not totally wrong in substance. See Rauschenbusch, *Theology*, 224–25; Matthews, "Approximating," 315–445.

20. Bainton, *Christian Attitudes*, 216.

"persistence of rational egoism," or humanity's "selfish and unselfish," "self-seeking and self-giving," "self-destructive as well as creative" impulses and powers.[21] It is within this theological mileu that cruciform kingdom service may be better comprehended and applied to the present moment.

A PROPHETIC VISION

Closely related to awareness of the theme of human brokenness is the potential prophetic role of not-yet eschatology, especially when wedded to a theology of the cross. The use of *prophetic* is not meant as predictive but proclamative. The not-yet conception is never fully satisfied with the status quo, even the status quo of individualistic existential despair, for the present always falls short of the future idea while ever moving toward Paradise regained. Jürgen Moltmann, when discussing the "sin of despair," criticizes the pessimism of existentialists such as Camus for abandoning hope in the name of realism. Moltmann argues, that "in adopting this so-called realism dictated by the facts [of reality] we fall victim to the worst of all utopias—the utopia of the *status quo,* as R. Musil has called this kind of realism."[22] A not-yet rejection of status quoism is consistent with Moltmann's concern and inherently biblical, for as Moltmann argues, "It is difficult to wage a revolution without the Bible (Ernst Bloch). It is even more difficult not to bring about a revolution with the Bible."[23] This observation is consonant with Wright's view of the cross as the day the revolution began. Wright's *The Day the Revolution Began* might have been augmented by such insights from Moltmann.

Moltmann correctly reasons, "Christian theology exists for the purpose not of following after the *Zeitgeist* and bearing its train, but for carrying before it the torch of hope and enkindling the fire of criticism in lazy humanity."[24] Carl Braaten, sympathetic to the Theology of Hope, speaks of the "heavenly critique of earthly existence. It [biblical eschatology] does not teach mere resignation in the face of exploitation, but liberation from oppression." The apocalyptic trend can prophetically lead to "the movement of protest in the revolutionary struggle against the established order."[25] Yet the "revolutionary struggle" itself is quite susceptible to a cancerous theology

21. Niebuhr, *Moral Man*, xix–xx, 25; *Man's Nature*, 106; *Christian Realism*, 6.

22. Moltmann, *Theology of Hope*, 23.

23. Moltmann, *Experiment Hope*, 6.

24. Moltmann, *Experiment Hope*, 46.

25. Braaten, *Eschatology and Ethics*, 130.

of glory and the replacing of oppression with a new form of oppression cloaked by the claim of liberation.

Hence, it is critical to remember that the revolutionary struggle itself, seeking to usher in the not yet, may and must be critiqued by the biblical not yet, for within the very struggle for liberation would be found the two seeds of both kingdom approximation and tribulational approximation (and antichrist). Neither progress nor decline is inevitable. Establishment figures and revolutionaries alike are subject to the critique of the prophetic message of cross and kingdom. The 1960s cultural revolution in America was instructive. Those opposing the establishment turned out to be subject to the same flaws as the establishment. Many cultural leaders of this American cultural revolution decried the loss of life in war, while encouraging a drug culture that destroyed countless lives, including their own. The Bolshevik and Cuban revolutions, and countless revolutions across the globe, are equally instructive. Conservative *or* liberal sentiments may be of antichrist, depending on the historical context and the nature of the sentiments.

A PURPOSE-FILLED VISION

Brown argues that the "belief that there is a fulfillment or a consummation, without trying to date it, safeguards belief in the meaningfulness of the whole historical enterprise. That is to say, one can affirm that human history under God has direction and purposiveness, that history is going somewhere."[26] Brown continues,

> Such an interpretation also safeguards against placing *all* of the meaning and significance of our existence within the temporal framework. We are rescued from the folly of placing all of our theological eggs in one utopian basket, only to have them smashed to bits when the bottom falls out of the basket. That the "fulfillment" is not simply the result of human striving, that it represents the activity of God rather than the activity of men, that it represents a judgment on our intentions and a fulfillment of God's intentions—such considerations help us even in the midst of our historical striving, to keep our attention where it needs to be: on what God can do both through us and in spite of us, for the furtherance of His mighty will. So the significance of our historical striving is seen in its relation to a more ultimate significance than can be measured in merely historical terms. Historical activity is intensely meaningful, but it is meaningful

26. Brown, "Eschatological Hope," 147.

because it is picked up, transformed, judged, purged, and fulfilled—by God.[27]

Postmillennialism, and even neo-postmillennialism or shrewd postmillennialism where the extreme difficulties of and significant time required for kingdom advance are acknowledged, seems inattentive to the intransigent and insidious presence of sin in history and, therefore, reflects an inadequate theological anthropology. The horror of the cross forever underscores the horror of humanity and civilization apart from grace. Not all postmillennialists are naïvely utopian, but they do perilously apply the millennial symbol to an era *prior* to the *Parousia*. A theology of cross and an already-not-yet kingdom questions whether any variety of postmillennialism is truly in touch with the depth of human social brokenness, from war to slavery to torture to human trafficking, or with a host of personal and social tragedies, the pain and agony of which defy the imagination. Kingdom approximation seems a more fitting description of pre-*Parousia* social and historical possibilities than *millennium, utopia, new society, new man or new humanity, Great Society, New World Order,* or *liberated existence.* And the New Age movement, with its emergent deified humanity and utopia, is especially out of touch with biblical reality and anthropology. The New Age movement lacks both a cross and an actual space-time *Parousia.*

Relative to all of these flawed visions, humanity would be better served by a cross and kingdom eschatology that shrewdly strives for utopian approximations rather than realizations. Such a vision is truly impressed, though not awestruck, with the dark side of existence and history. Cross and resurrection and Pentecost and already/not yet kingdom are critical norms and assumptions for theology and mission.

The already/not yet also avoids a similar weakness of some modern variations of postmillennialism, or neo-postmillennialism, which view millennial type realities as largely or solely developmental, or evolutionary possibilities or inevitabilities. Cross and kingdom millennial eschatology argues that some element of a catastrophic act of God is needed for the restoration of the creation, though the organic motif need not be entirely jettisoned. And the inaugurated kingdom perspective would quickly reject any postmillennial variation that considers progress as inevitable.

This cross and kingdom framework fills tedious, patient, daily kingdom service with needed hope and realism. We have seen how Moody's escapist hope severs eschatology from creation, incarnation, cross, kingdom, and consummation: "I look on this world as a wrecked vessel. God

27. Brown, "Eschatological Hope," 147.

has given me a life-boat, and said to me, 'Moody, save all you can.'"[28] Carl F. H. Henry accurately argues that any view of the future that undermines the "world-relevance" of the gospel is less than biblical. "Whatever in our kingdom views undercuts that relevance," he concludes, "destroys the essential character of Christianity as such."[29] Moody's fatalistic pessimism, as well as eschatological perspectives that negate the biblical verity that the next phase of God's kingdom work includes some measure of paradise regained, diminish the creation, history, cross, and kingdom.

Alva McClain brilliantly explores Cullmann's principle of continuity and makes the case for cruciform approximation in the present age by critiquing eschatological views laced with pessimism or escapism or any view that rejects the ultimate transformation of the present created order. This passage is truly *critical* for the argument of this work. Cruciform kingdom sacrifice really matters and all ahistorical future-visions, including some versions of neoorthodoxy, fail as follows:

> Thus [for many eschatological views] history becomes the preparatory "vestibule" of eternity, and not a very rational vestibule at that. It is a narrow corridor, cramped, and dark, a kind of "waiting room," leading nowhere *within* the historical process, but only fit to be abandoned at last for an ideal existence on another plane. Such a view of history seems unduly pessimistic, in light of Biblical revelation. While we . . . cannot, of course, accept the liberal illusion of human progress . . . [and its naïve anthropology], we must nevertheless reject likewise the "historical" despair of the theology of crisis.[30]

This critique applies both to neoorthodoxy and any amillennial view that affirms the annihilation of the creation or even a magical leap from the present order of things to a restored new creation. And the term *revolution* needs to be used most judiciously by those stepping into the participatory and approximative theology of cross and kingdom. In contrast to flawed views, unbounded love, meaning, and purpose overflow from McClain's vision of a future that fulfills rather than discounts the historical and civilizational process.

Jesus came proclaiming a global kingship and coming kingdom. He did not speak of the future or the presence of the future to ease human curiosity or merely supply a theological sedative. He demanded repentance. He called for change. His way is the way of the cross and the empty tomb.

28. Moody, "Return," 185.
29. Henry, *Uneasy Conscience*, 53.
30. McClain, "Premillennial Philosophy," 113.

His reign is a global reign with a future and already/not yet global manifestation. He spoke of and embodied the future in order to impact the present and transform the future of the entire cosmos. Jesus incarnated *via dolorosa* and kingdom.

Hence, the purpose of cruciform biblical eschatology is not merely to understand, predict, and interpret the future in various ways; the point is to *be it and change* it.[31] Webber illustrates this outlook with a call to action:

> Today Christians live in the recognition that the powers have been disarmed [by the cross and kingdom] and that Christ will ultimately destroy all evil. Christ's power over evil is both a present reality and a future hope. Consequently, we are called to a social involvement that seeks to transform [or, preferred, "impact and influence"] the present culture, moving it toward a greater approximation of the ideal. We ought not to expect a utopia to result. But we ought to believe that change is possible and that working for this change is a way of witnessing to the ultimate reality of God's kingdom. The Christian hope that sin will be destroyed and peace will reign is more than a dream. It is a task that we are to work toward even though we know it will be universally realized only by the consummation of Christ's work in [or, preferred, "in, through, and subsequent to"] His second coming.[32]

De Chardin, though utopian, essentially got it right concerning the passion or eschatological propellant that drives Christian mission: "expectation—anxious, collective and operative expectation of an end of the world, that is to say of an issue for the world—that is perhaps the supreme Christian function and the most distinctive characteristic of our religion."[33] Eschatology rules. Eschatology is the rocket fuel of kingdom advance.

---

31. This sentence, obviously, is a deliberate alteration of Marx's thesis XI in Marx, "Theses on Feuerbach," 158. Moltmann also alludes, though he makes no direct reference, to Marx's thesis: "The theologian is not concerned merely to supply a different *interpretation* of the world, of history and of human nature, but to *transform* them in expectation of a divine transformation" (Moltmann, *Theology of Hope*, 84). Schillebeeckx makes a similar statement as Moltmann: "We Christians used to interpret the world differently from non-Christians, but we did not transform it—and this is what really matters" (Schillebeeckx, *Schillebeeckx Reader*, 253). Marx's philosophy at least advocated for a better earthly future, though no attempt is being made here to sanction any, much less the whole, of his flawed political thought, or his implicitly naïve anthropology and utopianism. Indeed, someone has referred to Marxism as an eschatological heresy and distortion of Christian eschatology. Marxism's anthropology and eschatology are interconnected, and both fail miserably.

32. Webber, *Secular Saint*, 195.

33. Teillhard de Chardin, *Divine Milieu*, 151.

"Eschatophobia" robs the mission of the church of that fuel and stalls out the very *missio Dei*.[34] The prerequisite pillars of eschatologically animated kingdom advance are cruciform. Reality can and will change in the dawning of the new creation, especially *via dolorosa*. It will be helpful to clarify and explicate further the contours of this already/not yet cruciform kingdom framework.

A BIBLICAL ALREADY VISION

Beasley-Murray asserts, "Accordingly the *Kingdom of Christ is present among men in this world now*. Every line in the New Testament is written in the consciousness of the truth of that affirmation."[35] The kingdom already has been released as a force in history through the Christ-event, and while total victory is *Parousia*-dependent, temporary advances are attainable.

Cullmann's general orientation has been introduced in chapter 9, and he has, perhaps more so than any other scholar, delineated and elucidated the theological and eschatological foundation for a biblical theology of cross and kingdom. Cullmann recognizes the already aspect of New Testament teaching on the kingdom. For New Testament believers, the "characteristic thing" of "this present period" is that "the '*world*' *has already been drawn into the redemptive process*," meaning the kingdom has decisively invaded the present world order.[36] Note the contrast here on kingdom teaching with that which tends to locate Satan's defeat, social betterment, and the kingdom itself solely in the future. Pessimistic fatalism, date-setting, and rapture-escapism are closely related to an exclusively futuristic view of the kingdom and an escapist and solely transactional view of the cross. Isaac C. Rottenberg aptly draws attention to the social implications of this type of futurism: "When the 'not yet' is stressed at the expense of the 'already,' the world tends to be viewed as being under the rule of Satan, and a spirit of escapism and other-worldliness often prevails. There is much talk about heaven and the hopelessness of any human efforts to establish a more just social order."[37] In marked contrast to this excessive and despairing futurism, Cullmann synthesizes the future and present aspects of the kingdom. He explains, "The situation in redemptive history of the present, which lies between Christ's resurrection and *Parousia*, is a complex one; it is determined by the noteworthy tension between past and future, between 'already

34. Erickson, *Christian Theology*, 1152.
35. Beasley-Murray, *Highlights*, 76.
36. Cullmann, *Christ and Time*, 212.
37. Rottenberg, *Promise*, 48.

fulfilled' and 'not yet fulfilled.' The world is already ruled by Christ, and yet its present 'form' is passing away (1 Cor. 7:31)."[38]

Cullmann's theses, introduced in chapter 9, that the world has been drawn into the redemptive process, that the kingdom has decisively invaded the present, and that Christ's reign already has, in some sense, been established are strikingly pregnant with social relevance and serve as the foundation of Wright's theology of the revolutionary cross. Cullmann's recognition that the consummation is yet future guards against pre-*Parousia* utopianism and utopian triumphalism: "The decisive battle has already been won. But the war continues until a certain, though not as yet definite, Victory Day when the weapons will at last be still. The decisive battle would be Christ's death and resurrection, and Victory Day, his *Parousia*."[39]

In Cullmann's interpretation of the biblical teaching on the kingdom, there exists a powerful averment of the biblical doctrine of creation. The Christ-event, including the incarnation, cross and resurrection, is in time and in the creation. Consistent with Cullmann's thesis, in the New Testament, the resurrection, in contrast to Greek speculation, is historical and physical and paves the way for the eschatological consummation. Cullmann also observes that the world is "drawn into the redemptive process" as the result of the Christ-event at the center or midpoint of the Christian view of time.[40] The *Parousia* is not yet, but the cross and resurrection mean that already "Christ rules as Lord over all things on heaven and on earth!"[41] The *not yet* will occur on earth and in time and will transform the created order. Cullmann denounces the Platonic polarization of time and eternity, a polarization that still persists in theology. According to Cullmann the New Testament view is that eternity is extended unilinear time; it is transformed time: "Eternity is the endless succession of ages."[42] Time, Cullmann argues, "is conceived as a line upon which every section has its significance," thus ruling out both naïve "world affirmation" and "simple world denial."[43] Regardless of Cullmann's thesis about time, this vantage point is very pro-creation and pro-incarnation.

The past work of Christ is decisive. New Testament Christianity cannot be charged with thoroughgoing eschatomania, for in the New Testament, Cullmann contends, "The norm is no longer that which is to come; it

38. Cullmann, *Christ and Time*, 212.

39. Cullmann, *Salvation in History*, 44.

40. Cullmann, *Christ and Time*, 211–12.

41. Cullmann, *Christ and Time*, 211.

42. Cullmann, *Christ and Time*, 62.

43. Cullmann, *Christ and Time*, 213.

is He who has already come."[44] Still, victory awaits final consummation, in history, in time, in creation, and in the present cosmos.

Cullmann's view that eternity is unending time implies that the creation, likewise, will be granted eternality.[45] In light of these considerations, the doctrine of a transitional millennium as a next phase in creation restoration no longer seems particularly peculiar but instead serves as a reasonable assumption concerning the next stage of redemptive history in a fallen world. Postmillennial paradigms unrealistically ignore humanity's state of contradiction and affirm that this next stage of history can arrive without the next decisive act of God—the *Parousia*. Traditonal amillennialism often denies that there is a next stage of history and contends that either the entire cosmos will be annihilated or cataclysmically catapulted into the eternal state or the fullness of the new creation at the *Parousia*. Wright's amillennialism, as noted in this chapter, seems to be a more constructive new earth amillennialism. Cullmann's view strikes a reasonable and scripturally based balance and sound *via media* between all of these eschatological extremes and heralds kingdom approximation now and the already-not-yet restoration of a severely blemished creation and humanity.

A MORE PRECISE VISION CONTRA ALL FORMS OF UTOPIANISM

The appropriation of many of these movements or concepts and goals such as utopia, millennium, or new age implicitly assumes the attainability of that which is properly viewed in already/not yet thought as exclusively *Parousia*-dependent.[46] Spokespersons of some of these more post-Barthian move-

44. Cullmann, *Christ and Time*, 139.

45. Cullmann, *Christ and Time*, 62. Ladd summarizes, "In Hellenism people longed for release from the cycle of time in a timeless world beyond, but in biblical thought time is the sphere of human existence both now and in the future." (Ladd, *Theology*, 47). See the Greek on Rev 10:6. The authorized version of this verse is misleading and essentially Platonic.

46. Other utopianisms will be discussed, but an American evangelical form of shrewd utopianism, Greg Bahnsen's Christian reconstructionism, is instructive. His self-described "evangelical postmillennialism" recognizes some naïveté in earlier post-millennial formulations, though, he would argue, not as much as is often assumed to be the case. Bahnsen affirms that his postmillennialism is aware of the suffering of the saints in this age, the depth of opposition to the gospel, and the present perplexing problems in the world. He senses that America is in great trouble. He believes that most, not all, nations will be converted, and that this conversion is gradual and by God's grace operative through the church. The millennium is not ushered in by human effort alone. At this point there is much in common between his work and the position developed

ments do warn against naïve or triumphalistic utopianism.[47] Moltmann counsels, "Christian hope is no blind optimism. It is a discerning hope which sees suffering and yet believes in freedom."[48] Nevertheless, the cross and kingdom eschatology affirmed in this work would suggest that any perspective toying with the idea of a non-*Parousia*-dependent full realization of new creation realities in any strong sense—or even an overstatement of the longitudinal possibility of significant partial realizations (e.g., "world peace" or Wilson's "war to end all wars") is indeed utopian and subject to great disillusionment or total corruption in the crucible of historical experience. The world may become more peaceful overall prior to Christ's return, for seasons of unknown duration, with regional variations, but the abolition of all war is subsequent to Christ's Second Coming. To believe otherwise runs counter to the entire biblical narrative and touches the very edges of heterodoxy, heteropraxy, and heteropathy. False future-visions distort the beliefs, praxis, and passions of individuals, communities, the church, and civilization.

Numerous modern eschatologies, whether theistic, pantheistic-monistic, panentheistic, or secular, grant the possibility of something akin to a utopia or millennium prior to and apart from the biblical conception of the *Parousia*. Cullmann's perspective rejects the idea that the terms *millennium* or *utopia* can be applied in any sense to any historical period antecedent to Christ's return. There can be no new age, in the strong sense of the term, until Christ returns. There can be significant, long-lasting improvement or retrogression in the current age, but the expectation of arriving at a new level of historical existence, with a "new man" or new person or new humanity

---

in this chapter, with the main exception being that it would be better to speak of the conditional Christian influence on many nations rather than the conversion of many nations. The symbols he applies to pre-*Parousia* millennial possibilities, however, are simply too utopian, and unrealistic and in conflict with a sound biblical anthropology that recognizes realistic limits to fallen humanity under grace in the present era. Simply put, only another act of God in Christ of the magnitude of the Exodus or the Christ-event can actualize Bahnsen's entire list of pre-*Parousia* victories. His list includes the following: the universal Christianization and salvation of the world, not conceived in absolute terms but in terms of cultural dominance; the widespread conversion of the nations; the realization of the millennium of Rev 20; the vast numerical increase of believers; the moral improvement of all areas of life, such as just laws and charity for the poor; and, the universal diffusion of Christian knowledge (Heb 8:11) so that even the bells on the horses (Zech 14:20, RSV) will say, "Holy to the Lord." See Bahnsen, "In What Ways"; *No Other Standard*. It will be argued that the term *millennium*, which incorporates all of these ideas, is best applied to the era after the *Parousia*.

47. See, for example, Bonino, *Toward a Christian*, 138–39.

48. Moltmann, "Politics," 291. He clearly avoids a blind or naïve utopianism, but his "shrewd" utopianism still has dangerous idealistic tendencies.

or new society is a socially hazardous and naïvely utopian sentiment. Both end-times fatalism and aspirations for a perfect union now are poisonous to long-term cruciform kingdom melioration. Idealist semantics, relative either to theological anthropology or eschatology, frequently surfaced in theologies such as Liberation, Hope, and Process.[49] A vision of a more perfect union lies much closer to Scripture, common sense, historical data, and sound theology.

Utopianisms that motivate the oppressed to strive for that which is only *Parousia*-dependent are very vulnerable to manipulation of the masses, demonic corruption, and devastating disillusionment: "Because of man's very nature, therefore, Christian anthropology is Christian futurology and Christian eschatology."[50] Kingdom or already/not yet approximation in the present is cruciform and depends on grace, repentance, and sacrifice due to the fallen and contradictory nature of human existence. And anything remotely resembling new creation or millennial realization likewise requires epic grace, even the grace upon grace of the *Parousia*. Scripture clearly views the *Parousia* as flowing from the Christ-event but also as one of the main events of redemptive history; hence, it is of the theological, supernatural, and revelatory magnitude of other mega-events such as the creation, Exodus, or bodily and glorious resurrection.

Hence, the *Parousia*-dependent nature of the not yet kingdom is a helpful corrective to all forms of pre-*Parousia* utopianism, and clearly this truth needs much repetition. The worthy goal of utopia will not and cannot emerge entirely "from below," from the All who is God (pantheism), the all that is in God (panentheism), the dialectical forces of materialism evolving in history (Marxism), the inevitable progress of evolution, the realization of the Absolute (Hegel), or even from the grace-assisted ministry of evangelical Christian believers (nineteenth-century postmillennialism or twentieth-century Calvinistic Christian Reconstructionism). The greatest approximations of the future millennial fulfillment of history will always fall short of the ideal. History, therefore, awaits another mega-act of God in Christ as the spark that will ignite the millennial or transitional process to the fullness of the new creation. The return of Christ is the true and globally transformational revolution.

Lance Morrow perhaps states the situation best: "Pol Pot's Khmer Rouge sent to the killing fields all who spoke French or wore glasses or had

49. For overviews, see Nash, *Liberation Theology*; *Process Theology*. There are endless varieties of these movements; thus, all statements about these movements are generalizations. Some of these varieties may be consistent with the perspective developed in this chapter.

50. Rahner, *Foundations*, 431.

soft hands. The Khmer Rouge aimed to cancel all previous history and begin at Year Zero. *Utopia, this century has learned the hard way, usually bears a resemblance to hell.* An evil chemistry turns the dream of salvation into damnation."[51]

Webber makes a similar argument rooted in core Christian convictions:

> The Christian message *is* characterized by hope, but to assume that the new creation can become a reality apart from the second coming of Christ fails to consider the radical nature of sin and the biblical view of history. Certainly the more liberal notion of transformation and the nineteenth-century hope that the twentieth would be the Christian century are mocked by the deplorable events of the twentieth century. A view of transformation that neglects the ever-present reality of man's sinful nature and assumes that man is getting better ignores the teaching on sin. . . . The recognition that man is sinful and that Christ's victory over evil will not be complete until He returns and puts evil under his feet forever moderates all utopian idealism.[52]

Karl Barth twice witnessed the betrayal of Christian faith to forms of utopianism, first on the "black day" in 1914 when many of his former teachers proclaimed support of the war policy of Kaiser Wilhelm II, and then again in "the summer of 1933" when the German church began to fall under the sway of the German Christians who supported the "new heresy strangely blended of Christianity and Germanism," known as "National Socialism." Luther's theology of the cross and theology of glory seem especially relevant to Germany in the 1930s. Indeed, perhaps the latter sin that Barth witnessed under Hitler was greater than the former sin under Wilhelm II in view of the neo-orthodox critique of liberalism that was prior to this Nazi eschatological heresy known as the Third Reich, Realm, or Kingdom. Barth notes that he "could not very well keep silent but had to undertake to proclaim to the imperiled church what it must do to be saved."[53]

Contemporary events ceaselessly chasten the naïve optimism that Barth renounced. The daily news from across the globe is revealing. Hence, shrewd and neo-utopian hopeful eschatologies, rebuked by twentieth- and twenty-first-century blood-soaked realities, proliferating shameless spin, proliferating outrage, nuclear and terroristic actualities, at least recognize the difficulty, complexity, and setbacks involved in social transformation. Pierre Teilhard de Chardin, for example, takes seriously the issue of the

---

51. Morrow, "Evil," 51 (emphasis added).

52. Webber, *Secular Saint*, 186–87.

53. Barth, *How I Changed*, 45.

survival of the cosmos as it journeys toward the Omega point.[54] Jose Miguez Bonino rejects the idea that Liberation theology ignores sin or naïvely chases after utopia.[55] And Moltmann accepts the fact that there are limits to Christian influence in the world. He is quite explicit in rejecting Christian "triumphalism."[56]

Nevertheless, a softened, or shrewd pre-*Parousia* utopianism appears to remain in such hopeful eschatologies that directly conflicts with common sense and a biblical anthropology and a biblical theology of cross and kingdom. The Second Advent, according to Moltmann, is essentially the symbol for "a power which already qualifies the present—through promise and hope, through liberation and the creation of new possibilities. As this power of the future, God reaches into the present."[57] While the *Parousia* being a symbol or power in the present has critical significance for Moltmann, the actual event itself is almost marginal in his shrewd utopianism. With de Chardin, the *Parousia* appears to refer to the *telos* or ultimate consummation of the evolutionary process.[58] In these eschatologies something similar to utopia arrives prior to and apart from an actual *Parousia* through longsuffering and setbacks; nevertheless, utopia is not truly *Parousia*-dependent. The *Parousia* also seems redefined such that it moves into a new theological genre of symbol, allegory, existential aspiration, or the divine lure and process, drawing the cosmos toward its true future. The *Parousia* as *the* actual space-time, supernatural event ushering in the new creation becomes diminished and dissolved by the larger and more central philosophical and theological agenda. Biblical anthropology and eschatology are therefore undermined in such constructions.

Already-not-yet eschatology is not inherently inimical to some of the helpful insights of a Moltmann or Bonino if it is recognized that the power before us, invading or luring the present, can at best result only in kingdom approximation prior to Christ's return and that such approximation is typically wrought by cruciform sacrifice. If what they are saying is that utopia can be approximated now, with significant limitations requiring much semantic caution, and that our ultimate social hope is the King and his coming this-worldly global kingdom, then they are essentially adopting a millennial already/not yet outlook by default. Yet semantic caution seems muted. A conflict arises when someone claims that convergence at Omega

54. Teilhard de Chardin, *Phenomenon*, 22–72.

55. Bonino, *Toward a Christian*, 87–95.

56. Bauckham, *Moltmann*, 138–39.

57. Moltmann, "Hope and History," 376–77.

58. Teilhard De Chardin, *Phenomenon*, 163–273.

or some form of utopia can be realized solely via the developmental spirit of evolution or the power of hope in the present. Unfortunately, Moltmann's language is simply too utopian when he seems to predict the following apart from the *Parousia*: "Some day the biblical theology of 'it is written' will become an ontology of 'it has taken place.' Some day in nature, in history, and in society, we will no longer encounter temptations and contradictions but . . . promise and reality; hope and experience will be in accord."[59]

In like manner Moltmann affirms that God's kingdom "will come in its full identity into the world." The "ultimate liberation of the world," he contends, "is *already possible* through the faith-creating word," which is "nothing less than a messianic possibility."[60] It is in light of these statements that some have classified Moltmann as a somewhat secularized postmillennialist or neo-postmillennialist.[61] Moltmann's utopianism is more shrewd than, say, a Rauschenbusch's,[62] but such shrewdness is only to be expected after Nietzsche's predicted century of terror. Teilhard de Chardin's uncritical acceptance of evolution as the central metaphysical insight[63] so exalts the evolutionary utopian motif that he seems to accommodate to culture at times, as when he blessed repressive and totalitarian regimes.

This discussion of the perils of shrewd utopianism is required in view of the kind of clarity needed relative to Wright and Saler's eschatologies. Wright's revolution language needs to be better parsed in terms of what applies to the already and what applies to the not yet emanating from the day the revolution began. More specificity is essential. A biblical theology of cross and kingdom requires at least some precision *contra* perilous utopianisms.

Only a true, *theopnustos* utterance by a biblical prophet can set limitations on what degree of cultural and civilizational impact is realizable and viable *prior to the Parousia*, but Table 7 might assist with clarifying the desired eschatological precision needed to guide the cruciform, new creation mission of the church. The contrasts and comparisons of that which is

59. Moltmann, *Experiment Hope*, 45.

60. Moltmann, *Experiment Hope*, 45 (emphasis added).

61. Bloesch, *Essentials*, 193.

62. Rauschenbusch, however, also expressed caution, emphasized grace, and was not blindly utopian. See Rauschenbusch, *Theology*, 227.

63. Teilhard De Chardin, *Phenomenon*, 212–37. He writes that evolution is a "general condition to which all theories, all hypotheses, all systems must bow and which they must satisfy, henceforward, if they are to be thinkable and true. Evolution is a light, illuminating all facts, a curve that all lines must follow" (Teilhard De Chardin, *Phenomenon*, 218). He believes that modern humanity must see everything, including himself, in terms of biological space-time.

viewed as achievable prior to Christ's return are fallible, illustrative, and not exhaustive, and the three views briefly presented are, of course, representative of much more variety and diversity than what can be expressed in this didactic tool. This table compares and contrasts the affirmations or assumptions of naïve utopianism with shrewd utopianism and approximationism.

Table 7. Cross and Kingdom Eschatological Options

Naïve Utopianism or Post-millennialism	Shrewd Utopianism or Postmillennialism	Approximationism
Peace on earth in our time	The difficult, slow, and fitful but eventual realization of peace or the omega point (de Chardin)	A more peaceful earth in our time is possible but uncertain and true global peace is dependent on the *Parousia*
A war to end all wars in our time and make the world safe for democracy	Wars typically breed more wars, wars will likely continue for centuries if not millennia, peace will eventually emerge yet with many setbacks, and some shrewd utopians prefer socialistic alternatives to democracy (or democratic capitalism)	A more peaceful earth in our time is possible but uncertain and true global peace is dependent on the *Parousia* (and political and economic views vary)
The elimination of slavery in our time	Slavery could nearly be eradicated in our time if international cooperation obtained—yet this victory is more likely to come after countless centuries of struggle	Slavery can be (and has been) abolished in certain historical contexts, yet historical evidence, theological anthropology and eschatology suggest limitations prior to Christ's return (e.g., human trafficking numbers today may eclipse the slavery of the medieval and modern worlds)

The establishment of social justice and the elimination of poverty in our time	The establishment of social justice and the elimination of poverty can be greatly accelerated but are not fully realizable in our time	The establishment of social justice and the elimination of poverty can be greatly accelerated but are not fully realizable in our time, the church's role has been and could increasingly be significant, gains can easily become losses (apart from grace and vigilance), and programs for justice and the elimination of poverty can easily become diabolic
Prohibition of alcohol in our time	Such prohibition is not morally necessary, yet responsible usage of alcohol can increase century by century	Prohibition was bad eschatology, anthropology, and misread the entrenched culture of alcohol usage, yet the increase of responsible drinking, the decrease of alcoholic content and the decrease of pervasiveness of usage can be actualized over time ·
A *Christian Century*[64] in our time	A rather distant *Christian Century* or omega point may obtain (this could be framed in terms of religious pluralism or a more orthodox perspective such as Wright)	Enhanced Christian influence is challenging but possible, yet anything resembling a *Christian Century*, certainly on a global scale, prior to Christ's return, is dangerously naïve
A Christian theocracy in our time	A rather distant *Christian Century* or omega point may obtain (this could be framed in terms of religious pluralism or a more orthodox perspective such as Wright)	Enhanced Christian influence is challenging but possible, yet anything resembling a *Christian Century*, certainly on a global scale, prior to Christ's return, is dangerously naïve
The elimination of prostitution in our time	As with the abolition of war, significant progress may be made though the outcome is distant	The maintenance of prostitution laws and decrease of prostitution in some cultures is challenging but possible, and the elimination of all prostitution is naïve

64. The italics are intentional and draw attention to the magazine, *The Christian Century*, renamed as such in 1900 in the glow of utopianism. The magazine was originally founded in 1884 as *The Christian Oracle*.

The abolition of abortion in our time	For shrewd utopians who view abortion as immoral, what is achievable is analogous to other issues such as war and prostitution	The prohibition of late term abortions in some civilizational contexts is possible, the elimination of all abortion practices (and reversal of all legal decisions) is fraught with challenges, hard to sustain, yet the persuasion of indeterminate numbers to a pro-life culture is possible
The establishment of Christ's earthly kingdom prior to Christ's return within generations or centuries	The establishment of Christ's earthly kingdom lies in the distant future (and may be uncertain, as with process theology), and likely comes through many tribulations	Proleptic victories are possible, setbacks are to be expected, yet anything remotely resembling an earthly kingdom of Christ on earth is *not yet*

In summary, all forms of pre-*Parousia* utopianism, whether moderate or extreme, naïve or shrewd, tend to claim an absolute realization in the present that is inconsistent with historical evidence, biblical anthropology, and a biblical eschatology that reserves utopian manifestations for *the* future mighty act of God. Cross and kingdom eschatological approximation is the way forward.

A PROLEPTIC VISION

Perhaps Carl Braaten has, more than any other theologian, given direct attention to and clarified a concept closely akin to approximation. Braaten, who builds upon the work of Wolfhart Pannenberg, finds the "clue to the relationship of eschatology to ethics" in "the nature of the presence of the eschatological future in the person and activity of the historical Jesus. . . . [For Braaten the clue or] key term is *proleptic*; there is a proleptic presence of the eschatological kingdom in the activity of Jesus."[65] The basic meaning of proleptic, the adjectival form of prolepsis, is "the representation or assumption of a future act or development as if presently existing or accomplished."[66] The application of the proleptic model to a theology of cross and kingdom, where cruciform believers live in the shadow and dawning of the cross, resurrection, the *Parousia*, and the millennial phase of the

65. Bloesch, *Essentials*, 149–52.
66. Braaten, *Eschatology*, 110.

new creation, should produce socially relevant theology. Braaten explores the significance of the proleptic model:

> The kingdom of God which is really future retains its futurity in the very historical events which anticipate it in the present. Christian ethics is not to be understood as the means of producing the future kingdom of God, but only as annunciation, anticipation, and approximation, let us say as "signs of the coming kingdom." Christian ethics must be cast into the shape of eschatological Christology; for as the eschatological rule of God was proleptically present in the speech and actions of Jesus, so also this same eschatological reality can embody itself in the ethical actions of Christians who allow that rule swaying power in their lives. The right order is this: first, thy kingdom come, then thy will be done. The coming of the kingdom in its priority and power is the ground of the possibility of doing God's will on earth. Ethical actions are real, although never more than provisional representations of the ontologically prior and eschatologically future kingdom. Such ethical actions do not realize the kingdom; rather, the kingdom reveals itself through actions that prefigure its coming. The kingdom of God as the highest good may be said to be proleptically present in the ethical decisions and deeds that approximate its ultimate qualities.
>
> The proleptic structure of eschatological ethics has a twofold edge. On the one side, the futurity of the kingdom maintains a critical distance over against the present, so that every human effort and every social form are revealed to be imperfect and tentative ground for boasting [e.g., a false theology of glory] before the Lord who judges all things. On the other side, the presence of the future kingdom in proleptic form offers a real participation in its life, generating a vision of hope and the courage of action to change the present in the direction of ever more adequate approximations of the eschatological kingdom.[67]

Similar to cruciform love, the "ethics of eschatological love," which Braaten calls the "material reality" of the kingdom, "translates itself into an ethics of power and justice in a sinful world 'not yet' fully transformed." Eschatological ethics embraces the idea of a proleptic presence that "provides a bridge to the truth in dispositional ethics." A new state of being is the proleptic act of the God of the future that becomes "the source for a new stream of acts." Braaten views *eschatopraxis* as a more inclusive ethical orientation than dispositional, deed-oriented, or teleological ethics. For

---

67. Braaten, *Eschatology*, 110–11.

example, Marxism's exclusively teleological emphasis is criticized severely, for Braaten states, "The end that justifies is a future good that makes a present impact by bringing the means under judgment." The "ethics of the kingdom of God provide a single point of departure for personal, social and ecological ethics." No "dichotomy" exists "between personal and political ethics" when the kingdom is the "starting point for Christian ethics."[68] Braaten's "starkly simple recapitulation" of the relation between eschatology and ethics includes the following:

> The *leitmotiv* is the future eschatological kingdom of God that has become proleptically present in a definitive way in Jesus of Nazareth. This determines the goal of ethics—the kingdom of God as the highest good. The materially definitive content of the eschatological rule that is revealed in the ministry of Jesus is love. This determines the *norm* of ethics—the *agape* of God as the absolute norm underlying all principles of justice and equality, etc. The proleptic presence of the kingdom of God makes possible a real participation in the new reality that it brings. This determines the *motive* of ethics—the motivating force of the new being in Christ.
>
> Finally, there is the *context* of the ethical decision. Goals, norms, and motives converge upon a concrete context, not to invite us to groove in, but to challenge and to change the present conditions in the direction of a better approximation of the kingdom of God.[69]

Cross and kingdom approximation theology allows for a more prophetic and ethically robust revivification of the spirit of nineteenth-century postmillennialism, a powerful movement "for revival and reform . . . [viewed as] God's way of turning history into the millennium."[70] The church desperately needs eschatological propellant fuel drinkers, yet approximation theology is not disillusioned, defeated, or surprised by historical retrogression and tragedy.

Additionally, cross and kingdom approximation unites the best insights of biblical scholarship concerning the kingdom and then applies them to the social and ethical realm. In Christ the future has invaded the present. The powers of evil have received a debilitating frontal blow that ultimately disables darkness. The powers of evil are wounded, weakened but angry usurpers to Christ's earthly and cosmic throne. Sin is salient in the

---

68. Braaten, *Eschatology*, 116–22.

69. Braaten, *Eschatology*, 122.

70. Weber, "Premillennialism," 8.

present era, but so is the kingdom power of approximative transformation. The present is filled with meaning because of the presence and *telos* of the future. No naïve and doomed attempt is made to Christianize the planet entirely in the pre-*Parousia* era; instead, the church seeks to approximate the future as much as is realistically possible in given historical contexts—with a conscious awareness that the pillars of real change are cruciform.

In one's own life, and in the lives of all individuals, nations, and the global community, some measure of millennial approximation has become a historical possibility due to the impact of D-Day. The trajectory of approximated, but not yet consummated is intensely social and inherently cosmic in scope. This vision guides the church.

A FLUID, GRACE-BASED VISION FOR ECCLESIAL MISSION AND IMPACT

A discussion of key Arminian emphases, introduced in chapter 3, integrated with a theology of cross and kingdom, seem especially relevant at this juncture. The biblical witness and the evidence of history indicate that all such millennial approximation, or non-approximation (*Unheilsgeschichte*),[71] is conditioned upon humanity's response to the ever-present prevenient and common grace of God, and to the the convicting, saving, and sanctifying grace of his present kingdom. From Genesis to Revelation, neither personal nor social sin is viewed as necessary or distinct. Humanity is always held accountable for missing the mark and is never told, "You could not help yourself." The conditional nature of approximation or non-approximation emerges from the central biblical teaching of anthropological and historical conditionalism. Neither history nor humanity can be likened to a puppet an automaton. Why would a puppet be condemned to eternal reprobation? Why care about social justice if all is pre-determined? Because we are pre-determined to care? Such caring is not actually caring.

The tragedy of dark realties such as the Soviet gulag should be framed as abused freedom not predetermined or necessary history, lest God be considered the author of darkness. History is hard to interpret, but a very reasonable assumption is that history varies or fluctuates in terms of darkness or light, depending on time, local, and the human response to context and grace. History varies relative to its correspondence with the ontologically prior *telos* of the new creation. Simply put, history has its good times and bad times, or better and worse times. As my pastor often points out,

---

71. Cullmann speaks of the "history of disaster" due to "sin and judgment" (Cullmann, *Salvation*, 21).

every generation can affirm Dickens's famous quotation, to some degree, that we are living in the "best of times" and the "worst of times." To attribute these fluctuations entirely to divine predetermination reflects badly on God's character and rationality and ultimately makes God the author of *Unheilsgeschichte*. History is open and humanity is a free, grace-dependent agent contributing to this open-ended historical tapestry. Humanity and evil are to blame for tragedy. God's involvement in history is redemptive; he is the author of *Heilsgeschichte*, not *Unheilsgeschichte*.

Agape requires the grace-assisted church, the body of Christ, to experience the cross as it empties itself in the strain to avert endless repetitions of the surd, the demonic, the brutal, the oppressive, the antichrists, and the genocidal. There must be no more gas chambers or killing fields, yet there are no guarantees. The presence of the future demands striving for the liberation of the truly oppressed. The presence of the future requires the preservation and restoration of the present creation that will be the locus of the future. The condition for approximative transformation in the current age largely revolves around the effectiveness of the church of the cross and kingdom.

Crucifixion and sacrifice precede resurrection and transformation.

It is easier to take the non-cruciform and escapist route and be absolved of responsibility for world conditions. William F. Allman writes, "For some, it might be easier to make the single, big decision to abandon one world for the next than to make the countless, smaller, tougher [and cruciform] choices necessary to make this one better."[72] Likewise, the church naturally prefers not to be implicated in the atrocities of history and easily succumbs to socially passive or spectator eschatomania. Doubtless the church can never be held accountable for all the events of history, but surely the community of the future global kingdom bears some responsibility for the present state of the globe. And the legion so-called prophets who endlessly proclaim the arrival of the last generation bear guilt for corrosive civilizational self-fulfilling prophecies.

To be clear, the church cannot and should not pontificate on every conceivable social issue. The problem with such pontification is not that religion and politics don't mix, for theology is inherently political and cultural in scope. The error in such pontification is the assumption that anyone, save God, has the wisdom to speak for the church on the specifics of every imaginable social policy. There always will be a fine line between issues that should and should not be addressed by the church qua church. The church should err on the side of caution in such matters because cross

72. Allman, "Fatal Attraction," 13.

and kingdom anthropology ought to recognize that sin also is capable of invading the church and its movements and pronouncements prior to the *Parousia*. Yet the church of the future global kingdom should be directed towards an intense interest in the details of social policy and contribute, when possible, to the discussion of foundational values and assumptions for human flourishing that are also supportive of the freedom to evangelize and disciple biblically.

Hence, the proper function of the church in approximating the future is to reorient a people toward a life of conscious and cruciform commitment to the King and the coming kingdom of God. Evangelism and discipleship are aspects of this reorientation. The committed community should approximate the kingdom more than any other community. A prophetic witness to those outside the community should follow. Those within the community especially will be devoted to those genuinely oppressed and in need, not just in relief work but also in the attempted melioration of structures. The church will seek to influence those outside its fellowship by interjecting the values of the future, translated for the non-ecclesial context at all levels of society.

Arminian thought emphasizes prevenient or preventing grace and transforming unmerited grace and favor. This is the grace that makes the reception of the gospel possible. This is grace given to all that flows from a cross given for all. This is a universal grace mediated by the Spirit and given after the D-Day of cross, resurrection, and Pentecost. This is the grace that makes civilization and civilization amelioration possible. This is the grace that makes Christian mission possible.

This prevenient grace of cross and kingdom may have affinities with the insights of Carl Braaten. Braaten offers a possible common ground between those who are committed to the future kingdom and the church and those who may be unconsciously committed to a similar future. Braaten argues, "eschatological ethics has universal validity, and is not confined to the context of Christian *koinonia*."[73] His perspective has implications for how the church might partner with others in a post world characterized by philosophical and religious pluralism. He modifies natural law theology within the context of eschatology:

> The eschatological future of the kingdom is the power that draws all men, whether they know it or not. This power has been revealed in the Christ-event as the highest good which all men seek in the quest of personal identity-in-fulfillment. A philosophical analysis of the structure of human action discloses a

73. Braaten, *Eschatology,* 120.

striving for an envisioned good that is absent in the present. Ethical action is therefore constituted by the negation of evil here and now and an affirmation of a transcendent good that is future and yet to be fulfilled. This highest good which Jesus identified as the kingdom of God in his message can be seen retrospectively to be the power at work in every human quest for fulfillment. Therefore, the kingdom of God is proleptically present in all moral systems of mankind as the power of their end, and not only inside the ghetto of a Christian *koinonia*. This presence of the kingdom of God in the universal human striving for the good has been called the "natural law" in the classical tradition. The theory of "natural law" has fortunately been kept alive in the moral theology of Roman Catholicism, but regrettably in a thoroughly non-eschatological form. The values of this tradition can be taken up into the framework of eschatological ethics.[74]

Braaten's use of *natural law* may be controversial, but his observations can be appreciated within a grace-based kingdom framework of prevenient grace. Cullmann's eschatology is most unlikely to regress into a naïve anthropology that uncritically sees the kingdom in "every quest for human fulfillment" and assists with grounding Braaten's insights.

Braaten has touched on the valuable philosophical insight that many outside the church strive for something akin to millennial approximation or realization. Many outside the church understand the limits of progress while striving for a more perfect union. Hence, this striving may serve as a common ground for cultural engagement with those outside the church. Indeed, positive Christian influence on civilizations in the especially pluralistic postmodern context will require collaboration with those under the influence of prevenient grace who may be predisposed to dismiss anything remotely Christian.

Doubtless, some striving for a better future by unbelievers may be self-serving or misguided, arise out of fear, or represent a desire for a carnal kingdom. Yet base motives should not be too quickly attributed to all those outside the church or ignored by those in the church. Grace is universally operative. Those within the church are not exempt from the charge of having base motives, for some seek a present and future materialistic kingdom that requires no cost or cross with virtual or total disregard for the fate of others. The main point here is that the commonality of a *telos* of a better or more perfect future can be an open door for the church, especially in regions of the world where such striving is intense. The American experiment

---

74. Braaten, *Eschatology*, 120.

lauded by many evangelicals was clearly not led primarily by agnostics and anti-supernaturalistic Deists. However, even a quick trip to and review of materials, symbols, artifacts, and architecture in the Library of Congress will confirm that orthodox Christians, evangelical Christians, Rationalisitc Deists, Supernaturalisic Deists, and those influenced both by Christian orthodoxy and the Enlightenment often joined hands to quest for a more perfect union.

Whatever one thinks about the American experiment or any other civilization, prevenient grace is global and fosters common ground. Paul Tillich explores common ground when he speaks of the theological "method of correlation" that "explains the contents of the Christian faith through existential questions and theological answers in mutual interdependence," a method that salvages the "apologetic point of view."[75] All sincere seekers of a better future are asking questions for which the cruciform church of cross and kingdom have realistic, tangible, biblical, hopeful, and persuasive answers. Eschatology rules. All are on epic journeys; the core question is which journey is headed toward the true future.

Proleptic eschatology recognizes that the certain and future ideal is the present transformed, a certain future that already has surfaced in the present through the ministrations of Christ, cross, and church. At the grass roots or the highest levels of society, the church has an avenue of influence for the values of the true kingdom. The proleptic church, if attentive, has inspired advice from beyond for how best to improve the present and future.

The church is continually influenced by the world, and there is no reason why the process cannot be reversed even with recent challenges to the faith. Since the kingdom in its fullness is *Parousia*-dependent, the church will avoid utopian triumphalism while also rejoicing over all penultimate millennial approximations, even those approximations actualized by non-believers in the present age. Thus, the approximation concept, in contrast to the kingdom concept, may be more appropriately applied to the true accomplishments of unbelievers. There may be less theological difficulty in speaking of an unbeliever approximating a future global ideal than in speaking of an unbeliever approximating or advancing the kingdom rule of God, for the latter would imply that the unbeliever is, in some sense, in the kingdom whereas the former would only suggest that the unbeliever contributes to or mimics or is influenced by the future earthly ideal—and by grace.

75. Tillich, *Systematic Theology*, 60.

RECAPITULATION (OF THE CROSS AND KINGDOM THEOLOGICAL FOUNDATION AND VISION)

The cross and kingdom vision affirms the present, engages the present, avoids the tyranny of the future, and yet is centered in the ultimate future of the new creation. The present earth, social relations and activities, which are proleptically being transformed, are the environment and locus of the future millennium. The *telos* is not trans-historical, ethereal, subjective-existential, or totally transcendent reality. The present earth and social relations are not ephemeral on the cosmic time scale. The *telos* is a transformed present and a transformed and restored creation. The present earth is humanity's proper home, not some vague otherworldly form of existence. Christ *returns* to earth, which is a resounding affirmation of the creation. The body is resurrected in Christian thought, not a prison of the soul that is escaped or annihilated. Christianity is earthy, even worldly, though not in the sense of conforming to any present fallen world system. Christianity is about cosmos transformation and historical fulfillment, which inundates the present and the future with purpose, meaning, and value. The experience and realization of this meaning and value, however, is conditionally approximated but not yet consummated.

The cross and kingdom vision unites or unifies the doctrines of creation, fall, incarnation, cross, resurrection, and consummation, and the historical center and manifestation of this vision was the D-Day Christ-event of global transformation. As Robert Webber states, Christ "does not merely 'save souls.' His work affects the whole created order. [Christ] brought a new beginning to man and the whole creation."[76] Webber's thought is rooted in the theology of the ancient church and hints at the idea of the creation being pulled up into and healed by the Christ.[77] Irenaeus believes that the work of God in Christ "sums up all things into himself," including "the long roll of humanity."[78]

This approximation is not triumphalist; thus, no Christianized world or Christian nation, in the strong sense, is sought after or expected in this age. A Judeo-Christian-influenced nation is ever within our sights but not a theocracy. Just like leaven, the presence of the future can spread throughout the many cultures of the globe, impacting and influencing all of reality. Cruciform intellectual and cultural engagement is rooted in the true future and neither triumphalist nor escapist.

76. Webber, *Secular Saint*, 182.

77. See Athanasius, *On the Incarnation*, esp. xviii, 29–30.

78. Irenaeus, "Incarnation," 34–35.

In particular, and especially important for this present work, the motivation for cruciform approximation makes sense by realistically and optimistically grounding current and passionate missional and sacrificial service. What we do matters now. What we do matters eternally in the new creation. What we do matters for time and eternity, and a non-Platonic and biblical conceptualization of eternity is an eternity that shares significant continuity with the present.

In sharp contrast to otherworldly disengagement and escapism, McClain ponders why there is not a purposeful and impactful way forward: "Why should there not be an age in which all . . . unrealized and worthwhile dreams of humanity will at last come true on earth? If there be a God in heaven, if the life which he created on earth is worth-while, and not something evil per se, then there ought to be in history, some worthy consummation of its long and arduous course."[79]

McClain argues that eschatological views lacking such a consummation and approximation on earth and in history rob the present of meaning and direction. He provides the reader with this illustration: "It is like a man building a great staircase. Step by step he sets it up, laboring wearily, often suffering painful reverses because of tragic hazards and poor materials. And now at last it is finished. But lo, it is a stairway that goes no place!"[80] McClain prefers the following future-vision: "It says that life here and now, in spite of the tragedy of sin, is nevertheless something worth-while; and therefore all efforts to make it better are also worth-while. All true values of human life will be preserved and carried over into the coming Kingdom; nothing worthwhile will be lost."[81] McClain's line of thought is worth trailing, and a number of writers have hinted at this view.[82] Oscar Cullmann points out, "Just as the decision in Jesus Christ has already occurred upon earth, so even more must the completion take place precisely upon earth."[83]

---

79. McClain, "Premillennial Philosophy," 115.

80. McClain, "Premillennial Philosophy," 115.

81. McClain, "Premillennial Philosophy," 116.

82. See Beasley-Murray, "Premillennialism," 33; Snyder, "Holy Reign," 83–84; Ladd, "Can the Kingdom?" 70–71. Ladd defines the *Parousia* as "beyond history" in Ladd, *Presence of the Future*, 337. See also Beasley-Murray, *Highlights*, 76; Richard, "Elements," 108–18; Hoyt, "Dispensational Premillennialism," 68–69; Cullmann, *Christ and Time*, 141. McClain does contrast notably, however, with Cullmann. McClain is somewhat Platonic in his view of the eternal when he asserts, "History can deal with the present life, which is temporal. History can have nothing to do with the world to come which is eternal" (McClain, "Premillennial Philosophy," 112). See Cullman, *Christ and Time*, concerning his view of time and eternity and eternity as unending time.

83. Cullmann, *Christ and Time*, 142.

Cross and kingdom approximation, then, advocates the fulfillment and not the abolition of history. It bristles at understandings of the *Parousia* and consummation that suggest a final redemption above or beyond the present cosmos and history. The proleptic view of the kingdom certainly views the fullness of the new creation future as qualitatively superior to the present, but the future is not of a wholly other quality or category. An incarnational view of the consummation negates an exclusively transcendent emphasis that eradicates immanence. Transcendence and immanence meet in the God in Christ of the past and the future. Thus, there is nothing profane or trivial in the plodding historical process, or an earthly consummation, just as there is nothing profane or trivial about present earthly existence.

Such cross and kingdom cruciform approximation is an operative and programmatic theodicy with a crowning eschatological verification. John Hick, heterodox on much, was correct when he said, "We thus have to say, on the basis of our present experience, that evil is really evil, really malevolent and deadly and also, on the basis of faith, that it will in the end be defeated and made to serve God's good purposes."[84] History is the crucible of approximation and new creation. The pain of history will be transformed into joy on the very plane of history, and the transformational process already has enveloped the present: "Thy kingdom come. Thy will be done, on earth as it is in heaven."

Dietrich Bonhoeffer encapsulates this spirit in comments he made just prior to the arrest that would eventuate in his cruciform execution:

> For most people, the compulsory abandonment of planning for the future means that they are forced back into living just for the moment, irresponsibly, frivolously, or resignedly; some few dream longingly for better times to come, and try to forget the present. We find both these courses equally impossible, and there remains for us the very narrow way, often extremely difficult to find, of living every day as if it were our last, and yet living in faith and responsibility as though there were to be a great future. . . . Thinking and acting for the sake of the coming generation, but being ready to go any day without fear or anxiety—that, in practice, is the spirit in which we are forced to live. It is not easy to be brave and keep that spirit alive, but it is imperative.[85]

---

84. Hick, *Evil*, 400.

85. Bonhoeffer, *Letters*, 15. Similar ideas can be found in Bonhoeffer's discussion of living between the penultimate and the ultimate in Bonhoeffer, 84–91.

The cruciform church, in this understanding, must prepare for the possibility of a lengthy marriage with history, a marriage that may last for many thousands of years, if not for eternity (Cullmann). The church is in history for the long haul—for the duration—and should prepare accordingly. Yet the church also must live and preach as if it, and the whole of humanity, will be held accountable during any generation for how consistently life is lived with the *telos* of a new creation as framed by the glory of the cross.

Neither presumptuously optimistic Prometheus nor pessimistically despairing Sisyphus[86] is the patron saint of cross and kingdom approximation but the coming and victorious Lion and him crucified in history as a Lamb.

The clear rejection of all forms of pre-*Parousia* utopianism implies a shrewd and unending discontent with all social forms prior to the Second Advent. It also recognizes that antichrist easily lurks behind lofty and allegedly cruciform programs for peace, justice, and progress. On the other hand, the presence of the future now means that millennial approximations are possible, should be applauded (even when achieved by unbelievers or those working outside the normal parameters of the church),[87] and that life in history and on earth has deep and abiding value, meaning, purpose, and joy. The task of the church is to help ensure that it is something akin to the millennium, and not the tribulation, that is approximated as redemptive history advances in anticipation of Christ's return.

Both setbacks and victories are to be expected as history moves from D-Day to V-Day. Everyone can make an eternal contribution to the unfolding historical process and future consummation. Every believer's life should be epic. Every act of love and justice, every cruciform sacrifice, every true cultural achievement, every majestic symphony and artistic endeavor, and every restorative scientific or medical breakthrough blends into and contributes to the exquisite panorama of the earthly restoration and new creation. And some day faith will become sight, and hope will become reality when the future is no longer merely approximated but is fully and finally consummated. The Revelator speaks of this great day, when "The kingdom of the world has become the kingdom of our Lord and of his Christ, and he shall reign forever and ever" (Rev 11:15, RSV).

---

86. Moltmann, *Theology of Hope*, 24.

87. Schillebeeckx laments the fact that "in this age, God seems to be accomplishing more through men like Martin Luther King, for example, than through the church" (Schillebeeckx, *Schillebeeckx Reader*, 253). It should be noted that King did not operate entirely outside the church and was trained within the church although Schillebeeckx's point is well advised.

13

Theologia Crucis Post Post

POSTMODERN, POST-CHRISTIAN, POST-CHRISTENDOM, AND ANTI-CHRISTIAN

IT HAS BEEN SUGGESTED that a modified theology of the cross has special relevance and ministry applicability today. The *post* referenced in this chapter's title refers to the present era characterized as post-Christian, post-Christendom, post-critical,[1] and postmodern (or ultramodern,[2] as per Tom Oden). Post-Christian and post-Christendom are perhaps the easiest concepts to define, though not without challenges. Clearly, Christian influence is waning in many cultures and regions of the globe. Post-Christian will be used here to refer to a civilization and culture that is no longer or only marginally influenced by Christian beliefs, values, assumptions, and ethics, and which often views Christianity in an unfavorable light, or at least as an irrelevancy. Europe and America are at different stages in the process of post-Christianizing culture. Europe is largely post-Christian and has been for some time, perhaps since the eighteenth century or earlier. America is increasingly post-Christian relative to Judeo-Christian influence on civilization. Other areas of the globe are experiencing tremendous Christian growth with Christian influence on culture varying greatly between countries.

1. Post-critical here refers generally to post-critical philosophical thought, and the attempt to move beyond the methodology and intellectual modes and attitudes of the Enlightenment.

2. See below in this chapter concerning Oden's use of "ultramodern."

Anti-Christian seems to be the trajectory in the West, with Europe leading the way. When I was in graduate school, the common discussion was *secularization*, often presented as a morally neutral cultural, intellectual, and sociological trend. Enlightenment values (i.e., reason, science, scientific objectivity, toleration, progress) naturally marginalized partisan Christian influence.

One of the benefits of the postmodern situation or consciousness is that ideologies have often been unmasked as claiming modern or universal objectivity when in reality these ideologies are often extremely contextual, biased, and prejudiced. This work rejects the thesis that all beliefs and values are matters of personal, cultural, or subjective preference. Indeed, if all beliefs and affirmations are subjective, then self-stultification is the result of making such universal and relativistic claims. This unmasking, however, allows for discussion as to whether the Enlightenment values and so-called Enlightenment rational objectivity were actually driven, in part, by a desire to replace Christian influence with other modernist ideologies and functional modernist religions. Hence, secularization for some may have been as much or more about replacing Christian influence with another ideology, often by means of cultural, verbal, or actual violence, rather than the natural consequence of rational and scientific progress. Secularization may have been, in part, a will-to-power civilizational ideological pivot.

Another benefit of the postmodern situation, if it is proper to speak of the benefits of postmodernity, is that in this age of postmodernism or ultramodern syncretism in the West, and increasingly in America, postmodernism has often unmasked itself. Not only has one key possible motivation for modernism been unmasked, replacing or even eradicating Judeo-Christian influence, but the so-called plurality, tolerance, relativism, perspectivalism, and inclusivism of postmodernism often means *anything but Judeo-Christian* beliefs and values. This is not just a rejection of the alleged naïve absolutism of Christianity as postmodernism is arguably very absolutistic in thought and in the use of power to squelch Christian influence. Postmodern absolutism and the quarantined absolutism of selected religions and other voices are allowed by postmodernity. The Judeo-Christian influence on culture must be eradicated above all else. Postmodernism could argue that the reason for opposition to Judeo-Christian influence is that the Judeo-Christian perspective is hegemonic and the locus of oppression in the West; hence, Judeo-Christian absolutism and the accompanying religion-cultural-political monolithic edifice must be blasted away. The West, it is implied, is sinning greatly with this oppressive Judeo-Christian theology of glory, to use Luther's terms. Regardless, singling out any ideology for negative sanction runs counter to the spirit of relativistic postmodernism. If the real target of postmodernism was absolutism, postmodernists would be less certain of their own conclusions, and they would be equally concerned about legion religious and philosophical absolutisms.

Apart from postmoderns failing to recognize or admit that many of these Judeo-Christian values greatly contributed to free and pluralistic civilizations, and their freedom to advocate for postmodernity, if anything is crystal clear today it is that postmodernism has now become a most powerful expression of a manipulative theology of glory. Indeed, relativistic postmodernism functions as a church-state philosophical and religious hegemonic edifice equivalent in law, entertainment, media, education, culture, and Western civilization. The contemporary examples of postmodern oppression are endless, especially on college and university campuses. At the University of Minnesota, in the summer of 2018, it was reported that a new gender identity policy was under consideration known as the "Pronoun Rule": "All students, faculty, and staff would have the right to use whatever pronoun they wish on campus—whether it's he, she, 'ze' or something else. And everyone from professors to classmates would be expected to call them by the right words or risk potential disciplinary action, up to firing or expulsion."[3]

This proposed policy may or may not be adopted or modified, but it reflects three realities in terms of the mind-set of some cultural and educational leaders. First, tolerant relativism is not always so tolerant or inclusive, and postmodern free speech is not always so free. Second, this policy reflects animus toward Judeo-Christian influence on culture, seeking to exclude and punish those who sincerely affirm a traditional understanding of gender. And third, the endless inherent relativistic postmodern contradictions, such as free but not free speech, or inclusive but not inclusive communities, or absolutistic anti-absolutism, all point to the inevitable collapse of a civilization built upon postmodern or ultramodern relativism. There is no longer a plumb line for truth or ethics, so all reduces to tribal power or self-assertion. The plumb line used to be informed by Judeo-Christian values and Enlightenment ideals of truth and the common pursuit of a more perfect union. Those measuring rods have vanished from many segments of culture and civilization. The trajectory today is to criminalize Judeo-Christian-influenced law, culture, behaviors, actions, and even thoughts and attitudes. Accommodationist Christianity or cruciform Christianity may be the only two options within a generation in this increasingly uncivilized and balkanized post-Christian era, which may be progressively similar to what happened in late 1930s Germany.

3. Lerner, "He, She, or Ze?"

One additional benefit of the postmodern situation is that we have looked behind the curtains of both modernism and postmodernism only to find that many of the rulers of Oz are simply posturing for a culture and civilization no longer influenced by Judeo-Christian assumptions or values. Some have an agenda far more comprehensive than just creating a post-Christendom world while wrapping themselves in self-righteousness pseudo-toleration, pseudo-inclusivism, and pseudo-compassion. They actually seem to desire a civilization entirely free from Judeo-Christian influence. This post-Christian movement is yet another pseudo-theology of the cross, claiming to liberate while actually engaging in oppression and self-glorification. Some want a world where their religious equivalent, even when avoiding overtly religious language, is the new edifice, and Christianity disappears, returns to the cultural margins or the closet. It is really not always helpful at this juncture of history to speak of Christianity as religious and, therefore, to be excluded from culture and civilization and postmodernism, relativism, and secularism as nonreligious and, therefore, acceptable in the public marketplace of law and culture as if these new winds are religiously neutral. The reality is that postmodernism functions as a state-allowed, if not approved, religion and plumb line for truth and ethics.

Many cultural trends are not simply post-Christian but anti-Christian and moving toward a use or abuse of power aimed at non-accommodationist Christians that is analogous to anti-Semitism. These postmoderns parasite off the Judeo-Christian influence that greatly contributed to the very freedoms they utilize in service of eradicating Christian influence. These parasites are increasingly being exposed for what they actually are—rather manipulative fundamentalists of the political left who want to impose the equivalent of a functional theocracy. Perhaps we should now speak of the coming *postocracy*? The reality is that in both modernity and especially postmodernity there is often a prejudice against Judeo-Christian assumptions and influence, and a new, powerful, and rather manipulative absolutism masquerading as inclusive tolerance is gaining momentum.

In contrast to the more general concept of post-Christian influence, post-Christendom refers to the collapse of the Christian-influenced state or the church-state union, especially in the West. Christendom refers more to how Judeo-Christian values, and sometimes the church became aligned with or united with the state, especially in nations with official church-state unions. Did some Christians use this Christendom edifice to repress and exclude others improperly, and should this be condemned? Of course, and that is why the solution is not to advance a new anti-ideological and pseudo-inclusivist edifice that falsely claims not to be absolutistic or ideological. The solution is open discourse about which religious and philosophical assumptions and values provide the most stable pillars for human flour-ishing and aspirational civilizations. The Judeo-Christian perspective has a sound and strong historical case at least to be at the discussion table, if not a major player or the major player when discussing the future of thriving civilizations.

In any event, the theology of the cross is especially relevant in post-Christian and overt or cloaked anti-Christian and post-Christendom con-texts where faithfulness to the gospel sometimes results in marginalization, persecution, and even martyrdom. The true God of Jesus Christ is often en-countered not in the false glory of the oppressive state but in the cruciform faithfulness of kingdom Christians. Of course, Luther would be quick to point out that even amidst Christendom the true God is often found where least expected. The theology of the cross and theology of glory may serve as prophetic critiques of both Christendom and post-Christendom, though one must carefully guard against a reactionary anti-cultural posture.

ULTRAMODERN SYNCRETISM AND THE TROJAN HORSE

Some additional clarification regarding postmodernism and ultramodern syncretism should advance the argument of this work and its application to evangelicalism. Relative to what is often referred to as postmodernism, the average evangelical Christian, even if familiar with the term, is often unfamiliar with the nuances of this discussion and simply identifies post-modernism with relativism concerning truth and ethics. Postmodernism is viewed as a sort of profound skepticism concerning modern reason, truth, and ethical norms.

This "I function as god and truth is personal truth just for me" senti-ment lies at the heart of what many have referred to as the current age of postmodernism or ultramodernism. I prefer to refer to the present as the age of ultramodern syncretism. *Post*, of course, means *after* modernism, and modernism refers to the Western, modernistic age characterized by the following:

- Western, (often) arrogant reason;
- the rejection of past superstitions (e.g., traditional superstitions such as Christianity);
- scientific reasoning as the path to rational truth;
- belief in rational, scientific, progress;

- toleration (but only the toleration of reasonable beliefs and progressive thought, of course); and,

- tremendous zeal and optimism concerning the future with some radical modernists citing the need to start history all over again (e.g., the French Revolution, or various forms and iterations of communism).

By way of contrast, the *Encyclopedia Britannica* properly and succinctly emphasizes these postmodern themes: "A late twentieth-century movement characterized by broad skepticism, subjectivism, or relativism; a general suspicion of reason; and an acute sensitivity to the role of ideology in asserting and maintaining political and economic power."[4] The *Stanford Encyclopedia of Philosophy* emphasizes the *telos* and origin of the movement as follows: the desire and program "to destabilize other concepts [and words] such as presence, identity, historical progress, epistemic certainty, and the univocity of meaning. The term 'postmodernism' first entered the philosophical lexicon in 1979, with the publication of *The Postmodern Condition* by Jean-François Lyotard."[5]

Lyotard, of course, provided the oft-quoted and classic bumper sticker definition of the movement: "Simplifying to the extreme, I define postmodern as incredulity towards metanarratives."[6] A narrative is a story, and a meta-narrative is the larger or deeper and more profound story that lies behind or under or beyond the smaller stories that we encounter most every day. "The basketball Warriors won the world championship" is a story. "Professional sports are part of a decadent bourgeoisie culture destined to collapse when the oppressed finally turn away from the sedative of religion and sports and throw off their capitalistic chains and set up a new economic order" moves the simple basketball story toward the level of a meta-narrative. Meta-narratives are more comprehensive and transcending stories. Simply put, meta-narratives are grand stories that guide one's life and attempt to explain most everything important or deny that anything can be explained. They typically include

- major affirmations about reality, truth, and ethics;

- conceptual frameworks for meaning and purpose or the lack thereof;

- affirmations of what we should love or desire in life and how we should live, if such can even be known or affirmed; and,

---

4. Duigman, "Postmodernism."
5. Aylesworth, "Postmodernism."
6. Lyotard, *Postmodern Condition*, xxiv.

- overarching perspectives on how to understand human experience and knowledge, if such knowledge is even possible.

By this definition, while postmodernism has many variations that we cannot address in this present work, it is fair to say that postmodernism, which often opposes meta-narratives, is itself a meta-narrative. And, as previously noted, postmodernism increasingly functions as a new, post-Christian, and hegemonic religion or postocracy.

These mega-stories or meta-narratives, such as atheistic Marxism, Deism, or Christian theism, also provide a framework of assumptions, affirmations, commitments, and passions for the usage, meanings, and definitions of words or terms. As meta-narratives change, so do word definitions, such as marriage or gender. They frame language and communication. For skeptics, words are often viewed as mere tools of gaining power and advantage over others and do not convey any kind of normative truth or ethics for civilization. Of course these skeptics often use words to redefine and undermine other words. Religions and worldviews and, as noted, even postmodernism itself would be classic examples of grand, overarching, totalizing, all-encompassing narratives, or "Stories" with a capital *S* that seek to use semantic narratives and semantic universes to interpret, explain, create, or dismiss the major questions of existence. Most meta-narratives and semantic universes seek to influence or even direct the future of human existence and history.

Oden seemed to prefer the terms "ultramodernism" or "mod rot" as a superior way to characterize the current and latter stages of the failed project of modernism. Oden dates the postmodern age in the West from 1989 and the fall of the Berlin Wall and modernistic communism. Modernistic communism turned on itself, which was lived out in the tearing down of the Berlin wall. Modernism, therefore, is now running on fumes; the pillared assumptions driving and supporting the movement have collapsed. Oden was skeptical of letting the advocates of postmodernism define themselves as postmodern when, in fact, they were really ultramoderns.[7] Modernism (reason and science) failed miserably at creating an ideal or utopian civilization, and likewise failed at creating a semantic framework and value system that could provide the social glue for a better civilization. Modernism's quest for scientific and rational truth led to the rejection of truth. "Mod-rot" means we are running, stalling, and floundering on modernistic fumes amidst widespread fragmentation and cultural decay. The new reality, then, is ultramodernism, meaning that we are in the last stages of the death of modernity. The assumptions of modernity are largely deceased,

7. Oden, *After Modernity.*

but the modernist culture remains. Modernism is exhausting itself. Post-modernists are still largely modernists in many respects and parasite off the political structures, democratic freedoms, science, reason, and medical breakthroughs partially birthed by modernity, even while many of their core convictions undermine everything about modernism. Postmodernists are conflicted ultramodernists.

This work affirms that ultramodern syncretism is much preferred as a late twentieth- and early twenty-first-century appellation and mental grid for positioning and applying the theology of the cross and glory today. "Post" tells us little other than after, and "ultra" only lets us know we are in the final or extreme *reductio ad absurdum* stages of mod rot. "Post-pregnant" has little value in capturing the radical new reality and experience of a woman in contrast to the term mother! Syncretism, the "truth for me or my tribe" reckless and often incoherent mixing of beliefs, values, and practices, including the ultimate syncretism of mixing a suspicion or disdain for modernism with a parasitical dependence on modernism, better captures the contemporary chaotic *Zeitgeist*. Ironically, some parasitical ultramodern syncretists fly on jets and use electronic tablets and words via the World Wide Web to denounce, in far more than "truth is just for me" creatively chosen words and narratives, the many and great evils of Western- and Christian-influenced civilization.

Thus, the actual theology of glory equivalent today, in many circles, is the so-called non-ideological ideology of ultramodern syncretism that often seeks to privatize or even crush Christian belief, practice, and influence entirely. This totalizing anti-meta-narrative meta-narrative often takes the form of very oppressive educational, economic, legal, political, and artistic, including media and entertainment, attacks on Judeo-Christian practices, beliefs, and attitudes. And this assault on orthodox Christianity often masquerades as liberation, inclusion, social justice, and compassion. Ultramodern syncretism, in some forms, is an anti-Christian Trojan horse, hiding under the cover of noble values such as toleration, inclusion, and social justice.

Perhaps even more ironic is the fact that the patron saint of postmodernism or ultramodernism is Nietzsche who viewed Christ and the cross as foolish and Christianity and Judaism as glorying in weakness in order to rationalize Christian and Jewish voluntary and cowardly subjection. In other words, the losers (Christianity and Judaism), according to Nietzsche, baptized the virtues of the weak (meekness, sacrifice, love, turning the check) in order to accept, justify, and glorify their own defeat. So Nietzsche's rejection of orthodox Christianity and his cultural hermeneutic of power that undermined Christendom contributed greatly to the contemporary context where in the name of helping the weak and marginalized Nietzsche's weak and marginalized Christians are being increasingly marginalized and oppressed. More than ironic, this strategy is also a deceptive Trojan horse.

ULTRAMODERN SYNCRETISM, CROSS, KINGDOM, AND GLORY

Hence, the present application of Luther's conceptual tools of the theology of the cross, theology of glory, and *Deus Absconditus* is becoming challenging and ultra-complex. The false way of the cross (e.g., utilizing the label of social justice) is now being used to prop up a false theology of glory that crushes the true way of the cross. For example, the maintenance of biblical standards of morality in today's context is met with the allegation that such morality is totalizing, lacking in compassion, socially unjust, hegemonic, non-inclusive, and lacking an identification with the oppressed. The historic or proper use of Luther's cross and glory would suggest that the true way of the cross today, total allegiance to biblical verities and morality, is being marginalized or oppressed by a false ultramodern and syncretistic version of the theology of the cross. The true theology of the cross is being crucified upside-down. Postmodernity, in many of its forms, is the equivalent of the oppressive church-state edifice that persecuted Luther and the embodiment of the corrupt theology of glory. And the true followers of the cross are portrayed by this new postocracy as the oppressors. Nietzsche often spoke of the inversion of values and we certainly have arrived.

The only way forward for the biblically faithful is truly and lovingly to model and advocate for a genuine theology of the cross, and graciously and tactfully to expose this false ultramodern syncretistic postocracy. This postocracy may turn out to be far more toxic to aspirational civilization than many of the worst expressions of the unbiblical theology of glory in the history of Christendom.[8] The bottom line is that the winds of change are accelerating rather rapidly such that the biblical cruciform theme of the theology of the cross has increasing application today and could be a potent prophetic witness against this syncretistic and relativistic postocracy.

In terms of semantic analysis and theological anthropology, the current winds of change should not be unexpected. Fallen human beings almost

---

8. Also see Brian's Barthian influenced solution (Barthian, *Covering Up*, 163–92) for navigating the current age, although, as noted, the Barthian approach has many limitations and has likely fueled the very ultramodern pathologies that it seeks to remedy by failing to proffer a civilizational norm for truth and ethics that does not require a commitment to the Christ or the authority of preaching about Christ.

always claim the moral and spiritual high ground when rebelling against biblical norms—and sometimes use the Bible to self-justify this rebellion. For example, Jesus' statement "do not judge" (Matt 7:1) has morphed in our postmodern culture into a condemnation of all moral judgments, rather than a rejection of moral hypocrisy which was clearly the original intent—Jesus made many moral judgments and called on his followers to do the same. Humanity justifies evil actions via narcissistic semantic universes. Lance Morrow's haunting words quoted previously in chapter 11 bear repeating: "Utopia, this century has learned the hard way, usually bears a resemblance to hell. An evil chemistry turns the dream of salvation into damnation."[9] Evil self-justifies. All is rationalized for the sake of *the working class*, for *the people*, because of victimhood or oppression, because of Manifest Destiny, due to divine rights, due to humiliation, due to abuse, due to poverty or privilege, due to religion, due to anti-religion, due to tolerance, for the sake of inclusion, or due to a legion of other so-called righteous causes. The theology of the cross is capable of exposing such utopian movements.

Within this context, especially in relatively free societies, the way of the cross is not to glory in the post-Christian situation and remain silent, withdraw, hunker down for the duration, or go the way of ghettoized or monastic evangelicalism. The freedom of speech in such societies is a privilege that should be energetically, lovingly and most tactfully utilized, even if unjustified allegations such as right wing, Nazi, totalitarian, intolerant, bigoted, and hegemonic are hurled at those who truly stand in the stead of the cross. Those claiming to be liberators may well turn out, yet once again, to be some of history's greatest oppressors of the people of the cross and kingdom.

Amidst these crosswinds, kingdom advance will not obtain apart from cruciform sacrifice, putting the kingdom first, and prioritizing the kingdom much more so than values such as 401(k)s, cultural acceptance, cultural accommodation, worldly success, and cozy retirements. All must be on the altar of the *via dolorosa* for authentic kingdom advance in the age of the post. The ground has shifted. The twenty-first-century orthodox and evangelical church will only make a difference for time and eternity if it is a cruciform church—if literally everything, including self, resources, and the church, is placed on the altar of God's future. Kingdom advance and civilizational amelioration requires a return to perceptive discourse, historical and philosophical awareness, theological norms, biblical norms, biblical semantics, biblical agape, and a biblically grounded, thoroughly eschatological, and integrated understanding and definition of a theology of cross, kingdom, and glory.

9. Morrow, "Evil," 51.

14

Conclusions and Possible Applications

LUTHER'S THEOLOGY OF THE cross and glory served as a masterful turning point in church history relative to soteriology, epistemology, and cultural and civilizational analysis. Barth's theological and cultural critique of Luther's *Deus Absconditus*, along with the already-not-yet kingdom eschatology of Cullmann, provide needed correctives and enhancements to Luther's theology. An enhanced and refined theology of the cross, integrating cross, kingdom, and glory, has immense relevance in the age of the post. And, as discussed especially in chapters 3 and 4, the revivalistic work of the triune Spirit is the bridge between the cross and the kingdom, and between cruciform mission and kingdom advance.

If the trajectory of this work is sound, the implications and possible applications are many and should be explored by the theological community. The theology of the cross forever *counters works righteousness* and preserves the singular nature of the cross as the central salvific act of God. This singularity is well expressed in hymnody such as Bennard's *The Old Rugged Cross*, Wesley's *O Love Divine*, or Watts's *When I Survey the Wondrous Cross*.

> O Love divine, what has thou done!
> The immortal God hath died for me!
> The Father's coeternal Son
> bore all my sins upon the tree.
> Th' immortal God for me hath died:
> My Lord, my Love, is crucified! (Charles Wesley)

> When I survey the wondrous cross
> On which the Prince of glory died,

My richest gain I count but loss,
And pour contempt on all my pride.

Forbid it, Lord, that I should boast,
Save in the death of Christ my God!
All the vain things that charm me most,
I sacrifice them to His blood.

See from His head, His hands, His feet,
Sorrow and love flow mingled down!
Did e'er such love and sorrow meet,
Or thorns compose so rich a crown?

Were the whole realm of nature mine,
That were a present far too small;
Love so amazing, so divine,
Demands my soul, my life, my all. (Watts)

So I'll cherish the old rugged Cross
Till my trophies at last I lay down
I will cling to the old rugged Cross
And exchange it some day for a crown. (Bennard)

The theology of the cross underscores *the fallen epistemological condition* of humanity such that the cross serves as the primary locus of triune revelation via grace and the work of the Spirit concerning theological anthropology, soteriology, and the gracious way of salvation. This epistemological conclusion is not to negate that, via prevenient grace, humanity is capable of some awareness of the desperate human condition and the need for grace from above and beyond. Many have noted that human depravity, especially after the twentieth-century collapse of utopian dreams, is the most empirically verifiable doctrine of the Christian faith. The almost universal presence of motifs and practices such as sacrifice, reform, atonement, guilt, and the need for enlightenment or moksha is most indicative of a general grace-assisted awareness of human brokenness and the urgent need for redemption. Yet the cross alone and grace alone bring authentic spiritual liberation and kingdom prolepsis.

The theology of the cross literally shouts *that human nature is radically flawed and culture and civilization are generally inverted*—even religious culture. In such an inverted world, the Christ and Christlike are crucified, often with the encouragement of religious leaders. Will believers continue to be astonished that the wicked often prosper, even for a long season, even in religious contexts, or that the meek and pure in heart are often demoted, crushed, and crucified? Will believers continue to misapply the promises and blessings of Scripture individualistically and ignore a corporate, kenotic, cruciform kingdom hermeneutic and theodicy? Will believers ignore

Wright's eschatological critique of limiting the cross to individualistic soteriology? The cross is for all. The cross is for the entire cosmos, a cosmic cross, not just those securing tickets to heaven. The cross is cosmic D-Day.

The theology of the cross forever *counters the malignant theology of glory* that seeks to glory in and establish kingdoms not rooted in Scripture and the cross of Christ, and not birthed by the grace of the *via dolorosa* and miraculous resurrection: "Jesus Christ is manifest to . . . [an upside-down world], not primarily [in the present age] in the form of theophany and power, but in the form of weakness and suffering; thus, in order to 'find God' and God's actions in the world, it is precisely in the everyday suffering of humanity and creation—even the most terrible suffering—that one should look."[1] Hence, we often find "God's truth and God's actions in the least likely places—the battered body of a crucified [and innocent] criminal, the ugly and marginalized places of our own worlds. . . . [This] sheer counter-intuitiveness . . . [reminds us to keep] our projections of our own agendas onto God in check."[2] The contemporary application of Saler's critique certainly includes the gospel of success, health and wealth, as well as utopian and liberationist projections. For example,

- In an upside-down world, the way of the Savior may lead to a cross rather than personal peace, promotion, popularity, and prosperity.

- Doing everything right may lead to a demotion, a reeducation camp, killing fields, trails of tears, a concentration camp, or the shame and gallows of the distorted history of the City of Man.

- The wrong individuals may be promoted or be placed in "glorious" positions of leadership and power, whether in the church, corporations, or the state. Cruciform, kingdom Christians should not be surprised.

- The wrong individuals may linger for decades in less than just or less than fulfilling employment or life situations.

- The wrong individuals may achieve incredible financial and career success, even by questionable means, and seemingly never face accountability in this life. The same is true of virulent organizations and governments—some of which may linger and fester for decades, or even centuries.

- Fiscal and numerical success, even in Christian organizations, may reflect the demonic and an inverted fallen kingdom, rather than divine

1. Saler, *Theologia Crucis*, 6.
2. Saler, *Theologia Crucis*, 9.

blessing. This is not to say that quantitative assessments have no value. This is to say that, relative to numbers, all that glitters is not gold.

- Genuine kingdom approximation in an upside-down world requires a cross, or a kingdom Christian on a cross, which appears upside-down to a broken world. The cross is actually or ontologically right side up in an inverted reality.

- In an inverted reality, the way to approximation of the already-initiated kingdom is typically by way of the cross. Kingdom approximation requires cruciform holiness—and holiness is one but includes the personal and social. This is not to say that kingdom approximations are only possible via cruciform suffering. This is to say that the darker the context, the more likely it will be that the light is resisted. This is to say that the abolition of systemically entrenched and financially rewarding evils such as slavery of any kind almost necessarily required and requires the ridicule and scandal of the way of the cross.

- The bridge between the cross and kingdom, as with the pietist and Wesleyan revivals discussed in chapter 4, is the triune work of the Spirit. The triune crucified Savior sends the Spirit, which animates kingdom service, sacrifice, work, and progress in this world.

- The amelioration of depraved culture and civilization almost always necessitates, to some degree, the way of the cross, Spirit, resurrection, and kingdom. Yet, as noted, grace is operative beyond the church relative to improving or sustaining civilizations.

- The moralistic notion that culture and civilization can be meliorated merely or solely by "love," dialog, assistance to the needy and oppressed, commitment to social justice, modeling compassion among believers, cooperation, understanding, or "making nice" with a fallen world rests on a very flawed theological anthropology. This is not to say that constructive dialog and compassionate service have no value in kingdom advance or influence. This is to say that authentic kingdom advance and genuine glory in this age also inevitably and inexorably encounter an inverted world that crucifies genuine love and truth. Luther went so far as to argue that the theologian of the cross must experience the cross.[3] True social melioration emanates from cruciform, Spirit-animated, kingdom influence.

- Much of the human flourishing in the present may be ultimately traced back to the cross and kingdom and those who chose to follow in his

---

3. See chapter 2.

steps (1 Pet 2:21). Even those not directly in the orb of the church often contribute most to actualizing aspirational communities, culture, and civilization through sacrifice.

However, as emphasized throughout this work, while the theology of the cross is certainly a critique of the presumptuous posture of a cancerous theology of glory, *a biblical theology of the cross symbiotically tethered to kingdom eschatology is also an approximative and hopeful note for true glory, even in the present age.*

- Luther's theology of glory has unfortunately been almost entirely associated with a negative critique of human glory. This negative or prophetic critique is biblical and appropriate but incomplete. It is deficient due to its lack of emphasis on resurrection, new creation, approximation, kingdom and Spirit.

- The kingdom is the bridge between Luther's positive formulation of the theology of the cross and his typically negative definition of the theology of glory. The biblical material on the kingdom crucifies false glory. Through the cross and resurrection, together, we have the dawning of the initiated and glorious kingdom. Through the cross, glorious kingdom approximation is possible now. Through cruciform, Spirit-enabled kingdom advance, we have a foretaste of the glorious future. The pain and shame of the darkness at the cross is, ironically, the first daybreak of a glorious new creation that is bursting forth in redemption and resurrection.

- Through cross and kingdom approximation, infanticide can be criminalized, hospitals of mercy can be (and have been) established, wars can be mediated, evil powers can be contained or overthrown, and the captives (spiritually, politically, and culturally) can be proleptically liberated—already. The already kingdom, if genuine, is a proleptic form of true glory. The cross and kingdom, by definition, are inseparable from the gracious triune work of the Spirit in the world. Approximation, by definition, is dependent on the Spirit who was sent into the world to convict the world "concerning sin and righteousness and judgment" (John 16:8).

- The experiential confession of "Oh what a foretaste of glory divine" should serve as far more than an emotionally based individualistic affirmation of and hope for a Platonic heaven. This confession should embrace the full-orbed reality of the glorious already-not-yet kingdom new creation and serve as a call to action now. The biblical theology of glory should serve both as a negative or prophetic theological construct (critiquing pseudo-glory) and a hopeful *telos* for the present age (the already kingdom). The triune Spirit mediates true glory through the advancing kingdom just as Jesus was glorified on the cross (John 12:23).

- The theology of the cross and kingdom counters false kingdoms but affirms authentic kingdom approximations. Hence, in contrast to more negative representations of the theology of the cross, a theology of the cross and kingdom is very affirming of the creation and history. The cross is for the world that God so loved and eventuates in the glorious new creation. Yet this glorious new creation is already emerging amidst the false or so-called glorious kingdoms and influences these kingdoms to a greater or lesser degree. Making moral and ethical distinctions between cultures and kingdoms is a biblical imperative, so the response to utopianism is not fatalism or relativism but discriminating approximation. Both civilizational/cultural imperialism and civilizational/cultural relativism are demonic. The orientation of the theology of the cross and kingdom is not unqualifiedly condemnatory, or escapist, but instead it is proleptically discerning and impactful.

- While human glory certainly can be false or fleeting (Hos 4:7; 9:11; Ps 49:17; 1 Pet 1:24), scriptural glory (or δόξα in the New Testament) is typically positive and even doxological. Cross, kingdom, Spirit, and true glory are unified.

- The biblical already-not-yet framework for glory is helpful for integrating the positive and negative nuances of glory. There is a false and fading glory and false, so-called glorious kingdoms, but there is also a glory, even in this age, that is affirmed in Scripture and applied directly or indirectly to biblical figures such as Jacob, Joseph, David, Jehoiakim, and Joshua, and their kingdom impact. Solomon's splendor, the vibrancy of young men, humanity's exalted status, the divine plagues of judgment, divine miracles, the Exodus pillar of cloud, Mt. Sinai, Mt. Carmel, the Tabernacle, the birth of Christ, the Transfiguration, and the New Jerusalem are all glorious. The biblical theology of glory is neither entirely futurist nor entirely hidden.

- A biblical theology of cross and kingdom reflects optimistic realism for the era prior to Christ's return, or what Wesleyans often refer to as the realistic optimism of grace.

- The famous glory chapter—2 Cor 3—is a treasured chapter of mine because it summarizes and recapitulates the entirety of Scripture concisely and powerfully, including the relationship between the old and new covenants. This key text clearly emphasizes a theology of glory and presents glory in a very positive light and even as a theological nexus. The references to glory are numerous and culminate at the summit: "But we all, with unveiled face, beholding as in a mirror the glory of the Lord, are being transformed into the same image from glory to glory, just as from the Lord, the Spirit." Luther's negative or prophetic use of the theology of glory is essential, relevant, and it was part of a message that changed the world. Nevertheless, the biblical integration of cross, kingdom (including Spirit procession), and glory is ultimately a proleptic and hopeful note for the present.

- Glory certainly and primarily applies to God and is both hidden and manifest[4] (e.g., Exod 24; 29; 33; Num 14; Job 37; Ps 29; Prov 25; Isa 40). Yet, via the D-Day Christ event, including cross, Spirit, resurrection, and kingdom, "God willed to make known what is the riches of the glory of this mystery among the Gentiles, which is Christ in you, the hope of glory" (Col 1:27).

- Additionally,

  > While the contrast is valid, therefore [as advocated by more negative conceptions of the theology of glory], between the sufferings of Christ and the glory (literally, the glories) to follow (1 Pet 1:11), John's Gospel reveals a further development, namely, that the sufferings themselves can be viewed as a glorification. Jesus was aware of this and expressed himself accordingly. "The hour is come that the Son of Man should be glorified" (John 12:23).

  > Thus, glory also "properly belongs to the [cruciform] finishing of the work which the Father had given him to do, since that work represented the perfect will of God."[5] And, as previously referenced, Peter's martyrdom also brought glory to God (John 21:19). We can share in the glory of the cross.

- To wit, a biblical theology of the cross and glory must always be framed within the context of the kingdom of God. False glory must be contrasted with true glory; true glory follows the way of the cross; and, glory includes already and not-yet dimensions and applications. The cross of Christ initiates and actualizes true glory.

---

4 See Harrison, "Glory," 443–44; Huttar, "Glory."

5. Harrison, "Glory," 444.

- An unbalanced theology of the cross easily falls prey to negativity and separatism, just as a malignant theology of glory easily falls prey to self-glorification, spiritual hubris, and theological and cultural accommodation. A balanced theology of the cross is rooted in the work of the Spirit and tethered closely to the eschatological theology of the kingdom.

- Hence, what is needed today is a comprehensive and nuanced theology of the cross, kingdom, and glory that transcends negative and reactionary responses to works righteousness and takes the form of triune kingdom Spirit approximation.

Reinhold Niebuhr's classic Serenity Prayer aligns well with a cruciform piety that grasps both the limits and possibilities of kingdom approximation prior to Christ's return:

> God, give me grace to accept with serenity
> the things that cannot be changed,
> Courage to change the things
> which should be changed,
> and the Wisdom to distinguish
> the one from the other.
> Living one day at a time,
> Enjoying one moment at a time,
> Accepting hardship as a pathway to peace,
> Taking, as Jesus did,
> This sinful world as it is,
> Not as I would have it,
> Trusting that You will make all things right,
> If I surrender to Your will,
> So that I may be reasonably happy in this life,
> And supremely happy with You forever in the next.
> Amen.[6]

The cross and resurrection, at the soteriological core of the Christ-event, including the sending of the Spirit,[7] serves as *the integrative nucleus*

---

6. Shapiro, "Who Wrote?"

7. "I will ask the Father, and He will give you another Helper, that He may be with you forever; *that is* the Spirit of truth, whom the world cannot receive, because it does not see Him or know Him, *but* you know Him because He abides with you and will be in you. I will not leave you as orphans; I will come to you" (John 14:16).

and anchor for the whole of Christian theology when framed within an eschatological kingdom context. As observed, when the theology of the cross is isolated from the kingdom context, it easily succumbs to narrow and reactionary distortions of the more balanced and robust biblical teaching on cross and kingdom. Yes, the upside-down cosmos spawns false kingdoms and pretentious theologies of glory, but the cross and resurrection also birth potential and glorious kingdom approximations already.

Kenotic cruciform holiness or Christlikeness is the Rosetta Stone relative to authentic kingdom approximation and liberation. Prior to Christ's return, an inverted world is not proleptically restored or righted merely by suffering or sacrifice but only by the full and complete identification of believers by the Spirit with Christ crucified and resurrected. When believers live as dead to sin and risen with Christ, the future envelops and engages the present. The Christ-event was impactful for the church and world history because it was far more than a soteriological transaction or sacrificial martyrdom. The Christ-event was cosmic in impact and rooted in who Christ was—the Lamb without blemish. The Christ-event was a triune event creating a called out, sent out, and holy people of God: the church of Jesus Christ (ἐκκλησία). Therefore:

- Kingdom approximation is contingent upon authentic kenosis and cruciform embodiment.

- Kingdom approximation is contingent upon cruciform Christlikeness, effected by the Spirit, meaning that an inverted world may be proleptically influenced through the inverted or lowered status of the redeemed (e.g., through ridicule, oppression, and the way of the cross): "If the world hates you, you know that it has hated Me before *it hated* you. If you were of the world, the world would love its own; but because you are not of the world, but I chose you out of the world, because of this the world hates you" (John 15:18)

- The cruciform kenosis of genuinely holy, Spirit-led, or Christlike believers truly advances the glorious kingdom. "If you are reviled for the name of Christ, you are blessed, because the Spirit of glory and of God rests on you. Make sure that none of you suffers as a murderer, or thief, or evildoer, or a troublesome meddler; but if *anyone suffers* as a Christian, he is not to be ashamed, but is to glorify God in this name" (1 Pet 4:14–16).

This emphasis on kenosis, of course, has implications for Christian holiness, which some refer to as Christian formation or spiritual formation or Christian piety and spirituality. Holiness (e.g., the claim to possess holiness or an experience of holiness/sanctification or Christlikeness) apart from kenosis and the cruciform life is self-evidently a disembodied and inauthentic holiness: "If someone says, 'I love God,' and hates his brother, he is a liar; for the one who does not love his brother whom he has seen, cannot love God whom he has not seen" (1 John 4:20). Kenotic cruciform holiness and genuine Christlikeness are one, and kingdom approximation and liberation in the present will most certainly surface wherever authentic holiness and overflowing kenotic love exist.[8]

Relative to authentic holiness and Christian or spiritual formation and piety, contemporary models, methods, and theologies of spiritual formation that do not eventuate in legitimate and demonstrable changed lives and cruciform kenosis are suspect. Holiness that does not eventuate in self-emptying and overflowing love for others, culture, and civilization is suspect. Intentionally modifying and recontextualizing a statement by John Wesley who, in many respects, modeled authentic holiness, "intellectually and culturally disengaged holy Christians" is a phrase no more consistent with the gospel of Jesus Christ than "holy prostitutes." Authentic cross and kingdom holiness in Scripture is more akin to an epic participatory drama than a separatistic ecstatic spirituality.[9]

Hence, a biblical theology of cross and glory is properly framed as eschatological and integrated with the biblical teaching on the kingdom. This modified theology of the cross and glory should endure, guide, and contribute to authentic kingdom advance. To modify Luther: Here I stand, at the foot of the cross, on the *via dolorosa*, and I can do nothing else.

---

8. Liberation in this work is not identified with a specific political agenda, especially Leviathan-like governmental and utopian alleged solutions to all human ills; indeed, such agendas often reflect Luther's negative nuance of the theology of glory.

9. This is not to negate the value of praise and worship or spiritual retreats but simply to ensure that such are framed scripturally by Christ's cross and kingdom.

Appendix of Key Scriptures[1]

CHRIST AND *THEOLOGIA CRUCIS* VERSUS THE THEOLOGY OF GLORY

- "He was despised and forsaken of men, A man of sorrows and acquainted with grief; And like one from whom men hide their face He was despised, and we did not esteem Him. Surely our griefs He Himself bore, And our sorrows He carried; Yet we ourselves esteemed Him stricken, Smitten of God, and afflicted. But He was pierced through for our transgressions, He was crushed for our iniquities; The chastening for our well-being fell upon Him, And by His scourging we are healed." (Isa 53:3–5; see entire chapter)

- "From that time Jesus began to show His disciples that He must go to Jerusalem, and suffer many things from the elders and chief priests and scribes, and be killed, and be raised up on the third day." (Matt 16:21)

- "But first He must suffer many things and be rejected by this generation." (Luke 17:25)

- "Now My soul has become troubled; and what shall I say, 'Father, save Me from this hour'? But for this purpose I came to this hour." (John 12:27)

- "If the world hates you, you know that it has hated Me before it hated you. . . . If they persecuted Me, they will also persecute you; if they kept My word, they will keep yours also." (John 15:18–20)

---

1. Arranged with the intent of enhancing reader understanding rather than presenting the material chronologically.

- "Jerusalem, Jerusalem, who kills the prophets and stones those who are sent to her! How often I wanted to gather your children together, the way a hen gathers her chicks under her wings, and you were unwilling." (Matt 23:37)

BELIEVERS AND *THEOLOGIA CRUCIS* VERSUS THE THEOLOGY OF GLORY

- "You will be hated by all because of My name, but it is the one who has endured to the end who will be saved." (Matt 10:22)
- "Therefore, behold, I am sending you prophets and wise men and scribes; some of them you will kill and crucify, and some of them you will scourge in your synagogues, and persecute from city to city." (Matt 23:34)
- "But you will be betrayed even by parents and brothers and relatives and friends, and they will put some of you to death, and you will be hated by all because of My name." (Luke 21:16–17)
- "Strengthening the souls of the disciples, encouraging them to continue in the faith, and saying, 'Through many tribulations we must enter the kingdom of God.'" (Acts 14:22)
- "Indeed, all who desire to live godly in Christ Jesus will be persecuted." (2 Tim 3:12)
- "For you, brethren, became imitators of the churches of God in Christ Jesus that are in Judea, for you also endured the same sufferings at the hands of your own countrymen, even as they *did* from the Jews, who both killed the Lord Jesus and the prophets, and drove us out. They are not pleasing to God, but hostile to all men." (1 Thess 1:14–15)
- "For to you it has been granted for Christ's sake, not only to believe in Him, but also to suffer for His sake." (Phil 1:29)
- "Do not fear what you are about to suffer. Behold, the devil is about to cast some of you into prison, so that you will be tested, and you will have tribulation for ten days. Be faithful until death, and I will give you the crown of life." (Rev 2:10)
- "By faith Moses, when he had grown up, refused to be called the son of Pharaoh's daughter, choosing rather to endure ill-treatment with the people of God than to enjoy the passing pleasures of sin, considering

the reproach of Christ greater riches than the treasures of Egypt; for he was looking to the reward." (Heb 11:24-26)

- "And others were tortured, not accepting their release, so that they might obtain a better resurrection; and others experienced mockings and scourgings, yes, also chains and imprisonment. They were stoned, they were sawn in two, they were tempted, they were put to death with the sword; they went about in sheepskins, in goatskins, being destitute, afflicted, ill-treated (*men* of whom the world was not worthy), wandering in deserts and mountains and caves and holes in the ground. And all these, having gained approval through their faith, did not receive what was promised, because God had provided something better for us, so that apart from us they would not be made perfect." (Heb 11:35-40)

- "Blessed are those who have been persecuted for the sake of righteousness, for theirs is the kingdom of heaven. Blessed are you when people insult you and persecute you, and falsely say all kinds of evil against you because of Me. Rejoice and be glad, for your reward in heaven is great; for in the same way they persecuted the prophets who were before you." (Matt 5:10-12)

- "So they went on their way from the presence of the Council, rejoicing that they had been considered worthy to suffer shame for His name." (Acts 5:41)

- "Therefore do not be ashamed of the testimony of our Lord or of me His prisoner, but join with me in suffering for the gospel according to the power of God." (2 Tim 1:8)

- "For you yourselves know, brethren, that our coming to you was not in vain, but after we had already suffered and been mistreated in Philippi, as you know, we had the boldness in our God to speak to you the gospel of God amid much opposition. . . . For you recall, brethren, our labor and hardship, *how* working night and day so as not to be a burden to any of you, we proclaimed to you the gospel of God . . . so that you would walk in a manner worthy of the God who calls you into His own kingdom and glory. . . . For you, brethren, became imitators of the churches of God in Christ Jesus that are in Judea, for you also endured the same sufferings at the hands of your own countrymen, even as they *did* from the Jews, who both killed the Lord Jesus and the prophets, and drove us out." (1 Thess 2:1-2, 9, 12, 14-15) "For this finds favor, if for the sake of conscience toward God a person bears up under sorrows when suffering unjustly." (1 Pet 2:19)

- "Beloved, do not be surprised at the fiery ordeal among you, which comes upon you for your testing, as though some strange thing were happening to you; but to the degree that you share the sufferings of Christ, keep on rejoicing, so that also at the revelation of His glory you may rejoice with exultation. If you are reviled for the name of Christ, you are blessed, because the Spirit of glory and of God rests on you." (1 Pet 4:12–16)

- "And if children, heirs also, heirs of God and fellow heirs with Christ, if indeed we suffer with Him so that we may also be glorified with Him." (Rom 8:17)

- "From now on let no one cause trouble for me, for I bear on my body the brand-marks of Jesus." (Gal 6:17)

- "Therefore, we ourselves speak proudly of you among the churches of God for your perseverance and faith in the midst of all your persecutions and afflictions which you endure. This is a plain indication of God's righteous judgment so that you will be considered worthy of the kingdom of God, for which indeed you are suffering." (2 Thess 1:4–5)

- "All discipline for the moment seems not to be joyful, but sorrowful; yet to those who have been trained by it, afterwards it yields the peaceful fruit of righteousness." (Heb 12:11)

- "In this you greatly rejoice, even though now for a little while, if necessary, you have been distressed by various trials, so that the proof of your faith, being more precious than gold which is perishable, even though tested by fire, may be found to result in praise and glory and honor at the revelation of Jesus Christ." (1 Pet 1:6–7)

- "Always carrying about in the body the dying of Jesus, so that the life of Jesus also may be manifested in our body." (2 Cor 4:10)

- "Now I rejoice in my sufferings for your sake, and in my flesh I do my share on behalf of His body, which is the church, in filling up what is lacking in Christ's afflictions." (Col 1:24)

- "For I will show him how much he must suffer for My name's sake." (Acts 9:16)

- "Except that the Holy Spirit solemnly testifies to me in every city, saying that bonds and afflictions await me. But I do not consider my life of any account as dear to myself, so that I may finish my course and the ministry which I received from the Lord Jesus, to testify solemnly of the gospel of the grace of God." (Acts 20:23–24)

- "For, I think, God has exhibited us apostles last of all, as men condemned to death; because we have become a spectacle to the world, both to angels and to men. We are fools for Christ's sake, but you are prudent in Christ; we are weak, but you are strong; you are distinguished, but we are without honor. To this present hour we are both hungry and thirsty, and are poorly clothed, and are roughly treated, and are homeless." (1 Cor 4:9–13)

- "Blessed be the God and Father of our Lord Jesus Christ, the Father of mercies and God of all comfort, who comforts us in all our affliction so that we will be able to comfort those who are in any affliction with the comfort with which we ourselves are comforted by God. For just as the sufferings of Christ are ours in abundance, so also our comfort is abundant through Christ." (2 Cor 1:3–5)

- "Not only so, but we also glory in our sufferings, because we know that suffering produces perseverance; perseverance, character; and character, hope." (Rom 5:3–4)

- "For our light and momentary troubles are achieving for us an eternal glory that far outweighs them all." (2 Cor 4:17)

- "Therefore, since Christ suffered in his body, arm yourselves also with the same attitude, because whoever suffers in the body is done with sin." (1 Pet 4:1)

- "For it has been granted to you on behalf of Christ not only to believe in him, but also to suffer for him." (Phil 1:29)

- "I want to know Christ—yes, to know the power of his resurrection and participation in his sufferings, becoming like him in his death." (Phil 3:10)

- "Whoever does not take up their cross and follow me is not worthy of me." (Matt 10:38)

- "Whoever finds their life will lose it, and whoever loses their life for my sake will find it." (Matt 10:39)

- "For what credit is there if, when you sin and are harshly treated, you endure it with patience? But if when you do what is right and suffer for it you patiently endure it, this finds favor with God. For you have been called for this purpose, since Christ also suffered for you, leaving you an example for you to follow in His steps, 'WHO COMMITTED NO SIN, NOR WAS ANY DECEIT FOUND IN HIS MOUTH'; and while being reviled, He did not revile in return; while suffering, He uttered no threats, but kept entrusting Himself to Him who judges righteously; and He Himself bore our sins in His body on the cross, so that we might die to sin and live to righteousness; for by His wounds you were healed. For you were continually straying like sheep, but now you have returned to the Shepherd and Guardian of your souls." (1 Pet 2:20–25)

- "And he took bread, and when he had given thanks, he broke it and gave it to them, saying, 'This is my body, which is given for you. Do this in remembrance of me.'" (Luke 22:19)

- "And those who belong to Christ Jesus have crucified the flesh with its passions and desires." (Gal 5:24)

- "I have been crucified with Christ. It is no longer I who live, but Christ who lives in me. And the life I now live in the flesh I live by faith in the Son of God, who loved me and gave himself for me." (Gal 2:20)

- "I appeal to you therefore, brothers, by the mercies of God, to present your bodies as a living sacrifice, holy and acceptable to God, which is your spiritual worship." (Rom 12:1)

- "If anyone comes to me and does not hate his own father and mother and wife and children and brothers and sisters, yes, and even his own life, he cannot be my disciple." (Luke 14:26)

- "Then the mother of Zebedee's sons came to Jesus with her sons and, kneeling down, asked a favor of him. 'What is it you want?' he asked. She said, 'Grant that one of these two sons of mine may sit at your right and the other at your left in your kingdom.' 'You don't know what you are asking,' Jesus said to them. 'Can you drink the cup I am going to drink?' 'We can,' they answered. Jesus said to them, 'You will indeed drink from my cup, but to sit at my right or left is not for me to grant. These places belong to those for whom they have been prepared by my Father.' When the ten heard about this, they were indignant with the two brothers. Jesus called them together and said, 'You know that the rulers of the Gentiles lord it over them, and their high officials exercise authority over them. Not so with you. Instead, whoever wants to become great among you must be your servant, and whoever wants to be first must be your slave—just as the Son of Man did not come to be served, but to serve, and to give his life as a ransom for many.'" (Matt 20:20–28)

Bibliography

Adams, James Luther. "Arminius and the Structure of Society." In *Man's Faith and Freedom: The Theological Influence of Jacobus Arminius,* edited by Gerald O. McCullough, 88–112. New York: Abingdon, 1963.

Alexander, Ruth. "Are There Really 100,000 New Christian Martyrs Every Year?" *BBC News,* November 12, 2013. http://www.bbc.com/news/magazine-24864587.

Allman, William F. "Fatal Attraction." *US News and World Report,* April 30, 1990, 12–13.

Althaus, Paul. *The Theology of Martin Luther.* Translated by Robert C. Shultz. Philadelphia: Fortress, 1966.

Anderson, Jane. "The Impact of Family Structure on the Health of Children: Effects of Divorce." *Linacre Quarterly* 81.4 (2014) 378–87.

Arminius, James. *The Writings of James Arminius.* Translated by James Nichols and W. R. Bagnall. 3 vols. Grand Rapids, MI: Baker, 1956.

Athanasius. *On the Incarnation.* Translated by Archibald Robertson. 2nd rev. ed. London: David Nutt, 1891.

Aylesworth, Gary. "Postmodernism." *Stanford Encyclopedia of Philosophy,* February 5, 2015. https://plato.stanford.edu/entries/postmodernism.

Bahnsen, Greg L. "In What Ways Is Christ's Kingdom to Be Evident Today." Paper presented at the Evangelical Theological Society, 43rd Annual Meeting, Kansas City, MO, November 22, 1991. Audiocassette EV91005.

———. *No Other Standard: Theonomy and Its Critics.* Tyler, TX: Institute for Christian Economics, 1991.

Bainton, Roland H. *Christian Attitudes toward War and Peace.* New York: Abingdon, 1960.

———. *Here I Stand: A Life of Martin Luther.* New York: New American Library, 1950.

Barth, Karl. *The Doctrine of the Word of God: Part 1.* Vol. 1 of *Church Dogmatics.* Edited by Geoffrey William Bromiley and Thomas F. Torrance. 2nd ed. London: T&T Clark, 1975.

———. *How I Changed My Mind.* Introduction and Epilogue by John D. Godsey. Richmond, VA: John Knox, 1966.

Bauckham, Richard J. *Moltmann: Messianic Theology in the Making.* Bastingstoke, UK: Marshall Pickering, 1987.

Bayer, Oswald. *Martin Luther's Theology: A Contemporary Interpretation.* Grand Rapids, MI: Eerdmans, 2008.

Beasley-Murray, George R. *Highlights of the Book of Revelation*. Nashville, TN: Broadman, 1972.

———. "Premillennialism." In *Revelation: Three Viewpoints*, edited by David C. George, 11–70. Nashville: Broadman, 1977.

Bloesch, Donald G. *Essentials of Evangelical Theology*. Vol. 2 of *Life, Ministry, and Hope*. San Francisco: Harper and Row, 1979.

Boissoneault, Lorraine. "'The True Story of Dunkirk, As Told through the Heroism of the 'Medway Queen.'" *Smithsonian*, July 19, 2017. https://www.smithsonianmag.com/history/true-story-dunkirk-told-through-heroism-medway-queen-180964105.

Bonhoeffer, Dietrich. "Cheap Grace and Discipleship." In *Readings in Christian Thought*, edited by Hugh T. Kerr, 348–52. Nashville, TN: Abingdon, 1966.

———. *The Cost of Discipleship*. Revised and Unabridged. New York: Macmillan Company, 1966.

———. *Ethics*. Translated by Neville Horton Smith. Edited by Eberhard Bethge. New York: MacMillan, 1955.

———. *Letters and Papers from Prison*. Edited by Eberhard Bethge. New York: Simon and Schuster-Touchstone, 1971.

Bonino, Jose Miguez. *Toward a Christian Political Ethics*. Philadelphia: Fortress, 1983.

Braaten, Carl E. *Eschatology and Ethics: Essays on the Theology and Ethics of the Kingdom of God*. Minneapolis: Augsburg, 1974.

Bradbury, Rosalene. *Cross Theology: The Classical Theologia Crucis and Karl Barth's Modern Theology of the Cross*. Eugene, OR: Pickwick, 2011.

Brian, Rustin E. *Covering Up Luther: How Barth's Christology Challenged the Deus Absconditus that Haunts Modernity*. Eugene, OR: Cascade, 2013.

Brown, Robert McAfee. "'Eschatological Hope' and Social Responsibility." *Christianity and Crisis* 13 (1953) 146.

Casper, Jayson. "How Libya's Martyrs Are Witnessing to Egypt." *Christianity Today*, February 23, 2015. http://www.christianitytoday.com/news/2015/february/how-libyas-martyrs-are-evangelizing-egypt.html.

Cell, George Croft. *The Rediscovery of John Wesley*. New York: Henry Holt and Co, 1934.

Chambers, Oswald. *My Utmost for His Highest*. Westwood, NJ: Barbour, 1973.

Chiaramonte, Perry. "Christians the Most Persecuted Group in World for Second Year: Study." *Fox News*, January 6, 2017. http://www.foxnews.com/world/2017/01/06/christians-most-persecuted-group-in-world-for-second-year-study.amp.html.

Collins, Kenneth J. *The Scripture Way of Salvation: The Heart of John Wesley's Theology*. Nashville, TN: Abingdon, 1997.

———. *The Theology of John Wesley: Holy Love and the Shape of Grace*. Nashville, TN: Abingdon, 2007.

Cullmann, Oscar. *Christ and Time: The Primitive Christian Conception of Time and History*. Translated by Floyd V. Filson. Rev. ed. Philadelphia: Westminster, 1964.

———. *Salvation in History*. Translated by Sidney G. Sowers. New York: Harper and Row, 1967.

Dillard, Raymond B. "Glory." In *Baker Encyclopedia of the Bible*, edited by Walter A. Elwell, 870–73. Vol. 1. Grand Rapids: Baker, 1988.

Dillenberger, John, ed. *Martin Luther: Selections from His Writings*. New York: Anchor, 1961.

Dochuk, Darren, et al., eds. *American Evangelicalism: George Marsden and the State of American Religious History*. Notre Dame, IN: University of Notre Dame Press, 2014.

Duigman, Brian. "Postmodernism." *Encyclopaedia Britannica*, October 25, 2018. https://www.britannica.com/topic/postmodernism-philosophy.

Erickson, Millard J. *Christian Theology*. Grand Rapids, MI: Baker, 1985.

Gorman, Michael J. *Inhabiting the Cruciform God: Kenosis, Justification, and Theosis in Paul's Narrative Soteriology*. Grand Rapids, MI: Eerdmans, 2009.

Grider, J. Kenneth. "Arminianism." In *Evangelical Dictionary of Theology*, edited by Walter A. Elwell, 79. Grand Rapids, MI: Baker, 1984.

———. *A Wesleyan Holiness Theology*. Kansas City, MO: Beacon Hill, 1994.

Habermas, Gary. *Beyond Death: Exploring the Evidence for Immorality*. Eugene, OR: Wipf and Stock, 2004.

Hamilton, Alexander, et al. *The Federalist*. Edited by Benjamin Fletcher Wright. New York: Barnes and Noble, 2004.

Harrison, E. F. "Glory." In *The Evangelical Dictionary of Theology*, edited by Walter Elwell, 443–44. Grand Rapids, MI: Baker, 1984.

Hauerwas, Stanley, and William H. Willimon. *Resident Aliens: A Provocative Assessment of Culture and Ministry for People Who Know That Something Is Wrong*. Nashville, TN: Abingdon, 1989.

Henry, Carl F. H. *The Uneasy Conscience of Modern Fundamentalism*. Grand Rapids, MI: Eerdmans, 1947.

Hick, John. *Evil and the God of Love*. London: MacMillan, 1966.

Hoehner, Harold. "Is Christ or Satan Ruler of This World?" *Christianity Today* 34 (1990) 42–44.

Hoonderdaal, G. J. "A Dutch Theology of Toleration." *Religion in Life* 41.1 (973) 449–55.

Hoyt, Herman. "Dispensational Premillennialism." In *The Meaning of the Millennium*, edited by Robert G. Clouse, 63–116. Downers Grove, IL: InterVarsity, 1977.

Huggins, Jonathan R. *Living Justification: A Historical-Theological Study of the Reformed Doctrine of Justification in the Writings of John Calvin, Jonathan Edwards, and N. T. Wright*. Eugene, OR: Wipf and Stock, 2013.

Huttar, David F. "Glory." In *Baker's Evangelical Dictionary of Biblical Theology*, edited by Walter Elwell. Grand Rapids: Baker, 1996. Online. https://www.biblestudytools.com/dictionaries/bakers-evangelical-dictionary/glory.html.

Irenaeus. "Incarnation, Recapitulation, Redemption." In *Readings in Christian Thought*, edited by Hugh T. Kerr, 34–35. Nashville: Abingdon, 1966.

"Is It Time for Evangelicals to Strategically Withdraw from the Culture: Four Evangelical Thinkers Consider What Rod Dreher's Benedict Option Means for the Church." *Christianity Today*, February 27, 2017. http://www.christianitytoday.com/ct/2017/february-web-only/benedict-option-evangelicals-strategically-withdraw-culture.html.

Juza, Ryan P. "The New Testament and the Future of the Cosmos." PhD diss., Asbury Theological Seminary, 2017.

Kadai, Heino O. "Luther's Theology of the Cross." *Concordia Theological Quarterly* 63.3 (1999) 169–204.

Kairos Theologians. *Kairos Document: Challenge to the Churches*. Grand Rapids: Eerdmans, 1986.

Kandiah, Krish. "God Turns Up in All the Wrong Places at Christmas." *Christianity Today*, December 20, 2017. https://www.christianitytoday.com/ct/2017/december-web-only/god-turns-up-in-all-wrong-places.html.

Keener, Craig S. *The IVP Bible Background Commentary*. 2nd ed. Downers Grove, IL: InterVarsity Academic, 2014.

Kirkpatrick, David D. "Evangelical Sales are Converting Publishers." *New York Times*, June 8, 2002. http://www.nytimes.com/2002/06/08/books/evangelical-sales-are-converting-publishers.html.

Kolb, Robert, and Timothy J. Wengert, eds. *The Book of Concord: The Confession of the Evangelical Church*. Minneapolis, MN: Fortress, 2000.

Ladd, George Eldon. "Can the Kingdom be both Future and Present?" In *Crucial Questions about the Kingdom of God*, by George Eldon Ladd, 63–74. Grand Rapids, MI: Eerdmans, 1952.

———. *A Theology of the New Testament*. Grand Rapids, MI: Eerdmans, 1974.

LaHaye, Tim, and Jerry B. Jenkins. *The Left Behind Collection I*. 4 vols. Carol Stream, IL: Tyndale House, 2001.

Lepore, Jill. "A Golden Age for Dystopian Fiction." *New Yorker*, June 5, 2017. https://www.newyorker.com/magazine/2017/06/05/a-golden-age-for-dystopian-fiction.

Lerner, Maura. "He, She, or Ze? Pronouns Could Pose Trouble under University of Minnesota Campus Policy." *Startribune*, July 14, 2018. http://www.startribune.com/he-she-or-ze-pronouns-could-pose-trouble-under-u-campus-policy/488197021.

Lull, Timothy. *Martin Luther's Basic Theological Writings*. 2nd ed. Minneapolis: Fortress, 2005.

Luther, Martin. *A Compend of Luther's Theology*. Edited by Hugh T. Kerr. Philadelphia: Westminster, 1966.

———. *D. Martin Luthers Werke: Kritische Gesamtausgabe (Weimarer Ausgabe)*. Weimar: Böhlau, 1883–1929.

———, trans. *Das Neue Testament, nach der deutsche Übersetzung D. Martin Luthers*. Philadelphia: National, 1956.

———. *Luther's Works*. Edited by Jaroslav Pelikan. 55 vols. American ed. St. Louis: Concordia, 1955–86.

———. *Martin Luther's Basic Theological Writings*. Edited by William R. Russell. 3rd ed. Minneapolis: Fortress, 2012.

———. *The Sermon on the Mount and the Magnificat*. Edited by Jaroslav Pelikan. Vol. 21 of *Luther's Works*. St. Louis, MO: Concordia, 1956.

Lutzer, Erwin W. *Hitler's Cross*. Chicago: Moody, 1995.

Lyotard, Jean-Francois. *The Postmodern Condition: A Report on Knowledge*. Translated by Geoff Bennington and Brian Massumi. Theory and History of Literature 10. Minneapolis: University of Minnesota Press, 1993.

Maddox, Randy L. *Responsible Grace: John Wesley's Practical Theology*. Nashville, TN: Kingswood, 1994.

Madsen, Anna M. *The Theology of the Cross in Historical Perspective*. Eugene, OR: Pickwick, 2007.

Marsh, Michael N. *Out-of-Body and Near-Death Experiences: Brain-State Phenomena or Glimpses of Immortality?* Oxford: Oxford University Press, 2010.

Marx, Karl. "Theses on Feurbach." In *Karl Marx: Selected Writings*, edited by David McLellan, 171–74. New York: Oxford University Press, 1977.

Matthews, Douglas K. "Approximating the Millennium: Toward a Coherent Premillennial Theology of Social Transformation." PhD diss., Baylor University, 1992.

McClain, Alva J. "A Premillennial Philosophy of History." *Bibliotheca Sacra* 113 (1956) 111–16.

McGrath, Alister E. *Luther's Theology of the Cross.* Malden, MA: Blackwell, 1985.

Middleton, H. Richard. "Does Tom Wright Believe in the Second Coming?" *Creation to Eschaton: Explorations in Biblical Eschatology,* June 2, 2014. https://jrichardmiddleton.wordpress.com/2014/06/02/does-tom-wright-believe-in-the-second-coming.

Moltmann, Jürgen. *The Experiment Hope.* Translated and edited by M. Douglas Meeks. Philadelphia: Fortress, 1975.

———. "Hope and History." *Theology Today* 25 (1968) 369–86.

———. "Politics and the Practice of Hope." *Christian Century* 87 (1970) 288–91.

———. *Theology of Hope: On the Ground and the Implications of a Christian Eschatology.* Translated by James W. Leitch. New York: Harper and Row, 1967.

Moody, D. L. "The Return of the Lord." In *The American Evangelicals 1800–1900: An Anthology,* edited by William G. McLoughlin, 180–85. New York: Harper and Row, 1968.

Morrow, Lance. "Evil." *Time* 137 (1991) 48–54.

Nash, Ronald H. *Evangelicals in America: Who They Are, What They Believe.* Nashville: Abingdon, 1987.

———, ed. *Liberation Theology.* Milford, MI: Mott, 1984.

———, ed. *Process Theology.* Grand Rapids, MI: Mott, 1987.

Nelson, Marcia Z. "Frank Peretti: The Father of Christian Fiction Doesn't Want to Look Back." *Publisher's Weekly,* September 25, 2013. https://www.publishersweekly.com/pw/by-topic/authors/profiles/article/59186-frank-peretti-the-father-of-christian-fiction-doesn-t-want-to-look-back.html.

Nelson, Vernon H. *Christian David, Servant of the Lord.* Bethlehem, PA: Archives of the Moravian Church II, 1962

Niebuhr, H. Richard. *The Kingdom of God in America.* New York: Willett Clark, 1937.

Niebuhr, Reinhold. *Christian Realism and Political Problems.* New York: Scribner's Sons, 1953.

———. *Man's Nature and His Communities.* New York: Scribner's Sons, 1965.

———. *Moral Man and Immoral Society: A Study in Ethics and Politics.* New York: Scribner's Sons, 1932.

Nietzsche, Friedrich. *The Antichrist.* Translated by H. L. Mencken. Tucson, AZ: Sharp, 1999.

Novak, Michael. *The Spirit of Democratic Capitalism.* Rev. ed. Madison, WI: Lanham, 1990.

Oberman, Heiko. *The Harvest of Medieval Theology: Gabriel Biel and Late Medieval Nominalism.* Grand Rapids, MI: Baker Academic, 1983.

Oden, Thomas C. *After Modernity . . . What? Agenda for Theology.* Grand Rapids, MI: Zondervan, 1990.

———. "The Long Journey Home." *Journal of the Evangelical Theological Society* 34.1 (1991) 77–92.

O'Malley, J. Steven. *Children at Prayer: Pietists, Pentecost, and the Origin of a Globalized Christianity in Protestantism.* Lexington, KY: Emeth, forthcoming.

———. *Pietism, Pentecost, and the Origin of a Globalized Christianity within the Protestant Tradition.* Eugene, OR: Wipf and Stock, forthcoming.

———. *Pilgrimage of Faith: The Legacy of the Otterbeins.* Metuchen, NJ: Scarecrow, 1973.

Open Doors. "World Watch List." 2019. https://www.opendoorsusa.org/christian-persecution/world-watch-list.

Outler, Albert C., ed. *John Wesley.* New York: Oxford University Press, 1964

Petersen, Johann. *Die Macht der Kinder.* Frankfurt: Heil und Liebezeits, 1709.

"Quick Facts about Global Christianity." Gordon-Conwell Resources. https://www.gordonconwell.edu/ockenga/research/Quick-Facts-about-Global-Christianity.cfm.html#7.

Radcliff, Kaylena. "A War Story: 'There is No Pit So Deep God's Love is Not Deeper Still.'" *Christian History Magazine* 121 (2017) 40–43. https://christianhistoryinstitute.org/magazine/article/there-is-no-pit-so-deep.

Rahner, Karl. *Foundations of Christian Faith: An Introduction to the Idea of Christianity.* Translated by William V. Dych. New York: Seabury, 1978.

Rauschenbusch, Walter. *A Theology for the Social Gospel.* New York: MacMillan, 1917.

Richard, Ramesh P. "Elements of a Biblical Philosophy of History: Parts 1–3 of Premillennialism as a Philosophy of History." *Bibliotheca Sacra* 138 (1981) 108–18.

Richardson, Joel. "N. T. Wright and Eschatology." Joel Richardson (Blog). June 24, 2014, https://joelstrumpet.com/6773.

———. "N. T. Wright's Perversion of Biblical Hope." Joel Richardson (Blog). November 23, 2018. https://joelstrumpet.com/n-t-wrights-perversion-of-biblical-hope.

Rogers, Jack, and Donald McKim. *The Authority and Interpretation of the Bible: An Historical Approach.* Eugene, OR: Wipf and Stock, 1999.

Root, Andrew. *Christopraxis: A Practial Theology of the Cross.* Minneapolis: Fortress, 2014.

Rottenberg, Isaac C. *The Promise and the Presence: Toward a Theology of the Kingdom of God.* Grand Rapids, MI: Eerdmans, 1980.

Saler, Robert Cady. *Theologia Crucis: A Companion to the Theology of the Cross.* Eugene, OR: Cascade, 2016.

Schaff, Philip. *The Creeds of Christian Christendom with a History and Critical Notes.* Vol. 3 Grand Rapids, MI: Baker, 1966.

Schillebeeckx, Edward. *The Schillebeeckx Reader.* Translated by Crossroad Publishing. Edited by Robert J. Schreiter. New York: Crossroad, 1987.

Shapiro, Fred R. "Who Wrote the Serenity Prayer?" *Chronicle Review*, April 28, 2014. https://www.chronicle.com/article/Who-Wrote-the-Serenity-Prayer-/146159.

Smith, Timothy L. *Revivalism and Social Reform: American Protestantism on the Eve of the Civil War.* Baltimore: John Hopkins University Press, 1980.

Snyder, Howard A. "The Holy Reign of God." *Wesleyan Theological Journal* 24 (1989) 83–84.

Sojourners. "Who We Are." https://sojo.net/about-us/who-we-are.

Spener, Philip Jakob. *Pia Desideria.* Edited by Theodore Tappert. Philadephia: Fortress, 1964.

Steinmetz, Johann Adam. *Der Versiegelung der Gläubigen mit dem heiligen Geist in Einigen Pfingst-Erbauungsstunden.* Frankfurt am Main: Heinrich Ludwig Brönner, 1857.

————. *Die "Sammlung auserlesener Materaien zum Bau des Reichs Gottes" zwischen 1730 und 1760*. Edited by Rainer Lächele. Tübingen: Verlag der Frankeschen Stiftungen Halle im Max Niemeyer Verlag, 2006.

Sweeney, Douglas. "Was Luther a Calvinist?" *Gospel Coalition*, July 15, 2014. https:// www.thegospelcoalition.org/article/was-luther-a-calvinist.

Swensson, Eric. *Kinderbeten: The Silesian Children's Prayer and Prophecy Revival*. Eugene, OR: Wipf and Stock, 2003.

Teilhard de Chardin, Pierre. *The Divine Milieu*. Translated by William Collins. New York: Harper Colophon-Harper and Row 1960.

————. *The Phenomenon of Man*. Translated by Bernard Wall. Introduction by Julian Huxley. New York: Harper and Brothers, 1959.

Tillich, Paul. *Reason and Revelation, Being and God*. Vol. 1 of *Systematic Theology*. Chicago: University of Chicago Press, 1951.

Tyson, John R. *Charles Wesley on Sanctification*. Grand Rapids, MI: Zondervan, 1986.

United Methodist Church. *The Book of Discipline*. Nashville, TN: Abingdon, 1984.

Urban, Linwood. "Was Luther a Thoroughgoing Determinist?" *The Journal of Theological Studies* 22.1 (1971). http://www.jstor.org/stable/23962345.

Volf, Miroslav. *Free of Charge: Giving and Forgiving in a Culture Stripped of Grace*. Grand Rapids, MI: Zondervan, 2005.

von Zinzendorf, Nicholas. *Christian David, Servant of the Lord*. Edited by Vernon H. Nelson. Bethlehem, PA: Archives of the Moravian Church II, 1962.

Walvoord, John. "Why Must Christ Return?" In *Prophecy and the Seventies*, edited by Charles Lee Feinberg, 31–44 Chicago: Moody, 1971.

Weaver, Richard. *Ideas Have Consequences*. Chicago: Phoenix, 1962.

Webber, Robert E. *The Secular Saint: A Case for Evangelical Social Responsibility*. Grand Rapids, MI: Zondervan, 1979.

Weber, Timothy P. "Premillennialism and the Branches of Evangelicalism." In *The Variety of Evangelicalism*, edited by Donald Dayton and Robert K. Johnston, 5–21. Downers Grove, IL: InterVarsity, 1991.

Wesley, Charles. *The Sermons of Charles Wesley: A Critical Edition with Introduction and Notes*. Oxford: Oxford University Press, 2001.

Wesley, Charles, et al. *Manuscript Journal of the Reverend Charles Wesley, MA*. 2 vols. Nashville: Kingswood, 2008.

Wesley, John. "From the Journal: Wednesday, May 24, 1738." Christian History 2 (1983). https://christianhistoryinstitute.org/magazine/article/john-wesley-journal.

————. "The General Spread of the Gospel." In *Sermons II*, edited by Albert Outler, 485–99. Vol. 2 of *The Works of John Wesley*. Nashville: Abingdon, 1985.

————. *John Wesley*. Edited by Albert C. Outler. New York: Oxford University Press, 1980.

————. *Journal and Diaries I*. Vol. 18 of *The Bicentennial Edition of the Works of John Wesley*. Edited by W. R. Ward and Richard Heitzenrater. Nashville: Abingdon, 1984.

————. *Journal and Diaries II*. Vol. 19 of *The Bicentennial Edition of the Works of John Wesley*. Edited by W. R. Ward and Richard Heitzenrater. Nashville: Abingdon, 1984.

————. *Letters I* (1721–1739). 32 vols. Edited by Frank Baker. Oxford, UK: Clarendon, 1980.

————. "Salvation by Faith." In *The Sermons of John Wesley: A Collection for the Christian Journey*, edited by Kenneth J. Collins and Jason A. Vickers, 125–33. Nashville, TN: Abingdon, 2013.

————. "A Short History of the People Called Methodists." In *The Bicentennial Edition of the Works of John Wesley*, edited by Rupert E. Davies, 425–503. Vol. 9 of *The Methodist Societies, History, Nature, and Design*. Nashville: Abingdon, 1989.

————. "What Is an Arminian?" In *Readings in Christian Thought*, edited by Hugh T. Kerr, 193–95. 2nd ed. Nashville, TN: Abingdon, 1966.

Wesley, John, and Kenneth Cain Kinghorn. *A Plain Account of Christian Perfection as Believed and Taught by the Reverend Mr. John Wesley: A Transcription in Modern English*. Lexington, KY: Emeth, 2012.

Whitford, David M. "Martin Luther." *Internet Encyclopedia of Philosophy*. http://www.iep.utm.edu/luther.

Wiley, H. Orton. *Christian Theology*. 3 vols. Kansas City, MO: Nazarene, 1940–43.

Wood, Laurence. *Pentecost and Sanctification in the Writings of John and Charles Wesley*. The Study of World Christian Revitalization Movements in Pietist and Wesleyan Studies. Lexington, KY: Emeth, 2018.

Wright, N. T. *The Challenge of Jesus: Rediscovering Who Jesus Was and Is*. Downers Grove, IL: InterVarsity Academic, 1999.

————. *The Day the Revolution Began: Reconsidering the Meaning of Jesus's Crucifixion*. San Francisco: HarperOne, 2016.

————. "NTWrightPage." 2019. http://www.ntwrightpage.com.

————. *Surprised by Hope: Rethinking Heaven, the Resurrection, and the Mission of the Church*. 2008. New York: HarperCollins, 2008.

Index of Scripture

Index of Subjects

Made in United States
Orlando, FL
06 February 2022